The EVERYTHING. Lactose-Free Cookbook

Dear Reader,

It is estimated that 75 percent of the world population suffers from Lactose Intolerance (LI) to some degree! You may not even be aware that this is why your tummy hurts sometimes.

This book is designed to help you in discovering where you fit on the "Richter Scale of Lactose Intolerance" with valuable information that hopefully will bring you some "ah-ha" moments, resulting in a clearer understanding of LI for you.

You may be surprised to learn that "lactose free" doesn't necessarily mean "dairy free"!

Becoming lactose savvy is the key to your comfort kingdom, and it doesn't mean you need to deprive yourself of the foods you love. This book is all about delicious options! You'll learn how to use your "lactose compass"—your own body—in discovering what works for you!

I hope you enjoy this book and the delightful variety of recipes and choices that are available to you in your lactose intolerant life. Remember, it's not all or nothing!

It brings my heart joy to have written this book for you!

In health and wellness,

Jan McCracken

Welcome to the EVERYTHING Series!

These handy, accessible books give you all you need to tackle a difficult project, gain a new hobby, comprehend a fascinating topic, prepare for an exam, or even brush up on something you learned back in school but have since forgotten.

You can read an *Everything*® book from cover to cover or just pick out the information you want from our four useful boxes: e-questions, e-facts, e-alerts, e-ssentials. We give you everything you need to know on the subject, but throw in a lot of fun stuff along the way, too.

We now have more than 400 *Everything*® books in print, spanning such wide-ranging categories as weddings, pregnancy, cooking, music instruction, foreign language, crafts, pets, New Age, and so much more. When you're done reading them all, you can finally say you know *Everything*®!

QUESTIONS?

Answers to
common questions

FACTS

Important snippets
of information

ALERTS!

Urgent
warnings

Quick
handy tips

Editorial

Director of Innovation: Paula Munier

Editorial Director: Laura M. Daly

Executive Editor, Series Books: Brielle K. Matson

Associate Copy Chief: Sheila Zwiebel

Acquisitions Editor: Kerry Smith

Development Editor: Elizabeth Kassab

Production Editor: Casey Ebert

Production

Director of Manufacturing: Susan Beale

Production Project Manager: Michelle Roy Kelly

Prepress: Erick DaCosta, Matt LeBlanc

Design Manager: Heather Blank

Senior Book Designer: Colleen Cunningham

Interior Layout: Heather Barrett, Brewster Brownville

Visit the entire Everything® *series at* www.everything.com

THE
EVERYTHING
LACTOSE-FREE
COOKBOOK

Easy-to-prepare, low-dairy
alternatives for your favorite meals

Jan McCracken
Technical Review by Linda Larsen

adamsmedia
Avon, Massachusetts

The nutritional information provided with all of the recipes
in this book was calculated using NutriBase Clinical Version 7.0.

An Everything® Series Book.
Everything® and everything.com® are registered trademarks of F+W Publications, Inc.

Published by Adams Media, an F+W Publications Company
57 Littlefield Street, Avon, MA 02322. U.S.A.
www.adamsmedia.com

ISBN 10: 1-59869-509-6
ISBN 13: 978-1-59869-509-0
Printed in the United States of America.

J I H G F E D C B A

Library of Congress Cataloging-in-Publication Data
available from the publisher.

This publication is designed to provide accurate and authoritative information with regard to the subject matter covered. It is sold with the understanding that the publisher is not engaged in rendering legal, accounting, or other professional advice. If legal advice or other expert assistance is required, the services of a competent professional person should be sought.

—From a *Declaration of Principles* jointly adopted by a Committee of the American Bar Association and a Committee of Publishers and Associations

Many of the designations used by manufacturers and sellers to distinguish their products are claimed as trademarks. Where those designations appear in this book and Adams Media was aware of a trademark claim, the designations have been printed with initial capital letters.

The Everything® Lactose-Free Cookbook is intended as a reference volume only, not as a medical manual. In light of the complex, individual, and specific nature of health problems, this book is not intended to replace professional medical advice. The ideas, procedures, and suggestions in this book are intended to supplement, not replace, the advice of a trained medical professional. Consult your physician before adopting the suggestions in this book, as well as about any condition that may require diagnosis or medical attention. The author and publisher disclaim any liability arising directly or indirectly from the use of this book.

This book is available at quantity discounts for bulk purchases.
For information, please call 1-800-289-0963.

Dedication

This book is dedicated to the millions of people who are lactose intolerant, whether it is a small bump in your road of life or a very large one. It is my hope that this book might enhance your lives with choices, making happier tummies everywhere!

Acknowledgments

Thanks to Kerry Smith and Elizabeth Kassab, my editors at Adams Media.

Big thanks to Grace Freedson for her ongoing support as my literary agent; she brings me to the most interesting options for writing.

Many thanks to the nutritional analyst, Linda Larsen, who made sure that all of the ingredients in the recipes in this book are in alignment for the most important person of all, you, the reader!

Blessings to my friends and family who are my biggest fans in my writing career with everlasting encouragement and rah-rahs.

Very special thanks to a very special lady who God has blessed me with, Cherie Davidson. Cherie has become the 'little sister' that I always wanted and never had and is such a blessing to me. Not only do I call her Lil' Sis, but she answers to other names like "web gremlin" as she diligently maintains my Web site, *www.janmc cracken.com*.

Many heartfelt thanks to all and God bless you every one with health and wellness!

Contents

Introduction

My goal in this book is to provide you with a "Lactose Intolerance Compass" to guide you through the paces of lactose intolerance. It's my hope for you that you'll take this LI Compass and make it an adventure in discovering your varied and delicious options!

I've never been a fancy cook, coming from good ol' Midwestern stock, so you'll find the recipes in this book very practical and user-friendly. You'll find most of the ingredients in your local grocery store. If you choose more exotic ingredients, the national health food stores are bound to have what you're looking for.

As you know, awareness is about 90 percent of the battle—and knowledge is power. It's my hope that this book will provide you with simple recommendations on lactose, lactase, milk, and dairy products to arm you with the awareness necessary to help you create a healthy, lactose-friendly lifestyle without tummy aches!

The Everything® Lactose-Free Cookbook is an easy-to-use guide for everyday use, not just for special occasions. You'll find recipes to get your day started with a great breakfast and lots of smoothies and nogs too. Snacks are important, and there are great snack recipes galore, along with quick breads and muffins. When you're in a hurry, flip to the quick meals for satisfying and easy-to-make meals. Lactose intolerance doesn't mean you can't enjoy creamy sauces, gravies, dips, salsas and spreads, and tasty homemade salad dressings, so recipes for those are included as well.

There is a special section on yogurt cheese that might just change your life! In this section you'll find the how-to's of making yogurt cheese with lots of recipes for you to enjoy. The entrée recipes work for everyday meals—or add a little pizzazz to the presentation and serve them at a party or family get-together. You'll also find recipes for special soups, slaws, salads, rice dishes, couscous, veggies, and other accompaniments.

Good-for-you beans and lentils have their own chapter, as does pasta. There are even a couple of recipes for pizza! Lest you fear a life without dessert, the sweets chapter is one of the most fun chapters in the whole book. Choose from dessert recipes made with tofu, decadent cheesecakes made with yogurt cheese, and some of your favorites like chocolate cake and brownies.

With your LI Compass and the recipes in this book, please feel free to substitute ingredients with your favorites that work for you. Experiment and become adventurous in your cooking! You'll find that pleasing your palate and your tummy is very satisfying!

Finally, the importance of becoming a label sleuth cannot be overstressed. Reading each and every label carefully for lactose ingredients as well as learning to look for hidden lactose are key to fixing pleasing meals. This book includes a section on what to look for. If you want to learn even more, surf the Internet for free information on lactose intolerance.

With this book, you won't feel at all deprived—you'll be too busy creating your new healthy lifestyle and enjoying your new recipes.

Chapter 1
Low Dairy or No Dairy?

Lactose intolerance is an opportunity to explore the wide world of food. Look at your LI lifestyle as a challenge to sniff out the tastiest, healthiest foods. Lactose intolerance doesn't necessarily mean you can't have any foods with lactose in them, but there are certain foods you will want to avoid. For every high-lactose ingredient you need to cut from your diet, there are half a dozen tasty alternatives for you to enjoy. This cookbook contains recipes designed to give you the nutrients you need and the tastes you crave.

Lactose Intolerance Defined

Lactose intolerance—often referred to as LI—concerns the digestion of dairy products in your daily diet. Sometimes LI is referred to as lactase deficiency; the terms mean the same thing, and in the medical community the condition is referred to as "primary lactose intolerance." LI is a very common condition that often goes undiagnosed. Many individuals are living in unnecessary discomfort, and simple diet changes could easily make a huge difference. There is no magic wand to cure LI and no medical procedure that will correct it. Your comfort zone in living with LI depends on what you put in your mouth.

FACT

Lactose intolerance is completely different from milk allergy. Milk allergy is an allergic reaction triggered by the immune system to protein components in milk. Lactose intolerance is related to the digestive system and the inability to break down milk sugar (lactose). In addition, LI is not a contagious disease, and even though LI's symptoms are distressing and sometimes uncomfortable, they do not cause damage to the intestine.

Lactose and Lactase

Lactose is a primary simple sugar found in milk and dairy. In order to digest lactose, the digestive enzyme lactase must be present in the small intestine. Lactase breaks down the milk sugar into two simpler forms of sugar, glucose and galactose, which allows absorption into the bloodstream. The following definitions may be of help to you in your understanding of lactose intolerance.

- Lactase: The enzyme present in the lining of the small intestine that is needed to digest lactose (milk sugar) in order for it to be absorbed by the body and used as nourishment.
- Lactose: The sugar that is found naturally in the milk of all mammals, which the human body breaks down into galactose and glucose. Lactose is not found anywhere else in nature.

- Lactase Deficiency: The lack of the enzyme lactase, which is the cause of lactose intolerance.
- Lactose Intolerance: Being unable to digest the sugar in milk (lactose), which occurs because the body doesn't produce enough of the lactase enzyme.

Symptoms of LI

If there's a shortage of lactase in the small intestine, lactose carries additional fluid as it moves down to the colon. Fermentation of lactose in the colon begins to take place, and gases form. (Think of the fermentation process of fine wines and champagne.) The gas bubbles can be very uncomfortable, causing gastrointestinal symptoms such as cramping, flatulence, nausea, diarrhea, and abdominal bloating.

FACT When toddlers are around age two, their bodies begin to produce less lactase. The symptoms of the lessening of lactase production may not be realized until a person is much older. In some cases it can be as late as the senior years.

Symptoms can range from severe pain to mild discomfort, depending on each individual's degree of lactase deficiency and the amount of lactose that's been consumed. It's common for symptoms to begin anywhere from thirty minutes to three hours after eating or drinking food containing lactose.

Who Is Lactose Intolerant?

As many as 75 percent of all adults worldwide are lactose intolerant, and more than 50 million Americans suffer from some degree of lactose intolerance. While 85 percent of children outgrow their intolerance, adults are not so lucky. Genetics can be a contributing factor, and LI can also be common among individuals who are alcoholic or ingest an abnormal amount of alcohol.

The numbers and percentages of lactose intolerant individuals are staggering. In fact, lactose tolerance is rarer than lactose intolerance. The National

Institutes for Health reports that between 80–100 percent of Asian Americans and Native Americans are lactose intolerant, and up to 80 percent of African Americans are lactose intolerant. On the bright side, LI is not life threatening. It can be easily controlled by diet, and it's not an all-or-nothing situation.

Ongoing research is conclusive in illustrating a genetic link to lactose intolerance. This may be useful in developing a genetic test to identify potential lactose intolerance in people whose parents are lactose intolerant.

Secondary Lactase Deficiency

Secondary lactase deficiency is caused by certain digestive disorders that damage the small intestine. The damage inhibits the body's ability to produce lactase and process lactose. Crohn's disease, celiac disease, and inflammatory bowel disease can all lead to secondary lactase deficiency.

Testing, Testing

Medical tests can be performed with your doctor's advice to accurately diagnose lactose intolerance. It's important that you confirm the discomfort that you're experiencing after eating a meal or a snack is not a more serious digestive disorder than lactose intolerance. Consult your physician for advice on what testing needs to be done to narrow your diagnosis so that you can get on with enjoying your life.

In medically testing and measuring the absorption of lactose in the digestive system, common measures include a stool acidity test, a lactose tolerance test, and a hydrogen breath test. Let your doctor be your guide because every LI case is unique to the individual.

One very simple test can be performed at home. Avoid all milk products for several consecutive days. On a weekend when you plan to be at home, don't eat any breakfast but instead drink two large glasses of milk. During the next four to five hours, if you experience LI symptoms you are a prime candidate for being lactose intolerant. At this point, see a doctor for confirmation of your symptoms.

Dancing Around LI

As with most things in life, there are tricks to living with LI! You might begin by avoiding meals with large amounts of lactose or eating foods containing lactose several times a day in small amounts to see if your unpleasant symptoms diminish. Dancing around LI will take a bit of trial and error, but it won't take you long to discover your own personal lactose culprits and avoid them!

It's helpful to meet with a registered dietician for assistance in setting up a lifestyle diet plan to restrict your lactose intake and make sure you're getting all the nutrients and the calcium your body requires. A dietician can help you set your lactose boundaries.

Discover What Works for You

No two cases of LI are the same. Some individuals may drink two glasses of milk without a problem, some may only be able to tolerate half a glass at a time, and some may not be able to drink milk at all! You are your own best lactose-level detective in determining your degree of tolerance for milk and dairy products. Try consuming different levels of lactose to determine how much and what foods you can eat and still feel comfortable.

If you love milk and it doesn't love you back, try drinking it in small amounts. In addition, drink milk with food so that the milk isn't the only thing in your digestive system. These little hints will make your body happier because they slow down digestion and make the absorption of the lactose easier! Milk seems to be the major culprit in lactose intolerance, but there are other foods in the dairy department that you may be able to handle.

Look for dairy products that are lower in lactose such as yogurt, many cheeses, and yogurt cheese, just to mention a few. In addition, there's a variety of special lactose-free milks available in the dairy case!

Other options include adding a lactase enzyme to milk or searching out a chewable lactase supplement before eating foods containing lactose. This works quite nicely for lots of folks who are lactose intolerant. This is another item to put on your list to discuss with your physician.

Obvious Lactose

A major key to your digestive comfort is being food label savvy. Read labels and look for the obvious lactose first. Naturally occurring lactose in milk is listed as sugar on the Nutrition Facts label on a milk carton but the ingredients section doesn't list any added sugar. Milk is often added to some of the commercial products in the list below:

- Bread and other baked goods
- Nondairy and whipped creamers
- Drink mixes and breakfast drinks
- Margarines
- Salad dressings
- Lunch meats and hot dogs
- Processed breakfast cereals
- Candies, cookies, and snacks
- Soups (especially cream soups)
- Mixes for pancakes, biscuits, cookies, and cakes
- Sugar substitutes
- Instant coffee and cocoa mixes
- Instant mashed potatoes and French fries
- Pie crusts and pie fillings
- Pudding mixes

Not all of the products listed above contain lactose, and that's why reading labels is so important. It's important to look not only for milk and lactose among the contents, but also for such terms as whey, curds, buttermilk, malted milk, milk by-products, dry milk solids, nonfat dry milk powder, sour cream, and sweet cream, all of which contain lactose. It doesn't have to be in the dairy section to contain lactose. Every product and brand varies. Just because you become accustomed to a particular brand you think is free of lactose, be sure to read the label periodically because ingredients do change.

Kosher products labeled "Parve" or "Pareve" are lactose free. However, if the product is just labeled "Kosher" you can't be guaranteed that the product is lactose free.

Lactose Lurkers

Beware of lactose lurkers! They show up in the darnedest places and you won't know it until they hit your tummy—ouch!

FACT

Would you believe that some medications contain lactose? More than 20 percent of prescription drugs contain lactose, and over-the-counter medications are not lactose free either. Lactose is found in many types of birth control pills and tablets for stomach acid. Medications generally contain small amounts of lactose and only affect people who are very lactose intolerant.

Canned tuna and salmon are innocent-looking packages that may also contain lactose. Some of the commercial fisheries add milk products to their canned fish products in the canneries. Lactose is also commonly applied to dried vegetables to prevent discoloration. If a dried veggie is treated with a small amount of lactose when it's re-hydrated it will have a brighter color and be more appealing. Learn to read labels; it's important and your tummy will thank you big time!

Calcium Is a Team Player

It just so happens that many of the foods LI individuals shy away from are prime sources of calcium, so keeping calcium in the diet is a primary concern for people with LI. Calcium is the primary mineral for the growth, mainte-nance, and repair of bones and teeth. Calcium needs to be teamed with vita-min D and phosphorus for maximum benefits. Phosphorus is important to bone structure, and vitamin D allows the absorption of calcium into the body. It's possible to have a calcium deficiency due to a lack of vitamin D; even if you are taking in enough calcium, your body can't do anything with it unless it has vitamin D.

Meeting Your Calcium Quota

The Institute of Medicine released a chart listing the requirements for daily calcium intake. The calcium required to maintain good health varies by age group. The recommendations made are shown in the following table.

Table 1-1	
Age Group	Amount of Calcium to Consume Daily
0–6 months	400 mg
6–12 months	600 mg
1–5 years	800 mg
6–10 years	1,200 mg
11–24 years	1,200-1,500 mg
25–50 years	1,000 mg
51–70+ years	1,500 mg

The National Digestive Diseases Information Clearinghouse (NDDIC) is a service of the National Institute of Diabetes and Digestive and Kidney Diseases (NDDK). NDDK is part of the National Institute of Health of the U.S. Department of Health and Human Services.

It was also noted that pregnant and nursing women need between 1,200 and 1,500 mg of calcium daily.

"Bone Up" Foods

There's a wide array of calcium-rich foods for you to choose from, and this book contains lots of recipes that are full of calci-yum! Here's a short list of foods that will help you make sure you're meeting your daily calcium quota:

- Dark leafy greens
- Dandelion and mustard greens
- Turnip and collard greens
- Kale
- Broccoli
- Orange juice fortified with calcium
- Whole almonds
- Sesame seeds
- Dried figs
- Blackstrap molasses
- Canned sardines and salmon with bones
- Ocean perch
- Shrimp
- Soybeans
- Beans
- Calcium-fortified soy milk
- Extra firm tofu
- Yogurt
- Yogurt cheese
- Low-lactose cheeses

Note that spinach is missing from the list. This is because it contains oxalates, which prevent the body from absorbing calcium.

Boney Good Calcium

Calcium's importance in preventing osteoporosis is nothing new, but recent studies show calcium can be helpful in preventing heart disease, stroke, high blood pressure, hypertension, and possibly colon cancer.

If your regular diet isn't quite enough to meet your body's calcium requirements, ask your doctor or dietician about calcium supplements. As always, getting your calcium naturally through your food is best; it's never a good idea to try to make up for a poor diet with supplements. Developing a healthy lifestyle is a win/win situation!

Don't Inhale Your Calcium

Another little tip on calcium: try not to inhale it all at one sitting. Calcium likes to be absorbed slowly throughout the day, so spread it out to get the most from your calcium intake!

FACT

If you're an orange juice lover, you're ahead of the game. Take just a minute and read the front of the carton and the Nutrition Label. Many great orange juices today are fortified with both calcium and vitamin D. You'll get your calcium and the vitamin D necessary for your body to absorb it—score!

Vitamin D

Vitamin D is present in some foods, but you can also soak some up simply by taking a walk outside! If you spend just a few minutes each day out in the sun for brief periods you will absorb much needed vitamin D. There are other sources of vitamin D besides the sun and—you guessed it—the key lies in reading labels! As with calcium, taking supplements to fill these gaps for vitamin D is not always the best answer. Consult with your doctor or dietician to make sure you're on the right path.

Who's Got My Cheese?

Did someone say cheese? But that's in the dairy department! There is some great news: most lactose intolerant folks can tolerate cheese in their diet.

Most of the lactose is removed along with the whey when cheeses are made. There are high-lactose and low-lactose cheeses. Only you will know which cheeses you can tolerate; however, the great news is that "lactose free" doesn't necessarily mean "cheese free."

The Kingdom of Cheeses

Including cheese in your LI lifestyle depends on two things: the kinds of cheese you eat and the amount. Start out small and see what your level of tolerance is. Read labels. You'll find the lactose content in cheeses under sugar; the milk sugar in cheese is lactose.

The standards on the Nutrition Facts label allow the cheese maker to list zero grams of sugar in cheese if the cheese contains no more than half a gram of lactose per ounce. There are cheeses available to you with just trace amounts of lactose and even more with low levels of lactose (1–2 grams or less per serving).

Cheese-y

Many lactose intolerant people are able to digest aged, natural cheeses. Here's a list of some of them, but remember the cheese world is huge so read your labels! Processed cheese spreads and cheese foods do contain lactose and most likely should be avoided.

Some cheeses with low lactose levels include but are not limited to:

- Brie
- Cheddar
- Colby
- Edam
- Parmesan
- Swiss
- Camembert
- Gouda
- Danish Blue
- Gorgonzola
- Roquefort
- Emmental

Eating cheese is another valuable way to make sure your body gets enough calcium. Eat it in moderation until you figure out how much your body can tolerate. Test lactose-reduced cheese products with your lifestyle, and look for nondairy alternatives if you need to limit the amount of real cheese but don't want it to interfere with your favorite snacks.

Yummy Yogurt Live Is In

Yes, yogurt is made from milk, but you may be delighted to know that it fits in with your LI lifestyle.

Enter stage left the culturing process that milk goes through to become yogurt. It's this process that allows most lactose intolerant folks to enjoy yogurt's nutritional benefits and satisfying taste. Yogurt is also a great boost to your calcium intake!

While you're label sleuthing, look for descriptions such as "contains active cultures," "living cultures," and "active yogurt cultures." This will tell you the cultures are live and not pasteurized. Live cultures are important because they help your digestive system process the lactose. Avoid yogurt if the label reads "heat treated after culturing."

In the Yogurt Culture

All yogurts are not created equal in the culturing process, and it's important to look for yogurts that contain live and active cultures. These pure bacterial cultures convert the lactose content to lactic acid, which lowers the intestine's pH, reduces harmful bacteria, and aids in digestibility and the absorption of key nutrients.

The bacteria in yogurt are a friendly sort and contribute to the health of your colon; they are thought to lower the risk of colon cancer. That's just one example of a long list of the good things the friendly bacteria in yogurt does for your health and nutrition.

Yogurt's Nutritional Benefits

Look at a few of the nutritional benefits in just 1 cup of plain low-fat yogurt:

- 450 milligrams of calcium
- 154 calories
- 13 grams of protein
- 574 milligrams of potassium
- 4 grams of fat

Reading labels is extremely important in the yogurt department because of the sheer quantity of yogurt on the market. Please note that fruit-flavored yogurts and added sugars can drive the calorie count up over the top of 300 calories for one serving of some brands of yogurt.

A Glimpse at Cooking with Yogurt

Cooking with yogurt may seem like a bit of a strange culinary approach at first, but you're in for a palate-pleasing surprise! You can use it as a replacement for milk, buttermilk, mayonnaise, cream cheese and sour cream in many of your favorite recipes. Not only does it fit in with your LI lifestyle, but in many cases it's better for your overall health.

QUESTION?

How do I get my mashed potatoes to be really fluffy?
Use yogurt in your homemade mashed potatoes. Not only are you forgoing the lactose, but you and your family will like them better with yogurt stirred in as a substitute for milk or cream!

In baking, yogurt lends a flavorful moistness to quick breads, muffins, yeast breads, and breakfast grains like pancakes and waffles. The protein in the flour and the acid in the yogurt react well and lends a very fine texture and tenderness to baked products.

More Adventures with Yogurt

You'll find recipes made with yogurt scattered throughout this entire book. Using yogurt as a marinade will enhance the flavor of chicken, beef, pork, and lamb and tenderize the meat at the same time. Try it in dips and dressings. There isn't much that yogurt doesn't go with, from smoothies to great veggie sauces.

Versatile Yogurt Cheese

Even lower in lactose than yogurt is yogurt cheese, which is sometimes referred to as yogo-cheese. Call it whatever you want, but make sure you include it in your lactose intolerant lifestyle!

Making yogurt cheese is a very simple process. The main component is the quality of the yogurt you choose. Select a natural, plain low-fat yogurt. Read the label, and make sure there is no gelatin in the yogurt. Avoid the custard yogurts; they don't separate from the whey very well because of the binding agents. Some flavored yogurts will work, but not the ones that contain chunks of fruit.

Line a strainer or a colander with a layer of cheesecloth or two layers of white paper towels or a coffee filter. Make sure the cheesecloth drapes over the sides of the draining device. Place the draining device over a bowl so the whey can drain efficiently. Pour the yogurt into the draining device, cover tightly with plastic wrap, and place in the refrigerator overnight. The whey will drain off the yogurt. One cup of yogurt yields ⅓ cup of yogurt cheese. The consistency of your yogurt cheese depends on the number of hours you allow it to drain. If you want the consistency of sour cream or cream cheese, then 18–24 hours is ideal. The longer it drains, the firmer the yogurt cheese becomes, so it depends on what you're going to use it for—as a replacement for cream cheese, in a recipe for an herb spread, or in a cheesecake recipe. You'll learn as you go along. Remove the yogurt cheese from the refrigerator and discard the whey. Cover it tightly and store it in the refrigerator. Yogurt cheese will keep for up to a week.

There are special funnels available that are specifically designed for making yogurt cheese. These are a good investment if you're going to be making yogurt cheese on a regular basis. Recipes made with yogurt cheese are extra creamy, and you'll wonder how you've ever cooked without it!

Got Soy?

In looking for nondairy alternatives you'll find all kinds of soy products readily available to you in most grocery stores and definitely in health food stores. Most soy products are free of lactose as well as milk protein. If you are using soy milk as a milk replacement, be sure to choose one that is fortified with calcium. Today there are literally thousands of soy products on the market. Soy milk, tofu, soy cheeses, soy yogurt, soy sour cream, miso, tempeh, and soy sauce are all made from soybeans.

Where Soy's "Bean"

Soy cultivation dates back to the Chou dynasty in the eastern half of Northern China. It wasn't until sometime in the 1760s that soybeans were planted and harvested in the United States. Soy milk is made by grinding the beans, cooking them briefly, squeezing them, and combining the extracted liquid with water.

Soy Nutrition

Soy contains no cholesterol and very little saturated fat. It is a good source of protein, vitamin B12, fiber, potassium, iron, vitamin D, and zinc. Check the labels as soy products do vary by brand and some are enhanced and fortified with calcium, some have higher B-vitamin content than others, and so on.

Soy Savvy

You can find soy milk in the dairy case and in aseptic packages on the unrefrigerated grocery store shelves. Don't be under the illusion that soy milk is going to taste like cow's milk; it has a sweet, beany taste. Soy milk comes in different flavors and varieties; it's possible to satisfy your craving for chocolate milk with a soy alternative.

Tofu for You!

Tofu is soybean curd made from soy milk. The process of making tofu is similar to that of making cheese. You'll find tofu in different textures, which is based on its water content. Keep in mind that the firm and extra-firm tofu contains less water and more protein. The recipes in this book call for firm and extra-firm tofu because it retains its shape in stir-fry and other dishes.

Edamame

Tasty, crunchy, and packed full of protein, edamame are green soybeans that are harvested just before their maturity. They're harvested in pods and are very similar in size and color to peas. You're usually served edamame in Japanese restaurants and at sushi bars as an appetizer. Edamame is also available in the frozen food section of health food stores and in some grocery stores. Edamame is good cooked according to the package directions and served as a veggie side dish and is a great addition to salads.

How to Use This Book

Two icons in this book make flipping through it to zero in on a recipe as easy as possible. The following recipe key tells you at a glance some of the ingredients in each recipe.

Recipe Key:

🌀 Made with Soy Milk

🌗 May Contain Lactose

The icon that denotes lactose content includes all recipes made with yogurt cheese even if lactose does not show up in the nutritional statistics. It also includes recipes that have even trace amounts of lactose from other sources. This is not a warning to stay away from these recipes; it is an invitation to adjust the ingredients to suit your level of lactose intolerance.

Personal Substitutions

Please feel comfortable to substitute ingredients in the recipes in this book. Some lactose intolerant folks can tolerate butter, for instance. If you like the taste of rice milk and don't like the taste of soy milk, soy what? It's your culinary creation; use rice milk or other nondairy alternatives that appeal to you!

You're Armed and Ready!

With the information in this book, you can make your lactose intolerant life easier. Use the recipes in the book as basic recipes. Once you get the hang of discovering where lactose lurks and pinpoint your own personal tolerances, you're armed and ready to adjust your favorite recipes to satisfy your tummy and your taste buds!

Chapter 2
Smoothies and Nogs

Passion Fruit Smoothie

Serves 4

Calories: 116.58
Fat: 1.32 grams
Saturated Fat: 0.68 grams
Carbohydrates: 26.47 grams
Calcium: 46.11 mg
Lactose: 0.0 grams

½ cup plain yogurt
Pulp of 2 passion fruits
2 bananas
6 strawberries
⅓ cup frozen raspberries
1 cup apple juice
2 ice cubes

If you have a passion for smoothies, this one will make you smile—and it's pretty to serve, too! Because the bacteria in the yogurt have already begun to break down the protein molecules into lactic acid, this smoothie should be easy for your LI body to assimilate.

1. Place all ingredients in blender.

2. Blend until mixture reaches a smooth consistency and serve at once.

Peachy Breakfast Nog

Serves 4

Calories: 153.09
Fat: 0.86 grams
Saturated Fat: 0.47 grams
Carbohydrates: 34.69 grams
Calcium: 106.25 mg
Lactose: 0.0 grams

1½ cups peach nectar, chilled
2 16-ounce cans peach slices
    in juice, drained
1 8-ounce carton vanilla
    yogurt
⅛ teaspoon almond or
    vanilla extract

Oh, this one is just peachy keen! Smoothies and nogs are a great way to kick-start the day, and this one gives you a jump on your daily calcium requirement!

1. Combine all ingredients in blender. Process until smooth.

2. Pour into glasses and serve immediately.

Lactose-Friendly Yogurt

Make your smoothies and nogs tasty, full-bodied, and healthy by adding some yogurt. Delicious eaten on its own as a meal or a snack, yogurt also makes a tasty topping for fresh fruits, works great in sauces, is a wonderful baking ingredient, makes a yummy addition to soups and casseroles, and transforms into delicious dressings and dips.

Chai Smoothie

If you're a fan of Chai tea, you're gonna love this smoothie! It can be a great treat or mid-day pick-me-up. You don't have to worry about dairy in this recipe because it's made specifically with LI in mind—hence the soy milk!

1. Pour the soy milk into a blender. Add banana, cinnamon, cardamom, coriander, cloves, black pepper, honey, and ice.

2. Blend on high speed until smooth.

3. Serve immediately with fruit garnish, if desired.

Frozen Tea Ice Cubes

If you want to add to the flavor of the Chai in this smoothie, prepare Chai tea and freeze it in ice cube trays. Use the Chai cubes in place of regular ice cubes in this smoothie so as not to dilute the great Chai flavor!

Serves 1

Calories: 282.88
Fat: 4.42 grams
Saturated Fat: 0.66 grams
Carbohydrates: 56.74 grams
Calcium: 375.56 mg
Lactose: 0.0 grams

1 cup soy milk
1 banana, cut in chunks
½ teaspoon ground cinnamon
⅛ teaspoon ground cardamom
⅛ teaspoon ground coriander
⅛ teaspoon ground cloves
⅛ teaspoon ground black pepper
1 tablespoon honey
6 ice cubes

Blueberry Banana Nog

The apple and the apple juice in this nog add a bit of natural sweetness to this purple-hued nog. Not peeling the apple keeps in those all-important nutrients that your body will make such good use of!

Serves 4

Calories: 134.39
Fat: 0.52 grams
Saturated Fat: 0.12 grams
Carbohydrates: 34.26 grams
Calcium: 13.56 mg
Lactose: 0.0 grams

2 bananas
½ cup frozen blueberries
1 cored, unpeeled red apple
1¼ cups apple juice
2 ice cubes

1. Combine all ingredients in blender. Blend until smooth.

2. Pour into serving glasses and serve immediately.

Frozen Bananas

Ripe bananas are perfect for blending. Before they get too old, peel them, put them into a resealable plastic bag, and pop them in the freezer. Frozen bananas are perfect for nogs and smoothies. If you use a frozen banana you won't need ice cubes, which dilute the flavor. Also, you'll find you don't waste bananas if you freeze them!

Kiwi Starter

If you don't have fresh pineapple, you can substitute drained, canned pineapple chunks in this recipe. The flavor will still be yummy, but fresh is always best.

Serves 4

Calories: 119.87
Fat: 0.58 grams
Saturated Fat: 0.06 grams
Carbohydrates: 29.92 grams
Calcium: 34.32 mg
Lactose: 0.0 grams

3 sliced kiwi fruit
1 cup fresh pineapple chunks
1 banana
1 cup tropical fruit juice
2 ice cubes

1. Combine all ingredients in blender. Blend until smooth.

2. Pour into glasses and serve immediately.

Almond Peach Nog

This is not only delicious but is also a beautiful peachy colored drink. Some folks with LI like the taste of almond milk better than soy milk—you make the call!

1. Pour almond milk into a blender. Add peaches, honey, vanilla and almond extracts, and top with ice.

2. Blend on high speed until smooth.

3. Serve with a fresh peach slice perched on the side of the glass.

Beta-Carotene Points

Peaches are a great source of beta carotene, which is a carotenoid that converts to vitamin A. By changing to vitamin A, beta carotene is a high performer in your overall health. As an antioxidant vitamin, it provides protection from disease and the degenerative aspects of aging.

Serves 1

Calories: 218.50
Fat: 3.73 grams
Saturated Fat: 0.06 grams
Carbohydrates: 47.35 grams
Calcium: 218.90 mg
Lactose: 0.0 grams

1 cup almond milk
2 large ripe peaches, peeled, pitted and diced
1 tablespoon honey or to taste
1 teaspoon pure vanilla extract
½ teaspoon pure almond extract
6 ice cubes
Fresh peach slices for garnish (optional)

Berry Jumble Smoothie

Fresh berries can always be substituted for frozen; however, you may actually prefer frozen berries. They make the smoothie thicker. And look at the calci-yum counts on this one—score!

Serves 2

Calories: 235.13
Fat: 3.75 grams
Saturated Fat: 1.43 grams
Carbohydrates: 48.17 grams
Calcium: 118.46 mg
Lactose: 0.0 grams

½ cup soy milk
½ cup plain yogurt
½ cup frozen blueberries
½ cup frozen raspberries
½ cup frozen blackberries
1 frozen banana, cut in chunks
Orange slices for garnish (optional)

1. Pour soy milk into a blender. Add yogurt, berries, and banana.

2. Blend on high speed until smooth.

3. Garnish with orange slices as desired and serve immediately.

Deluxe Daybreak Smoothie

This breakfast smoothie makes you feel like you're pampering yourself when it's actually packed with a ton of stuff that's really good for you!

Serves 4

Calories: 129.01
Fat: 3.13 grams
Saturated Fat: 0.66 grams
Carbohydrates: 21.75 grams
Calcium: 70.00 mg
Lactose: 0.0 grams

½ mango, cut in chunks
2 tablespoons oat bran
2 cups soy milk
2 tablespoons honey
¼ cup yogurt

1. Blend all ingredients together in blender until smooth.

2. Pour into glasses and serve with a spoon.

Breaking the Fast with Breakfast

Do your body and mind a big favor and don't skip breakfast—ever! Replenishing your body's blood sugar stores in the morning will help you sustain not only your physical activities throughout the day but also the mental work that you need to perform. It also improves concentration!

Pear Nog

Nogs are so versatile that you can use any of your favorite juices, nectars, or fruits. This one is just for you pear lovers!

1. Combine all ingredients in blender.

2. Process about 30 seconds or until smooth. Serve immediately.

Serves 2

Calories: 219.24
Fat: 3.71 grams
Saturated Fat: 2.38 grams
Carbohydrates: 44.69 grams
Calcium: 149.83 mg
Lactose: 0.0 grams

2 cups chilled pear nectar
1 8-ounce carton plain yogurt
¼ teaspoon almond extract

Nutty Straw-Nana Nog

This is a creamy and delicious nog that will even satisfy your sweet tooth. How can something so good for you also be loaded with lots of protein, minerals, and vitamins—but zero lactose? Double yum!

1. Combine all ingredients except strawberry in blender. Blend on high for 30 seconds.

2. Garnish with a whole strawberry if desired and serve immediately.

Serves 2

Calories: 271.05
Fat: 8.67 grams
Saturated Fat: 1.49 grams
Carbohydrates: 42.89 grams
Calcium: 82.45 mg
Lactose: 0.0 grams

1 banana
1 cup soy milk
1 cup orange juice
10 strawberries, sliced
4 teaspoons natural peanut butter
Whole strawberries for garnish (optional)

Peanut Butter Banana Flip

Serves 2

Calories: 218.30
Fat: 10.64 grams
Saturated Fat: 2.01 grams
Carbohydrates: 24.70 grams
Calcium: 56.83 mg
Lactose: 0.0 grams

1 cup soy milk
2 tablespoons natural peanut butter
1 teaspoon pure vanilla extract
1 frozen banana, cut into chunks
6 ice cubes

Small kids, medium kids, big kids, and adults love peanut butter and bananas together. Here's a great tasting and energizing smoothie for a snack or a morning boost. And this one has zero tolerance for lactose!

1. Pour soy milk into blender. Add peanut butter, vanilla, banana, and ice cubes.

2. Blend on high speed until smooth and serve immediately.

Read Those Labels!

Read the labels on those peanut butter jars to see how much salt or sugar has been added to enhance the flavor—and diminish the nutritional value!

Banana Fig Nog

Serves 3

Calories: 186.04
Fat: 5.92 grams
Saturated Fat: 1.07 grams
Carbohydrates: 31.17 grams
Calcium: 64.87 mg
Lactose: 0.0 grams

1 cup soy milk
6 fresh ripe small black figs, cut in half
1 medium frozen banana, cut in chunks
3 tablespoons roasted cashews
1 teaspoon pure vanilla extract
½ teaspoon ground nutmeg
4–6 ice cubes

Variety is the spice of life—and that includes a variety of fruits. There are so many ways for you to have a lip-smacking variety of recipes that don't aggravate your LI!

1. Pour the soy milk into blender. Add figs, banana, cashews, vanilla, nutmeg, and ice cubes.

2. Blend until smooth and serve immediately.

Orange Coconut Dreamsicle-in-a-Glass

If you want to enhance the delight of this delectable Dreamsicle-in-a-Glass, freeze some orange juice ice cubes ahead of time. Use the juice ice cubes in place of the plain ol' ones. And remember when you're buying orange juice to look for the calcium-fortified variety.

Serves 3

Calories: 201.09
Fat: 7.39 grams
Saturated Fat: 5.11 grams
Carbohydrates: 31.69 grams
Calcium: 107.84 mg
Lactose: 0.0 grams

2 oranges, peeled, cut into chunks
1 cup soy milk
½ cup grated coconut
2 teaspoons pure vanilla extract
2 teaspoons honey
6 ice cubes

1. Place orange chunks into blender and blend on high to break up. Add milk and blend oranges and milk together just until combined.

2. Add coconut, vanilla, honey, and ice cubes.

3. Blend on high speed until smooth. Serve immediately.

Beyond Bones and Teeth

Calcium is crucial to building strong bones and teeth, but it's responsible for so much more. It helps your blood clot, your heart keep beating, and your nervous system send messages. Unfortunately, being LI makes it a challenge to get as much calcium as your body needs. Smoothies and nogs are the perfect way to combat this shortage.

Tropical Soy Nog

*Be sure to peel your papaya before you cut it into chunks
and throw it in the blender—the skin isn't edible!*

Serves 1

Calories: 177.45
Fat: 3.82 grams
Saturated Fat: 0.52 grams
Carbohydrates: 29.66 grams
Calcium: 120.22 mg
Lactose: 0.0 grams

*¾ cup soy milk
1½ cups papaya, cut in
    chunks and frozen
1½ teaspoons fresh lemon
    zest
1 teaspoon pure vanilla
    extract*

Pour soy milk into blender. Add peeled papaya, lemon zest, and vanilla. Blend on high speed until smooth and serve immediately.

Papaya Trivia

Papayas can grow to weigh up to 20 pounds! Now that's some fruit. It's deliciously tart, yet its sweet flavor complements many dishes. The papaya is a great addition to tossed salads, and you can use it as a base in refreshing smoothies for breakfast or an energy drink.

Fruity Yogurt Smoothie

*Why not experiment with frozen tea ice cubes? Just make
your favorite flavored tea and make it into ice cubes—it will
add flavor to your LI-healthy and calcium-fortified smoothie!*

Serves 2

Calories: 231.07
Fat: 1.79 grams
Saturated Fat: 0.90 grams
Carbohydrates: 49.68 grams
Calcium: 188.37 mg
Lactose: 0.0 grams

*1 cup orange juice
1 cup fruit-flavored yogurt
1 frozen banana
4 ice cubes*

1. Combine all ingredients in blender.

2. Mix well until smooth. Serve immediately.

Chapter 3
Bountiful Breakfasts

Fresh Mushroom Scramble

*Simple and fresh ingredients come together to create this
tasty and satisfying breakfast scramble. If you'd like it to be totally
free of anything that reads "milk," simply leave out the soy milk!
The consistency of the eggs will change just a tad.*

Serves 4

Calories: 207.84
Fat: 12.58 grams
Saturated Fat: 3.46 grams
Carbohydrates: 5.31 grams
Calcium: 71.67 mg
Lactose: 0.13 grams

4 egg whites
8 whole eggs
2 tablespoons soy milk
Salt and pepper to taste
*2 tablespoons Worcestershire
sauce*
2 small cloves garlic, crushed
2 teaspoons olive oil
*12 fresh mushrooms, washed
and stemmed*
*2 tablespoons chopped
parsley*
*Freshly ground pepper
to taste*

1. Lightly whisk the egg whites in a large bowl. Add the whole eggs and soy milk and whisk until combined. Season lightly with salt and pepper.

2. Combine the Worcestershire sauce, garlic, and olive oil. Brush the mushrooms lightly with the Worcestershire sauce mixture, then grill or broil on medium heat for 5–7 minutes or until soft. Remove and keep warm.

3. Heat a nonstick frying pan and add the egg mixture, scraping the bottom gently with a flat plastic spatula to cook evenly. Cook until the egg is just set.

4. To serve, divide the scrambled eggs and mushrooms among four serving plates. Sprinkle the eggs with the chopped parsley and freshly ground pepper. Serve immediately.

Spinach Omelet

The Parmesan cheese enhances the flavor of this omelet. The harmony of spinach and eggs makes this omelet not only pretty to look at but tasty and pleasing to even an LI tummy!

Serves 6

Calories: 168.79
Fat: 11.02 grams
Saturated Fat: 3.57 grams
Carbohydrates: 3.46 grams
Calcium: 164.34 mg
Lactose: 0.10 grams

1 10-ounce package frozen chopped spinach, thawed and undrained
3 tablespoons chicken broth
1 clove garlic, crushed
⅛ to ¼ teaspoon pepper
¼ cup grated Parmesan cheese
10 eggs
2 tablespoons water
2 teaspoons margarine, divided
Nonstick cooking spray

1. Combine spinach, broth, garlic, and pepper in a small saucepan; cover and simmer 20 minutes. Stir in Parmesan cheese; cook 1 minute or until cheese is melted, stirring constantly. Set aside.

2. Combine eggs and water; beat lightly. Coat a 10" omelet pan or heavy skillet with cooking spray; add 1 teaspoon margarine. Place pan over medium heat until just hot enough to sizzle a drop of water.

3. Pour half of egg mixture into pan. As mixture starts to cook, gently lift edges of omelet with a spatula and tilt pan so uncooked portion flows underneath.

4. As mixture begins to set, spread half the spinach mixture over half the omelet. Loosen omelet with a spatula; fold in half and slide onto a warm serving platter.

5. Repeat procedure with remaining ingredients.

Spinach Rating

Spinach is a great source of vitamins A and C, and it has lots of minerals, iron, potassium, and beta-carotene. Spinach has a high calcium count as well; however, spinach contains substances called "oxalates" which stop calcium absorption.

Veggie Omelet

Colorful veggies add to the crunch and the appeal of this easy-to-prepare omelet. Keep that rainbow of veggies coming into your LI lifestyle every day. Not only is it an LI-friendly thing to do, but it will also improve your overall health.

Serves 2

Calories: 161.81
Fat: 10.46 grams
Saturated Fat: 2.85 grams
Carbohydrates: 6.61 grams
Calcium: 48.33 mg
Lactose: 0.08 grams

½ cup thinly sliced mushrooms
¼ cup chopped green pepper
¼ cup chopped onion
1 tablespoon diced pimiento
3 eggs at room temperature, separated
2 tablespoons mayonnaise
¼ teaspoon salt
⅛ teaspoon pepper
Nonstick cooking spray

1. Combine mushrooms, green pepper, onion, and pimiento in a 1-quart casserole; cover loosely with heavy-duty plastic wrap and microwave on high for 3 to 3½ minutes or until vegetables are tender. Drain and set aside.

2. Beat egg whites until stiff peaks form. Combine egg yolks, mayonnaise, salt, and pepper; beat well. Gently fold egg whites into egg yolk mixture.

3. Coat a 9" glass pie plate or quiche pan with cooking spray. Pour egg mixture into pie plate, spreading evenly. Microwave at medium (50 percent power) for 8 to 10½ minutes or until center is almost set, giving pie plate a half-turn after 5 minutes.

4. Spread vegetable mixture over half of omelet. Loosen omelet with spatula and fold in half. Gently slide the omelet onto a warm serving platter.

Veggies and Lactose

You will be delighted to know that all fresh veggies and fruits are totally lactose free in their natural state. Grow your own, pick your own, or buy them fresh from the market—it doesn't matter as long as you cook with the freshest fruits and vegetables possible.

Eggs En Cocotte with Tomato Sauce

*En cocotte is French and means cooked in a casserole.
In this case, the casseroles are tiny ramekins. Remember eggs contain
that all-important vitamin D that helps you absorb calcium!*

Serves 4

Calories: 231.70
Fat: 13.15 grams
Saturated Fat: 2.86 grams
Carbohydrates: 19.13 grams
Calcium: 67.30 mg
Lactose: 0.06 grams

*1 tablespoon olive oil
1 clove garlic, crushed
3 vine-ripened tomatoes,
    peeled, seeded and
    chopped
½ teaspoon olive oil
4 eggs
Tabasco sauce to taste
2 tablespoons chives, snipped
    with scissors
Salt and pepper to taste
4 slices thick multigrain bread
1 tablespoon margarine*

1. Preheat the oven to 350°F.

2. To make the sauce, heat 1 tablespoon oil in a heavy frying pan or iron skillet. Add the garlic and cook for 1 minute or until it starts to turn golden. Add tomatoes. Cook over medium heat until thickened, approximately 15 minutes.

3. Grease four ½-cup ramekins with 1 tablespoon olive oil. Break one egg into each, trying not to break the yolk. Pour the tomato sauce evenly around the outside of each egg so the yolk is still visible. Add a little Tabasco sauce and sprinkle with chives. Season lightly with salt and freshly ground black pepper.

4. Place the ramekins in a deep baking tray and pour enough boiling water into the pan to come halfway up the sides of the dishes. Let the eggs bake for 15 minutes for soft eggs and another 3 minutes if you prefer your eggs to be more set. Serve with bread and margarine.

Cheaper by the Dozen

With their low price and high protein, eggs are the best buy around. They come dressed in their own little cases that protect them until you're ready to use them. Best of all, eggs are lactose free and friendly!

Skillet Breakfast

*Skillet meals are quick and easy and you have only one pan to wash.
Potatoes are lactose free and give some heft to this dish.*

1. Sauté chopped pepper and onion in olive oil. Add potatoes and brown slightly.

2. Add tomato and garlic, cooking until mixture is warm.

3. Top with cheese. Serve with eggs of your choice.

Serves 4

Calories: 248.79
Fat: 12.77 grams
Saturated Fat: 2.97 grams
Carbohydrates: 30.44 grams
Calcium: 73.98 mg
Lactose: 0.02 grams

1 bell pepper, chopped
½ onion, chopped
3 tablespoons olive oil
3 medium sized white potatoes, cooked and diced
1 fresh tomato, chopped
1 clove garlic, chopped
¼ cup Cheddar cheese, grated

Breakfast Potatoes

Potatoes are great for breakfast and these will wake up your taste buds as well as your metabolism. There's no lactose in this recipe, so your tummy will be full and happy.

1. Scrub potato and pat dry. Prick several times with a fork. Place potato on paper towel in microwave oven. Microwave on high for 5–6 minutes, turning potato after 3 minutes.

2. Let potato stand 5 minutes to cool before checking for doneness. Cut potato into ¾" cubes and set aside.

3. Place margarine in a 1½-quart casserole. Microwave 30 seconds or until melted.

4. Stir celery salt, paprika, and pepper into margarine. Add potatoes and parsley. Toss all together.

5. Cover with casserole lid. Microwave on high for 2 minutes. Stir before serving.

Serves 2

Calories: 173.69
Fat: 3.87 grams
Saturated Fat: 0.79 grams
Carbohydrates: 31.83 grams
Calcium: 27.67 mg
Lactose: 0.0 grams

1 large baking potato
1½ tablespoons margarine
¼ teaspoon celery salt
¼ teaspoon paprika
⅛ teaspoon pepper
¼ cup finely chopped fresh parsley

Waffles

No wafflin' with this recipe. The flour and cornmeal combo give the waffles a great texture, the old-fashioned rolled oats give them a bit of a crunch, and the egg whites make them almost float away. Top your waffles with 2 teaspoons of blackstrap molasses; the molasses alone meets almost 12 percent of your daily calcium needs.

1. In a large bowl, combine the flour, oats, cornmeal, and baking powder.

2. In another large bowl, whisk the yogurt cheese, water, margarine, and egg whites until well combined. Stir into dry ingredients and allow to stand for 15 minutes.

3. Preheat a 7" waffle iron on medium setting and pour batter to cover about two-thirds of grid. Bake until steam stops escaping. Waffles will be golden in 3 to 4 minutes.

Serves 7

Calories: 335.84
Fat: 9.84 grams
Saturated Fat: 3.05 grams
Carbohydrates: 43.74 grams
Calcium: 258.14 mg
Lactose: 0.07 grams

1 cup all-purpose flour
1 cup old-fashioned rolled oats
½ cup yellow cornmeal
5 teaspoons baking powder
2 cups yogurt cheese
¾ cup water
6 tablespoons melted margarine or oil
3 large egg whites

Strawberry Banana French Toast

This is a show-stopper for a Sunday brunch and pretty enough to be a dessert!

1. Cut a horizontal pocket in the bread. Combine strawberries and mashed banana. Fill pocket with strawberry-banana mixture.

2. Combine eggs, soy milk, and cinnamon. Soak both sides of stuffed bread in milk mixture.

3. Melt butter in a nonstick skillet over medium heat. Cook bread about 3–5 minutes on each side, making sure it is cooked through. Bread will turn golden.

4. Garnish with fresh sliced strawberries if desired.

Serves 1

Calories: 301.00
Fat: 8.45 grams
Saturated Fat: 3.22 grams
Carbohydrates: 48.37 grams
Calcium: 89.96 mg
Lactose: 0.03 grams

2" thick slice of whole grain bread
⅓ cup sliced strawberries
½ banana, mashed
2 eggs, beaten
¼ cup soy milk
½ teaspoon cinnamon or to taste
1 tablespoon butter
Strawberries for garnish (optional)

Buckwheat Pancakes

Yields 12 pancakes

Calories: 342.64
Fat: 10.33 grams
Saturated Fat: 1.05 grams
Carbohydrates: 54.70 grams
Calcium: 80.55 mg
Lactose: 0.0 grams

1 cup buckwheat flour
1 cup unbleached white flour
2 teaspoons baking powder
1 teaspoon baking soda
½ teaspoon salt
½ pound soft tofu
2½ cups water
2 tablespoons oil
2 tablespoons honey

1. In a large mixing bowl, combine buckwheat flour, white flour, baking powder, baking soda, and salt.

2. In a blender, combine tofu, water, oil, and honey. Blend together until mixture reaches a smooth consistency. Make a well in dry ingredients and pour in contents from blender. Stir until ingredients are just combined; there will be lumps, but don't worry about them.

3. Heat griddle or large skillet over medium-high heat. Lightly oil. Pour ¼ cup batter onto griddle for each pancake.

4. The tops of the pancakes will bubble and begin to look dry when it's time to flip them over. Flip and brown the other side 2 minutes or until golden.

5. Serve hot with warm syrup, your favorite fruit sauce, or fruit preserves.

Stack 'Em

A pancake stack makes a deliciously edible centerpiece for a brunch or special breakfast. Place a large hot pancake on a warm serving dish and spread generously with your choice of filling. Repeat, using 4 or 5 pancakes. Top with fruit sauce that will run down the sides, fresh blueberries, and a large dollop of nondairy whipped topping.

German-Style Apple Pancakes

It just doesn't get any easier or more scrumptious than these fresh apple pancakes.

❧

1. Preheat oven to 450°F.

2. Combine apples, sugar, cinnamon, and lemon juice in a bowl. Toss to coat the apples. Melt 2 tablespoons of margarine in a large, heavy-bottomed pan over medium-high heat. Add the apple mixture and sauté the apples for 6 minutes or until just soft.

3. Place the remaining 3 tablespoons of margarine in an 8" × 11" × 2" baking dish. Put baking dish in the oven until the margarine is melted. Spread apples evenly over the bottom of the dish.

4. Prepare the batter by whisking together the eggs and soy milk in a bowl until well blended. Add flour and salt. Stir until just combined. The batter will be slightly lumpy. Slowly pour batter over apples.

5. Bake for about 20 minutes or until the pancake is golden brown and puffed. Sprinkle with confectioners' sugar. Cut into pieces and serve immediately with warm maple syrup.

Serves 4

Calories: 384.10
Fat: 19.37 grams
Saturated Fat: 10.44 grams
Carbohydrates: 44.95 grams
Calcium: 51.40 mg
Lactose: 0.04 grams

1 pound Granny Smith apples, peeled, cored, and thinly sliced
3 tablespoons sugar
½ teaspoon cinnamon
2 tablespoons freshly squeezed lemon juice
5 tablespoons margarine
3 large eggs
¾ cup vanilla soy milk
¾ cup flour
¼ teaspoon salt
Confectioners' sugar
Maple syrup, warmed

Cocoa Pancakes

Calories: 260.47
Fat: 9.91 grams
Saturated Fat: 5.21 grams
Carbohydrates: 40.01 grams
Calcium: 65.34 mg
Lactose: 0.0 grams

*1½ cups whole wheat pastry
flour*
*½ cup unsweetened cocoa
powder*
*2 tablespoons granulated
sugar*
1 teaspoon baking powder
½ teaspoon baking soda
½ teaspoon salt
2 cups chocolate soy milk
1 tablespoon vegetable oil
1½ teaspoons vanilla extract
½ cup carob chips

*Who said that you can't satisfy your chocolate craving without
suffering with your LI! If you're not a fan of carob chips, there are
some decadent chocolate chips on the market that are definitely
lactose free, so do your homework if you want the real thing!*

1. Sift flour, cocoa, sugar, baking powder, baking soda, and salt into mixing bowl. Add chocolate soy milk and oil, whisking until just combined. Stir in vanilla extract. Let batter sit 5 minutes before cooking.

2. Spray a large nonstick skillet with cooking spray. Heat skillet over medium heat. Pour ¼ cup batter on skillet for each pancake. Sprinkle pancakes with carob chips if desired.

3. Cook for 2 minutes, turning when tops begin to bubble and edges begin looking dry. Cook 2 minutes more and remove from skillet, placing on a warm plate. Serve with syrup or yogurt and fresh fruit.

Cocoa and Antioxidants

The word cocoa *doesn't necessarily bring healthy thoughts to mind. Well, the fact is that 1 tablespoon of cocoa powder contains as many antioxidants as ⅔ cup of fresh blueberries. Cocoa contains more antioxidants than green tea and red wine!*

Tart Apricot Syrup

Shock your taste buds with this tart syrup!

1. Combine chopped dried apricots and 1 cup water in a small saucepan. Bring to a boil, cover, and simmer for 20 minutes.

2. Allow to cool. Whip contents in a blender. Add 1½ cups of water or enough to reach syrup consistency.

3. Store in refrigerator.

Yields 3 cups

Calories: 39.16
Fat: 0.08 grams
Saturated Fat: 0.0 grams
Carbohydrates: 10.18 grams
Calcium: 8.94 mg
Lactose: 0.0 grams

1 cup chopped dried apricots
2½ cups water

Blueberry Syrup

Venture away from the usual maple syrup with this easy homemade blueberry syrup.

1. Combine sugar and cornstarch in a saucepan. Stir in boiling water. Cook over medium heat until mixture comes to a full boil, stirring constantly.

2. Reduce heat and simmer for 1 minute, stirring constantly. Remove from heat. Fold in blueberries and lemon juice.

3. Serve warm or chilled.

Fruit . . . Naturally

Fruit is naturally sweet. When you're making syrups and sauces, try to use fresh fruit whenever possible. Frozen unsweetened fruit or canned fruit packed in its own juice are good runners-up. All of these options help reduce the intake of both sugar and calories.

Yields 2¼ cups

Calories: 39.53
Fat: 0.24 grams
Saturated Fat: 0.02 grams
Carbohydrates: 9.79 grams
Calcium: 3.17 mg
Lactose: 0.0 grams

¼ cup sugar
1 tablespoon plus 1½
   teaspoons cornstarch
1¼ cups boiling water
1 16-ounce package frozen
   unsweetened blueberries,
   thawed and drained
1 tablespoon lemon juice

Pineapple Syrup

This is a very sweet syrup that your sweet tooth is sure to love.
Watching calories is always important, so make a little go a long way!

Yields 2½ cups

Calories: 42.39
Fat: 0.09 grams
Saturated Fat: 0.01 grams
Carbohydrates: 11.18 grams
Calcium: 6.63 mg
Lactose: 0.0 grams

1 cup dried pineapple
2 cups water

1. Combine the dried pineapple with 1 cup water in a small saucepan. Bring to a boil and simmer, covered, for 20 minutes. Remove from heat and cool.

2. Whip contents in blender and add 1 cup of water. Blend to syrup consistency. Add more water sparingly, until desired syrup consistency is reached.

3. Store covered in refrigerator.

Strawberry Sauce

Strawberries are a favorite, so spread this sauce around! This sauce
has it all—great taste and lots of vitamin C and folic acid.

Yields 1⅓ cups

Calories: 31.49
Fat: 0.21 grams
Saturated Fat: 0.01 grams
Carbohydrates: 7.66 grams
Calcium: 11.15 mg
Lactose: 0.0 grams

3 cups fresh strawberries,
*   halved*
2 tablespoons orange juice
*   concentrate*
1 tablespoon sugar
1 teaspoon grated orange
*   rind*
½ teaspoon grated lemon
*   rind*

1. Place all ingredients in blender. Process until smooth, scraping sides as necessary.

2. Pour mixture in a small bowl. Cover and thoroughly chill.

Fresh!

This recipe is very versatile. Spooned over waffles with a dollop of yogurt and topped with a whole fresh strawberry, it turns an everyday waffle into an LI celebration with zero grams of lactose. This same fresh sauce is great on meringues and as a dip for other fruits.

Chapter 4
Quick Breads and Muffins

Nutty Bran Bread

*Blackstrap molasses gives the bread a sassy sweetness
and bones up your calcium at the same time!*

Yields 2 loaves

Calories: 108.98
Fat: 3.26 grams
Saturated Fat: 0.36 grams
Carbohydrates: 17.56 grams
Calcium: 15.34 mg
Lactose: 0.0 grams

2 tablespoons yeast
1½ cups warm water
4 tablespoons olive oil
*1 tablespoon blackstrap
    molasses*
½ cup soy milk
4 cups unbleached white flour
1 cup whole wheat flour
1 cup bran cereal
1 tablespoon sugar
1 tablespoon salt
½ cup walnuts

1. Preheat oven to 400°F.

2. Dissolve yeast in warm water. Add olive oil, molasses, and soy milk, mixing well.

3. Combine dry ingredients and walnuts. Add molasses mixture and knead for at least 20 minutes.

4. Round up dough in greased bowl. Let dough rise in warm place until double. Punch down, divide into 2 loaves.

5. Flatten dough and roll up into loaf shapes. Place in loaf pans. Let rise until double. Bake for 30 minutes.

Whole Wheat Flour

Whole wheat flour is natural and made from whole wheat. It isn't bleached and retains its golden brown color. Unlike other processed flours, whole wheat flour contains all the wheat germ and bran of the original grain. A heavy flour, it can be lightened by simply whisking it or sifting it.

Whole Wheat Banana Bread

This recipe adds a bit of a healthy crunch to a long-time favorite. It's a tasty breakfast on the run with some fresh fruit, and a snack to look forward to. This particular recipe is lactose friendly and a real energy booster!

Yields 1 loaf

Calories: 131.77
Fat: 4.57 grams
Saturated Fat: 0.54 grams
Carbohydrates: 20.99 grams
Calcium: 10.58 mg
Lactose: 0.01 grams

2 cups whole wheat flour
¼ cup wheat germ
1 teaspoon baking soda
½ teaspoon salt
1½ cups mashed ripe banana
¼ cup oil
¼ cup honey
2 eggs
1 teaspoon vanilla extract
Nonstick cooking spray

1. Preheat oven to 350°F.

2. In a large bowl combine flour, wheat germ, baking soda, and salt. Make a well in center of mixture.

3. Combine banana, oil, honey, eggs, and vanilla. Add to dry ingredients. Stir together until just moistened.

4. Coat a 9" × 5" × 3" loaf pan with cooking spray. Spoon batter into pan. Bake for 60 minutes or until a wooden pick inserted in center comes out clean.

Grains Give Your Body Fuel

Not only do grains supply your body with fuel, they're packed with fiber, iron, and B vitamins. Whole grains are the most nutritious. When you're baking, substitute different whole grain flours in your recipes. Incorporate them slowly by substituting ½ cup of whole grain flour for ½ cup all-purpose flour.

Zucchini Carrot Bread

Yields 2 loaves

Calories: 171.55
Fat: 9.72 grams
Saturated Fat: 0.78 grams
Carbohydrates: 19.42 grams
Calcium: 17.79 mg
Lactose: 0.01 grams

3 eggs
1 cup oil
1½ cups brown sugar, packed
1 cup zucchini, grated,
    squeezed, and tightly
    packed
1 cup carrots, grated
2 teaspoons vanilla
2½ cups all-purpose flour
1 teaspoon baking soda
1 teaspoon baking powder
1 teaspoon salt
3 teaspoons cinnamon
½ cup bran cereal
1 cup chopped nuts

The water content of fresh zucchini makes this bread incredibly moist while the grated carrots add a natural sweetness. This recipe is healthy and LI friendly. Try substituting a portion of the all-purpose flour with a whole grain flour of your choice for added crunch, not to mention nutrition!

1. Preheat oven to 350°F.

2. Prepare two 9" × 5" loaf pans by greasing well. Set aside. Beat eggs together with oil in a large mixing bowl. Stir in sugar, zucchini, carrot, and vanilla.

3. Sift together flour, baking soda, baking powder, salt, and cinnamon. Gradually add dry mixture into zucchini mixture, beating after each addition. Blend remaining ingredients into mixture, adding nuts and bran cereal last.

4. Bake 1 to 1½ hours or until top splits and is golden brown.

Pumpkin Applesauce Bread

*This bread is bursting with flavor, crunch, and moistness.
It's sure to become a favorite breakfast and snack bread.*

1. Preheat oven to 350°F.

2. Combine sugar, molasses, pumpkin, applesauce, oil, eggs, and yogurt in a large mixing bowl. Beat at medium speed using an electric mixer.

3. Sift flour, baking powder, baking soda, cinnamon, and nutmeg together. Add gradually to first mixture, beating after each addition. Add vanilla, nuts, and raisins. Mix well.

4. Pour into two well-greased 9" × 5" loaf pans. Bake for 60 minutes.

5. Cool in pans for 10 minutes and then remove from pans. Wrap in foil and store overnight for best flavor.

Playing with Ingredients

If you don't care for raisins, add dates instead! Combine whole wheat flour with unbleached flour for a different consistency. Don't be afraid to be adventurous in your cooking and baking! In your additions and subtractions, try substituting blackstrap molasses for sugar as often as you can to sweeten the recipes in your LI lifestyle.

Yields 2 loaves

Calories: 205.63
Fat: 7.60 grams
Saturated Fat: 0.69 grams
Carbohydrates: 32.39 grams
Calcium: 22.00 mg
Lactose: 0.01 grams

2 cups sugar
⅓ cup blackstrap molasses
1 cup canned pumpkin
1 cup applesauce
⅔ cup oil
3 eggs
⅓ cup yogurt
3⅔ cups flour
1½ teaspoons baking powder
2 teaspoons baking soda
2 teaspoons cinnamon
1 teaspoon nutmeg
1 teaspoon vanilla
1 cup chopped nuts
1 cup raisins

Oatmeal Poppy Seed Bread

*This is a delicious and nutritious bread that makes a great
healthy snack with an extra treat of poppy seeds tucked in!*

Yields 2 loaves

Calories: 99.38
Fat: 2.09 grams
Saturated Fat: 0.36 grams
Carbohydrates: 17.79 grams
Calcium: 13.75 mg
Lactose: 0.0 grams

*1 cup plus 3 tablespoons
    rolled oats*
¼ cup molasses
¼ cup margarine
2 teaspoons salt
1½ cups water
1 tablespoon poppyseeds
1 package dry yeast
¼ cup warm water
3 cups whole wheat flour
1¼ cups all-purpose flour

1. Preheat oven to 375°F. Grease a large baking sheet with sides and sprinkle lightly with 1 tablespoon oats. Set aside.

2. Using a heavy-bottomed large pan, combine molasses, margarine, salt, and water and bring to a boil. Combine 1 cup oats and poppy seeds in a heat-proof bowl. Pour boiling mixture over oats and poppy seeds. Let cool to room temperature, stirring occasionally. Dissolve the yeast in the warm water and add to the oat mixture when cool.

3. Combine flours and add to oat mixture. Turn onto a floured board and knead vigorously 6–8 minutes. Place in a greased bowl, cover, and let rise in a warm place until doubled in volume, about 60 minutes. Turn out onto a lightly floured surface. Knead dough well. Divide into two equal pieces.

4. Shape bread into long, pointed ovals. Place on prepared baking sheet. Chop 2 tablespoons of oats and sprinkle over the tops of the loaves. Cover loosely with waxed paper and set aside to let rise again, just short of doubling.

5. Slash each loaf diagonally 4 times with a very sharp knife. Bake for 45 minutes. The oatmeal on top will be crispy and browned.

Irish Soda Bread

This bread is best if you eat the whole thing the day that it is made! It doesn't store well, so make a big pot of soup to enjoy with fresh baked bread.

Yields 1 loaf

Calories: 125.95
Fat: 0.75 grams
Saturated Fat: 0.10 grams
Carbohydrates: 24.98 grams
Calcium: 13.50 mg
Lactose: 0.0 grams

1½ cups soy milk
1½ tablespoons white vinegar
4 cups unbleached all-purpose flour
1½ teaspoons salt
1 teaspoon baking soda
½ teaspoon baking powder

1. Preheat oven to 375°F. Lightly oil a baking sheet and set aside.

2. Measure soy milk in a large measuring cup. Add vinegar and set aside.

3. Combine flour, salt, baking soda, and baking powder in a large bowl. Mix until well blended. Add the milk mixture a little at a time to make a soft dough that isn't too sticky. Knead on a floured surface, just until dough is smooth, about 3 minutes. Shape dough into a round loaf.

4. Using a sharp knife, cut an "X" in the top. Place loaf on prepared baking sheet. Bake on center oven rack about 45 minutes or until golden brown.

Apple Raisin Bread

This bread freezes very well and is a great breakfast bread toasted or warmed quickly in the microwave. Need something to tide you over in the middle of the afternoon? Take a slice of this bread with you and have it with a cup of afternoon tea.

Yields 2 loaves

Calories: 214.79
Fat: 10.44 grams
Saturated Fat: 0.89 grams
Carbohydrates: 28.82 grams
Calcium: 8.63 mg
Lactose: 0.01 grams

3 cups flour
2½ cups sugar
1¼ cups oil
4 eggs, beaten
1 tablespoon plus 1 teaspoon vanilla
2 teaspoons cinnamon
1½ teaspoons salt
1½ teaspoons baking soda
1 teaspoon ground cloves
1½ teaspoons baking powder
3 cup chopped, unpeeled apples
⅔ cup raisins
½ cup chopped nuts

1. Preheat oven to 325°F. Lightly grease bottoms of two 9" × 5" × 3" baking pans.

2. Combine all ingredients except apples, raisins, and nuts in mixer bowl. Beat on low speed, scraping bowl, for 1 minute. Beat on medium speed for another minute. Fold in apples, raisins, and nuts. Pour into prepared pans.

3. Bake about 60 minutes or until wooden toothpick inserted in center comes out clean. Cool 10 minutes and remove from pans. Refrigerate to store.

Orange Blueberry Bread

The combination of grated orange peel and blueberries will wake up your taste buds for sure.

Yields 1 loaf

Calories: 186.49
Fat: 6.53 grams
Saturated Fat: 1.13 grams
Carbohydrates: 30.32 grams
Calcium: 12.30 mg
Lactose: 0.0 grams

Nonstick cooking spray
1 cup blueberries
1¾ cups plus 2 tablespoons whole grain pastry flour
¼ cup cornmeal
1½ teaspoon baking powder
½ teaspoon baking soda
½ teaspoon salt
¾ cup sugar
6 tablespoons soft margarine
1 large egg
½ cup orange juice
2 tablespoons grated orange peel

1. Preheat oven to 350°F. Coat an 9" × 5" loaf pan with cooking spray. Set aside.

2. Mix blueberries with 2 tablespoons of the flour in a small bowl. Set aside. Mix remaining 1¾ cups flour, cornmeal, baking powder, baking soda, and salt in a medium bowl. Set aside.

3. Place sugar and margarine in a large mixing bowl. Beat for 3 minutes on high with an electric mixer until light and fluffy. Add egg and beat well. Continue beating and add orange juice and orange peel. Place mixer on low speed, adding flour mixture gradually and blending well. Fold in blueberries.

4. Pour into prepared loaf pan. Bake about 60 minutes or until wooden toothpick comes out clean when inserted in center. Cool on wire rack for 5 minutes in pan. Remove pan and place back on wire rack to cool completely.

Whole Wheat Pastry Flour

If you haven't baked with whole wheat pastry flour, you're in for a treat! It feels almost like silk when you rub it between your fingers. It makes your home baking adventures light and airy. You may have to add a bit of unbleached white flour or regular whole wheat flour if the consistency of your dough isn't quite right.

Corn Muffins

Corny muffins! These are delicious served warm with a hot bowl of soup. The moist texture yogurt cheese adds is a little different and quite delightful. The brown sugar adds a bit of sweetness.

1. Preheat oven to 425°F. Prepare 12 muffin cups with paper liners.

2. In a large bowl, combine cornmeal, flour, sugar, baking powder, and salt. Set aside.

3. Combine yogurt cheese, egg whites, oil, and water in a small bowl, whisking until well blended. Add to dry ingredients, stirring until just moistened.

4. Fill muffin cups about three-fourths full. Bake 15–18 minutes or until golden brown.

Yields 12 muffins

Calories: 157.41
Fat: 5.53 grams
Saturated Fat: 0.80 grams
Carbohydrates: 21.93 grams
Calcium: 57.82 mg
Lactose: 0.0 grams

1 cup yellow cornmeal
1 cup all-purpose flour
3 tablespoons light brown sugar
1 tablespoon baking powder
¼ teaspoon salt
¾ cup yogurt cheese
2 egg whites
¼ cup oil
¼ cup water

Whole Wheat Muffins

Anything in the ingredients list that doesn't strike your fancy? Take it out or substitute it with something else. These whole wheat muffins are like nothing you've had before!

1. Preheat oven to 400°F. Prepare miniature muffin pan with paper muffin cups.

2. Combine flours, baking powder, baking soda, caraway seeds, poppyseeds, salt, and walnuts in a medium bowl. Set aside.

3. In a small bowl, combine yogurt cheese, water, egg whites, oil, and honey. Whisk until well blended. Add to dry ingredients stirring until just moistened.

4. Spoon into muffin cups and bake for 15 minutes.

Yields 12 muffins

Calories: 74.17
Fat: 2.88 grams
Saturated Fat: 0.46 grams
Carbohydrates: 9.06 grams
Calcium: 38.82 mg
Lactose: 0.0 grams

½ cup whole wheat flour
⅓ cup all-purpose flour
1 teaspoon baking powder
¼ teaspoon baking soda
¼ teaspoon caraway seeds
½ teaspoon poppy seeds
¼ teaspoon salt
3 tablespoons chopped walnuts, optional
½ cup yogurt cheese
2 tablespoons water
2 egg whites
1 tablespoon oil
1 tablespoon honey

Lemon Ginger Poppy Seed Muffins

Don't be surprised if strangers knock on your front door when you're baking these fragrant muffins! With the freshly squeezed lemon juice and fresh ginger you'll be delighted with their fresh taste.

Yields 10 muffins

Calories: 199.51
Fat: 6.26 grams
Saturated Fat: 1.15 grams
Carbohydrates: 30.86 grams
Calcium: 20.55 mg
Lactose: 0.01 grams

2 cups flour
1 tablespoon baking powder
½ teaspoon baking soda
¼ teaspoon salt
½ cup sugar
2 tablespoons poppy seeds
3 tablespoons grated fresh ginger
2 large eggs
1 cup soy milk
1 tablespoon freshly squeezed lemon juice
¼ cup margarine, melted and cooled
2 tablespoons chopped lemon zest

1. Preheat the oven to 400°F. Baking rack in oven should be in the center position. Line muffin tins with paper muffin cups. Set aside.

2. In a large bowl, combine flour, baking powder, baking soda, salt, sugar, poppy seeds, and ginger. Mix together with a whisk until blended.

3. In another bowl, whisk together eggs, soy milk, lemon juice, margarine, and zest until well blended. Gently stir egg mixture into flour mixture until just combined. Batter will be lumpy.

4. Spoon the batter into prepared muffin tins, filling each cup two-thirds full. Bake 20 minutes until golden brown.

5. Let cool for about 10 minutes in pan then remove from pan and let cool completely on a wire rack.

Poppy Seed Trivia

And you thought those little black specs were just that! Poppy seeds are a source of calcium and magnesium and may help prevent high blood pressure and osteoporosis. Osteoporosis is always a concern but more so when paired with lactose intolerance. Go poppy seeds!

Blueberry Muffins

How low can you go? This healthy remake of a classic favorite contains only 0.01 grams of lactose. Lots of family favorite recipes can be updated very easily with substitutions that make sense for you and your family.

1. Preheat oven to 350°F. Prepare muffin pan with large paper muffin cups.

2. Sift flour and sugar together in a bowl. Add egg, soy milk, and oil. Beat well. Fold in blueberries.

3. Spoon mixture into muffin cups. Bake for 20–25 minutes until risen and golden. Place on a wire rack to slightly cool. Serve warm.

Yields 8 muffins

Calories: 224.91
Fat: 7.40 grams
Saturated Fat: 0.90 grams
Carbohydrates: 36.06 grams
Calcium: 34.19 mg
Lactose: 0.01 grams

1¼ cups self-rising flour
⅔ cup brown sugar
1 egg, beaten
1 cup soy milk
3½ tablespoons sunflower oil
⅔ cup blueberries, rinsed

Blueberry Oat Muffins

Blueberries are great on hot oatmeal, so just imagine how tasty this combination is in a muffin.

1. Preheat oven to 400°F. Prepare 12 muffin cups with paper liners.

2. Place oats in a food processor or blender. Process about one minute. Transfer to a large bowl.

3. Add brown sugar, baking powder, cinnamon, lemon peel, and salt. Fold in blueberries.

4. In a small bowl, whisk the egg whites until foamy. Add yogurt cheese, oil, and water, whisking until well blended. Add to the dry ingredients. Stir until just moistened.

5. Fill muffin cups almost full. Bake 20 minutes or until golden brown.

Yields 12 muffins

Calories: 209.86
Fat: 5.17 grams
Saturated Fat: 0.95 grams
Carbohydrates: 33.73 grams
Calcium: 73.01 mg
Lactose: 0.0 grams

2½ cups quick or old-fashioned rolled oats
½ cup firmly packed dark brown sugar
2 teaspoons baking powder
½ teaspoon cinnamon
½ teaspoon grated lemon peel
¼ teaspoon salt, or to taste
1 cup fresh blueberries
2 egg whites
⅔ cup yogurt cheese
2 tablespoons oil
3 tablespoons water

Cranberry Muffins

*Happiness is a cranberry muffin with a splash
of tart apple flavor and a zing of orange zest.*

Calories: 225.65
Fat: 6.67 grams
Saturated Fat: 1.06 grams
Carbohydrates: 37.40 grams
Calcium: 48.85 mg
Lactose: 0.0 grams

*1 cup rolled oats
1 cup yogurt
1 egg, lightly beaten
¾ cup brown sugar
¼ cup oil
2 teaspoons orange zest
1¼ cups unbleached white
 flour
1 teaspoon baking powder
½ teaspoon baking soda
½ teaspoon salt
1 cup cranberries
2 tablespoons sugar
1 tart apple, cored and
 chopped*

1. Preheat oven to 375°F.

2. In a medium bowl, combine oats with yogurt. Add egg, brown sugar, oil, and orange zest. Stir together.

3. In another bowl, combine flour, baking powder, baking soda, and salt. Sift dry ingredients over yogurt mixture. Fold in until just combined.

4. Toss cranberries with sugar. Fold in cranberries and apples. Spoon into prepared muffin tins. Bake for 20–25 minutes.

Cranberries and Cholesterol

These colorful, bright berries may just help control cholesterol. When you pick out cranberries at the market, look for firm-skinned fruits and a deep red color. Cranberry juice has the same cholesterol-lowering qualities.

Bran English Muffins

*Have your favorite fresh fruit purée ready to spread on
one of these warm homemade English muffins.*

1. Combine milk, margarine, and salt in a small pan. Cook over low heat until margarine melts. Add cereal, stirring well. Let cool at room temperature. Dissolve yeast in warm water in a large bowl. Allow to stand for 5 minutes. Stir lukewarm milk mixture into dissolved yeast.

2. Gradually stir in 3½ cups flour. Knead in enough remaining flour to make soft dough. Place dough in a large bowl coated with cooking spray. Cover and let rise in a warm place, free from drafts, for 60 minutes or until doubled in bulk. Turn dough onto a lightly floured surface.

3. Roll dough out to ½" thickness. Cut into rounds with a 3" biscuit cutter dipped in flour. Cover and let rest on a floured surface 30 minutes.

4. Coat an electric skillet with cooking spray. Heat at medium (350°F). Sprinkle lightly with cornmeal. Transfer muffins to skillet. Cook partially covered for 12 minutes. Turn and continue cooking, partially covered, an additional 12 minutes.

5. Transfer to wire racks. Allow to completely cool. Split muffins, and toast until lightly browned. Store in an airtight container.

Yields 16 muffins

Calories: 152.51
Fat: 2.31 grams
Saturated Fat: 0.36 grams
Carbohydrates: 28.15 grams
Calcium: 17.12 mg
Lactose: 0.0 grams

1⅔ cups soy milk
2 tablespoons margarine
½ teaspoon salt
*1½ cups wheat bran flakes
    cereal*
1 package dry yeast
¼ cup warm water
*3½ to 4¼ cups all-purpose
    flour*
Nonstick cooking spray
1 teaspoon cornmeal

Breakfast Muffins

Gotta grab breakfast on the run? Reach for these healthy muffins. Add more or less raisins and walnuts according to your personal preference.

Yields 24 muffins

Calories: 115.44
Fat: 2.56 grams
Saturated Fat: 0.45 grams
Carbohydrates: 20.88 grams
Calcium: 32.57 mg
Lactose: 0.0 grams

1 cup unbleached white flour
1 cup rye flour
1 teaspoon baking powder
1 teaspoon salt
1 teaspoon baking soda
2 tablespoons sugar
¼ cup molasses
1¼ cup plain yogurt
1 cup rolled oats
1 cup raisins
½ cup walnuts (optional)
Nonstick cooking spray

1. Preheat oven to 350°F. Prepare two muffin tins with paper muffin liners. Set aside.

2. Sift together all dry ingredients except oats. Set aside.

3. Beat together molasses and yogurt until smooth. Stir in dry ingredients. Fold in oats, raisins, and walnuts (if desired), stirring until blended.

4. Allow to stand for 20 minutes. Fill muffin cups with batter. Bake for 45 minutes until golden brown.

Yogurt Yodel

Yogurt comes to the rescue by helping you create truly mouth-watering creations that you can enjoy with your LI lifestyle. These muffins are delightfully moist, and you can thank the yogurt for that! Cooking with yogurt gives you flexibility, great texture, and taste!

Honey Oat Bran Muffins

Made with oat bran, these muffins are a great breakfast-to-go and a dandy treat with a cup of tea. Don't expect them to last long when you bake them. In fact, they may not even have a chance to get cold!

1. Heat oven to 425°F. Place 12 paper liners in muffin tin.

2. In a large bowl, mix oat bran, sugar, baking powder, and baking soda.

3. Add yogurt, egg whites, honey, and oil. Stir until ingredients are just moistened. Stir in raisins and nuts.

4. Spoon batter into muffin cups. Bake until golden brown, about 15 minutes.

5. Place individual muffins on a wire rack to cool.

Oat Bran Blessings

Oat bran is the outermost layer of the oat kernel. Not only is it a rich source of B complex vitamins, protein, minerals, and heart healthy soluble fiber, it helps to lower blood cholesterol levels, possibly reducing the risk of heart attacks. It helps the body use insulin more efficiently—a huge asset in controlling diabetes.

Yields 12 muffins

Calories: 146.02
Fat: 6.11 grams
Saturated Fat: 0.94 grams
Carbohydrates: 25.15 grams
Calcium: 41.74 mg
Lactose: 0.0 grams

2 cups oat bran
¼ cup packed dark brown sugar
1 tablespoon baking powder
½ teaspoon baking soda
1 cup plain yogurt
2 egg whites, slightly beaten
¼ cup honey
2 tablespoons oil
⅓ cup raisins
⅓ cup chopped walnuts

Cinnamon Apple Muffins

Yields 12 muffins

Calories: 164.35
Fat: 5.13 grams
Saturated Fat: 1.22 grams
Carbohydrates: 26.73 grams
Calcium: 31.47 mg
Lactose: 0.0 grams

2 medium Granny Smith
    apples
1 cup all-purpose flour
¾ cup yellow cornmeal
½ cup white sugar
2 teaspoons baking powder
½ teaspoon baking soda
¼ teaspoon salt
½ teaspoon cinnamon
1 cup plain yogurt
1 teaspoon vanilla
¼ cup margarine, melted and
    cooled
1 egg

Granny Smith apples are great for baking and cooking, but you can substitute any other cooking apple. Feel free to combine some whole wheat flour with your regular flour or if you prefer, totally substitute with wheat flour!

1. Preheat oven to 350°F. Place 12 paper liners in muffin tin. Peel, core, and dice apples. Set aside.

2. Mix flour, cornmeal, sugar, baking powder, baking soda, salt, and cinnamon in a large bowl. Using a separate bowl, gently toss diced apples in ½ cup of the flour mixture until well coated.

3. In a small bowl, whisk together yogurt, vanilla, margarine, and egg. Fold yogurt mixture into flour mixture until just moistened. Fold in apples.

4. Spoon batter into prepared muffin cups. Bake until toothpick inserted in the center comes out clean, about 25 minutes.

5. Allow to cool in pan for 5 minutes. Transfer to wire rack to finish cooling.

Chapter 5
Snacks

Sunflower Coconut Granola

The good stuff in this granola mix just keeps on going.
Use this mix as a snack or as a topping for yogurt.

Yields 32 servings

Calories: 400.90
Fat: 23.55 grams
Saturated Fat: 3.28 grams
Carbohydrates: 42.48 grams
Calcium: 63.69 mg
Lactose: 0.0 grams

5 cups rolled oats
1½ cups sunflower seeds
1½ cups wheat germ
1½ cups coconut, shredded
1½ cups flaked bran
1½ cups pecans, chopped
1½ cups walnuts, chopped
1½ cups slivered almonds
¾ cup sesame seeds
¾ cup oil
¾ cup honey
¾ cup molasses
1½ teaspoons almond
*   flavoring*
1½ teaspoons vanilla
*   flavoring*
1 cup raisins

1. Preheat oven to 350°F.

2. Mix dry ingredients in a large bowl. Set aside. Combine oil, honey, molasses, and flavorings in a saucepan. Bring to a boil and keep boiling until well blended, about 4 minutes. Pour slowly over the dry ingredients.

3. Divide evenly on two sheet pans with sides. Bake for 5–8 minutes. Remove from oven and turn all ingredients with a large spoon or spatula.

4. Return to oven for 4 minutes, remove, and turn ingredients. Repeat 4–5 more times every 4 minutes to ensure granola is evenly browned. Cool thoroughly.

5. Sprinkle with raisins. Store in an air tight container.

Energizing Granola

When you find a granola recipe you love, hang on to it and use it as a base. Keep adding different ingredients to the same recipe for variations. Nutritious granola can hold off hunger for long periods of time. The chewy crunch and great flavor of granola packs a ton of health benefits and keeps your energy level up.

Healthy Homemade Granola

Mix your own nuts or buy a commercial bag of mixed nuts. Almonds, walnuts, and pine nuts work well with this recipe. Choose your favorite dried fruits as well. Apples, pears, cherries, apricots, and raisins are all good choices.

1. Preheat the oven to 300°F.

2. Combine oats, coconut, sesame seeds, and wheat germ in a large non-plastic bowl.

3. Warm the oil and honey in a medium saucepan until bubbly. Pour the liquid over the oat mixture and stir to coat. Stir in nuts.

4. Spread the entire mixture in shallow baking pans with sides.

5. Bake for 25 minutes or until granola turns a golden brown.

6. Remove from oven and let cool. Stir in the dried fruits. Store in an airtight container.

Yields 24 servings

Calories: 352.64
Fat: 17.97 grams
Saturated Fat: 3.10 grams
Carbohydrates: 42.96 grams
Calcium: 36.75 mg
Lactose: 0.0 grams

4 cups old-fashioned oats
1 cup shredded coconut
⅓ cup sesame seeds
1 cup wheat germ
½ cup safflower oil
½ cup honey
3 cups mixed nuts
2–3 cups dried fruits, diced

Quick Granola Bars

*If a granola bar is easier to tote around for
a snack than loose granola, try this recipe.*

Yields 16 bars

Calories: 214.72
Fat: 6.27 grams
Saturated Fat: 1.09 grams
Carbohydrates: 33.29 grams
Calcium: 56.92 mg
Lactose: 0.01 grams

Nonstick cooking spray
*2 cups old-fashioned rolled
    oats*
*1 cup light brown sugar,
    firmly packed*
*1 cup dry roasted unsalted
    peanuts, coarsely
    chopped*
½ cup raisins
½ cup yogurt cheese
*½ cup egg whites
    (approximately 7 egg
    whites)*
1 teaspoon vanilla extract

1. Preheat oven to 350°F. Spray a 9" × 9" baking pan with nonstick cooking spray.

2. In a large bowl, combine oats, brown sugar, peanuts, and raisins. In a medium bowl, combine yogurt cheese, egg whites, and vanilla, whisking until well blended. Stir into dry ingredients.

3. Firmly press mixture into prepared baking pan.

4. Bake about 30 minutes or until lightly browned. Cool on rack for 10 minutes before cutting into bars.

Making Your Own

Making your own granola bars is kind of like being the captain of your own ship! You are in total control of all the ingredients, which helps you control your LI destiny as well as the flavor and taste of the granola bar. Experiment with homemade granola bars until you find a combination of ingredients that you love!

Peanut Butter Granola Bars

This makes for a healthy snack or a lunch box treat. Peanut butter combined with dried apricots is a taste bud pleaser, and the sunflower seeds provide a natural crunch—all held together with natural honey!

Yields 24 bars

Calories: 261.94
Fat: 11.68 grams
Saturated Fat: 2.08 grams
Carbohydrates: 36.91 grams
Calcium: 25.71 mg
Lactose: 0.0 grams

3 cups granola
1 cup chopped dried apricots
½ cup chopped peanuts
½ cup sunflower seeds
½ cup smooth peanut butter
2 cups honey
2 eggs
4 tablespoons margarine

1. Coat a 9" square dish with margarine and set aside. In a mixing bowl, combine the granola, apricots, peanuts, and sunflower seeds. Set aside.

2. In a nonstick saucepan, combine the peanut butter and honey. Stir with a wooden spoon until mixture becomes a smooth liquid. Beat eggs and add one at a time, stirring continuously, until the mixture begins to boil. Remove from heat. Stir in margarine. Allow to cool.

3. Pour the honey and peanut butter mixture over granola mixture. Stir to coat thoroughly. Spoon peanut butter mixture into prepared pan.

4. Refrigerate for three hours. Cut into 2" squares. Store bars in the refrigerator between waxed paper to keep fresh.

Sesame Bars

This recipe is fun for the kids to make and the bars will keep well when stored in a covered container.

1. Preheat the oven to 350°F. Grease a large baking pan. Set aside.

2. Mix ingredients together. Keep working the mixture even though it will seem dry.

3. Empty the bowl into the prepared pan. Firmly press the mixture evenly into the pan. Bake for about 30 to 40 minutes. The bars should be nice and brown.

4. Let cool and cut into bars.

Cinnamon Raisin Oat Bars

Choose your favorite type of jelly to add flavor to these tasty squares.

1. Preheat oven at 350°F.

2. Combine oats, flour, brown sugar, cinnamon, and baking soda, mixing well. Stir in melted margarine. Mix well.

3. Set aside 1 cup crumb mix. Pat remaining mix into greased 9-inch square pan. Warm jelly over medium heat. Add raisins to jelly and toss with reserved crumb mix.

4. Sprinkle evenly on top of layer in pan. Bake at 350°F for 30 minutes or until edges are golden brown. Allow to cool and cut into squares while still warm.

Fig Bars

If you are a fig bar lover, then homemade fig bars will make your day!

Yields 32 bars

Calories: 93.64
Fat: 3.22 grams
Saturated Fat: 0.53 grams
Carbohydrates: 17.14 grams
Calcium: 21.73 mg
Lactose: 0.0 grams

Nonstick cooking spray
10 ounces dried figs without stems
¾ cup raisins
1½ cups plus 3 tablespoons water
⅓ cup granulated sugar
¼ teaspoon ground cardamom
1¼ cups whole grain pastry flour
1 cup oat bran
¼ cup brown sugar
¼ teaspoon salt
8 tablespoons cold margarine

1. Preheat oven to 400°F. Prepare two large baking sheets with cooking spray.

2. Coarsely chop figs. Place in a food processor. Add raisins, and pulse until somewhat smooth. Place mixture in a medium saucepan. Add 1½ cups of the water plus sugar and cardamom. Bring to boil over medium-high heat. Reduce heat to medium-low and cook for 15 minutes, stirring occasionally until mixture thickens. Remove from heat.

3. Combine flour, oat bran, brown sugar, and salt in the food processor. Briefly pulse. Cut margarine into small pieces and add to processor. Process until fine crumbs form. Slowly add remaining water, one tablespoon at a time, until mixture forms a ball.

4. Turn mixture onto a floured surface. Divide in half. Roll each half into a rectangle 24" × 3". Spoon half of fig mixture down center of each rectangle and carefully fold sides over mixture. Pinch edges together in center. Cut into 1½" long pieces. Place pinched edges down on prepared baking sheets. Leave about 1½" between pieces.

5. Bake one sheet at a time for 10 minutes or until very lightly browned. Remove from oven. Place on wire rack and allow to cool completely.

Figgy Trivia

Figs are fat-free, low in sodium, and, like other plant foods, cholesterol free. They provide more dietary fiber per serving than any other common dried or fresh fruit. Figs have the highest overall mineral content of all common fruits. A small ¼ cup serving of figs contains 53 mg of calcium and is sweet enough to satisfy your sweet tooth.

Yields 48 biscotti

Calories: 42.47
Fat: 2.24 grams
Saturated Fat: 0.29 grams
Carbohydrates: 4.88 grams
Calcium: 3.53 mg
Lactose: 0.0 grams

⅔ cup chopped walnuts
8 tablespoons sugar
1¼ cups whole grain pastry
   flour
¼ cup cornmeal
1 teaspoon baking powder
¼ teaspoon salt
4 tablespoons margarine, at
   room temperature
2 large eggs
2 teaspoons grated orange
   peel
½ teaspoon orange extract

Orange Biscotti

*Biscotti is for dunking! Brew your favorite cup of joe or tea
and dunk away without worrying about lactose creeping in!*

1. Preheat oven to 350°F. Line a baking sheet with parchment paper.

2. Combine walnuts and 2 tablespoons of sugar in food processor. Pulse until walnuts are coarsely ground but not paste. Place in a large bowl. Stir in flour, cornmeal, baking powder, and salt.

3. Place margarine and remaining 6 tablespoons of sugar in a large bowl. Beat with an electric mixer on medium speed until light and fluffy. Beat in eggs, orange peel, and orange extract. Beat in flour mixture gradually until smooth and thick. Cover. Refrigerate about 60 minutes, making sure dough is firm.

4. Divide dough in half. Form each half into a 12" log. Place logs 5" apart on the baking sheet. Slightly flatten each log to ½" thick. Bake 25 to 30 minutes or until tops are firm to the touch.

5. Remove from oven. Let cool on wire rack for 3 minutes. Using a serrated knife, cut each log diagonally into ½" thick slices. Place slices cut side down on baking sheet. Return to oven and bake 10 to 15 minutes, turning slices halfway through baking. Biscotti will be golden brown. Cool on wire rack until completely cool.

Honey-Sesame Snack

*This simple and quick snack will warm your tummy. It's a
great treat when you have a hankering for something sweet.*

1. Preheat oven to 400°F.

2. Quarter tortilla into wedges. Place on an ungreased baking sheet.

3. Bake for 3 minutes. Brush each wedge with honey. Sprinkle with sesame seeds. Bake an additional 2 minutes or until golden brown.

Serves 4

Calories: 50.25
Fat: 1.51 grams
Saturated Fat: 0.31 grams
Carbohydrates: 8.19 grams
Calcium: 15.60 mg
Lactose: 0.0 grams

*1 8" whole wheat flour tortilla
1½ teaspoons honey
1½ teaspoons sesame seeds,
    toasted*

Homemade Pretzels

*You can make this whole batch of pretzels for less than what one costs
at the mall, plus you can be sure there's no hidden lactose in them.*

1. Preheat oven to 425°F.

2. Mix together yeast, water, and sugar. Add salt and flour.

3. Place on a floured board. Knead a few times and pinch off a small lump of dough. Roll into desired shape.

4. Place on an ungreased cookie sheet and sprinkle with salt. Repeat with remaining dough. Bake 12–15 minutes until golden brown.

Yields 4 pretzels

Calories: 237.97
Fat: 0.68 grams
Saturated Fat: 0.11 grams
Carbohydrates: 49.83 grams
Calcium: 10.35 mg
Lactose: 0.0 grams

*½ tablespoon yeast
¾ cup warm water
½ tablespoon sugar
½ teaspoon salt
2 cups flour
Coarse salt to taste*

Mix It Up!

*Don't be afraid to try other flours for pretzels in place of all-purpose
unbleached white flour. You might want to combine whole wheat pastry
flour with some rye flour for a different-tasting pretzel. Use cracked
whole wheat flour for crunch.*

Apple Banana Sandwich

Serves 1

Calories: 284.07
Fat: 10.09 grams
Saturated Fat: 1.78 grams
Carbohydrates: 46.69 grams
Calcium: 53.44 mg
Lactose: 0.0 grams

2 slices whole wheat bread
2 teaspoons margarine
1 apple, peeled, cored, and thinly sliced
½ banana, sliced
1 teaspoon brown sugar
Pinch of ground cinnamon

You might want to substitute the margarine with your favorite peanut butter and spread a thin layer on one slice of the bread. Peanut butter banana sandwiches aren't new, but add the crunch of an apple with a tad of brown sugar and cinnamon and you almost have dessert!

1. Lightly toast both slices of bread. Spread margarine on one slice. Cover with apple and banana. Sprinkle with brown sugar and cinnamon.

2. Place in toaster oven. Broil for one minute. Bread should be fairly soft. Remove from toaster oven. Cover with the other piece of toast and slice diagonally.

Frozen Applesauce Fruit Cups

Serves 4

Calories: 125.14
Fat: 0.35 grams
Saturated Fat: 0.06 grams
Carbohydrates: 32.01 grams
Calcium: 28.02 mg
Lactose: 0.0 grams

1 cup chunky applesauce
1 10-ounce package frozen strawberries, thawed
1 11-ounce can mandarin oranges, drained
1 cup green seedless grapes
2 tablespoons orange juice concentrate

If you have old-fashioned sundae glasses, use them for this great fruit snack. Serving this in a clear crystal glass or bowl makes it very pretty. You can also freeze it in small paper cups or plastic bowls if you want to pack it in your lunch.

1. Combine all ingredients in a medium bowl. Spoon fruit mixture into old-fashioned sundae glasses.

2. Cover with plastic wrap and freeze until firm.

3. Remove from freezer about 30 minutes before serving.

Fruit Dip

When your sweet tooth is screaming, grab some fresh fruit and start dipping! You'll be surprised how it can be tamed with fresh fruit and a special dip like this one!

1. In a small bowl, stir together yogurt, juice, honey, and cinnamon. Cover tightly.

2. Refrigerate for up to 5 days until ready to serve with assorted fresh fruit for dipping or topping.

Yields 8 servings

Calories: 29.23
Fat: 1.01 grams
Saturated Fat: 0.64 grams
Carbohydrates: 4.18 grams
Calcium: 37.80 mg
Lactose: 0.0 grams

1 cup plain yogurt
3 tablespoons orange juice
1 tablespoon honey
*¼ teaspoon ground
   cinnamon*

Ambrosia Salad

This versatile treat makes an ideal snack, meal, or light lunch.

1. Mix all the fruits together in a large bowl. In a small bowl, combine honey, yogurt, and vanilla. Mix well.

2. Pour dressing over fruit. Toss to coat evenly.

3. Cover and chill overnight. If desired, sprinkle coconut on top at serving time.

Serves 12

Calories: 138.72
Fat: 0.58 grams
Saturated Fat: 0.22 grams
Carbohydrates: 34.44 grams
Calcium: 53.17 mg
Lactose: 0.0 grams

*2 cups pineapple chunks,
   drained*
2 bananas, sliced
*2 small apples, peeled, cored,
   and chopped*
*2 oranges, peeled, sectioned,
   and cut into pieces*
2 cups strawberries, sliced
*2 peaches, peeled, stoned,
   and sliced*
1 cup seedless grapes
½ cup raisins
¼ cup honey
1 cup vanilla yogurt
½ teaspoon vanilla extract
Shredded coconut (optional)

Lemon-Roasted Fruit

*Keep adding a rainbow of fruits to your diet. This roasted
fruit recipe will be a treat for an afternoon snack with a cup
of tea, especially if you share it with a good friend.*

❧

Serves 6

Calories: 82.90
Fat: 3.88 grams
Saturated Fat: 0.63 grams
Carbohydrates: 13.15 grams
Calcium: 12.05 mg
Lactose: 0.01 grams

*2 tablespoons melted
    margarine
2 tablespoons freshly
    squeezed lemon juice
1 tablespoon honey
3 cups pineapple chunks
Fresh mint sprigs, optional*

1. Preheat oven to 350°F.

2. In a medium bowl, combine margarine, lemon juice, and honey. Toss
   pineapple to coat. Let stand at room temperature for a minimum of
   30 minutes or up to 2½ hours.

3. Grease a shallow glass baking dish. Place pineapple in prepared baking dish. Bake for 30 minutes or until fruit is thoroughly warmed and
   tender.

4. Serve cooked pineapple on individual dessert plates topped with a dollop of Fruit Dip (page 67). Top with a fresh mint sprig if desired.

Variations

*You can substitute any fruit of your choice for the pineapple or use a
variety of fruits. Peaches, pears, apples, whole strawberries, black cherries, green grapes, papaya, or mango slices all work well with this
recipe. All are naturally lactose free!*

Chapter 6
Lunches and Light Meals

Basic Dough

Look, no yeast! This recipe makes great pizza crust,
breadsticks, homemade bagels, twists, and rolls.

1. Sift flours, baking powder, salt, and baking soda together.

2. In a large bowl, combine egg whites, yogurt cheese, and margarine. Whisk until well blended.

3. Add dry ingredients, stirring until smooth dough forms. Turn dough onto a floured surface. Knead for 30 seconds. Use in your favorite recipe or choose one in this chapter!

Veggie Pizza

Fresh crunchy and colorful veggies with scrumptious seasonings make this
pizza pretty enough to devour. If you don't want "raw" veggies on your pizza,
simply blanch them for one minute or steam them ever so slightly.

1. Preheat the oven to 450°F.

2. Roll out the dough with a rolling pin, patting into a 10" round. Place on an ungreased pizza pan or cookie sheet, and prick with a fork. Bake for about 15 minutes until browned.

3. Remove pizza to a rack to cool. In a medium-sized bowl, combine yogurt cheese and seasoning. Whisk until well blended. Spread on cooled pizza shell.

4. Scatter fresh veggies on top. Cut into 8 wedges and enjoy!

Cheese Pizza

*If you can't tolerate the cheeses in this recipe, substitute
options that your stomach is more comfortable with.*

Yields 10 wedges

Calories: 115.54
Fat: 4.74 grams
Saturated Fat: 2.44 grams
Carbohydrates: 10.27 grams
Calcium: 150.71 mg
Lactose: 0.01 grams

Nonstick cooking spray
2 tablespoons plus 2
 teaspoons light
 margarine
⅔ cup yogurt cheese
4 egg whites
½ cup all-purpose flour
¼ cup whole wheat flour
1 teaspoon baking powder
½ cup tomato sauce
½ teaspoon dried oregano
½ teaspoon dried basil
1 large clove garlic, minced
4 ounces part-skim
 mozzarella cheese,
 grated
1 tablespoon grated
 Parmesan cheese

1. Preheat the oven to 375°F. Spray a 10" deep-dish pizza pan with non-stick cooking spray. Set aside.

2. Melt margarine. Cool. In a medium bowl, combine with yogurt cheese and egg whites, whisking until well mixed.

3. Combine flours with baking powder. Whisk dry mixture into the yogurt mixture. Spread on bottom and up the sides of the pizza pan.

4. Combine tomato sauce, oregano, basil, and garlic, mixing well. Spread evenly over pizza crust, leaving a ½" border around the edge. Sprinkle with mozzarella and Parmesan.

5. Bake 20–25 minutes. Cool 5 minutes. Cut into 10 wedges.

Cheese, Please!

This recipe certainly depends on your own individual tolerance; the cheeses in this recipe are lactose intolerant friendly. This recipe has 0.01 grams of lactose per serving. However, remember that every body runs differently and tolerates different fuels to keep it in running order!

Pita Lasagna

Serves 4

Calories: 240.21
Fat: 6.27 grams
Saturated Fat: 3.75 grams
Carbohydrates: 29.51 grams
Calcium: 358.39 mg
Lactose: 0.0 grams

1 cup yogurt cheese
2 tablespoons tomato paste
½ small onion, minced
1 clove garlic, minced
½ tablespoon grated
*   Parmesan cheese*
½ tablespoon minced parsley
1 teaspoon dried mixed
*   Italian herbs*
Salt to taste (optional)
4 5" rounds pita bread, split
*   open*
2 ounces mozzarella cheese

*You can make this ahead of time and keep it refrigerated until you're
ready to serve it. Make it for a light lunch for four and serve it with a
fresh, crisp side salad. If the suggested cheese ingredients don't set
with your LI level, just use the cheese that pleases your tummy.*

1. Preheat broiler.

2. In a medium bowl, combine yogurt cheese, tomato paste, onion, garlic, Parmesan cheese, parsley, and seasonings. Whisk until well blended.

3. Spread about ¼ cup of the mixture over the bottom of each pita bread round. Sprinkle tops with grated mozzarella.

4. Broil briefly just until cheese melts, about a minute. Replace tops and press together. Broil a few moments longer and serve immediately.

Tuna and Raisin Coleslaw Pitas

Try toasting your pita bread in this recipe; however, you may sometimes want a totally cold pita pocket. If so, just skip the "toasty" part.

1. Preheat broiler or toaster oven.

2. In a medium bowl, mix together grated carrot, cabbage, yogurt, vinegar, and raisins. Fold in the tuna and half the sesame seeds. Season to taste with freshly ground pepper.

3. Lightly toast the pita breads under broiler or toaster oven. Let cool. Using a sharp knife, slice each pita in half. Divide filling evenly. Sprinkle remaining sesame seeds on top of the filling.

4. Cut apples into wedges. Serve at once with the filled pita breads.

Tuna Alert!

Be sure to read the labels on canned tuna and salmon to be sure there are no lactose lurkers that were added at the packing houses. On the up side, eating canned tuna is one way to get the calcium you need.

Serves 4

Calories: 217.52
Fat: 4.36 grams
Saturated Fat: 1.03 grams
Carbohydrates: 31.35 grams
Calcium: 53.20 grams
Lactose: 0.0 grams

½ cup grated carrot
¾ cup white cabbage, thinly sliced
⅓ cup plain yogurt
1 teaspoon cider vinegar
⅛ cup raisins
1 6-ounce can tuna in water, drained
2 tablespoons sesame seeds
Freshly ground black pepper to taste
4 whole-wheat pita breads
4 apples, cut in wedges

Meat Loaf Pockets

These kid-pleasers are tasty and can be made ahead of time. Be sure to read the label on the store-bought spaghetti sauce to look for lurking lactose.

❧

Serves 4

Calories: 445.52
Fat: 16.98 grams
Saturated Fat: 5.06 grams
Carbohydrates: 37.00 grams
Calcium: 78.96 mg
Lactose: 0.02 grams

1 pound lean ground beef
1 egg
½ cup dry bread crumbs
½ onion, chopped
½ cup ready-made spaghetti
    sauce
¼ teaspoon Worcestershire
    sauce
¼ teaspoon liquid hickory
    smoke (optional)
⅛ teaspoon dried marjoram
⅛ teaspoon dried thyme
1 tablespoon chopped
    parsley
4 pita bread rounds
1 avocado, sliced
1 tomato, sliced

1. Preheat oven to 350°F.

2. Grease one small loaf pan. Place all ingredients except bread, avocado, and tomato in a large bowl. Mix well.

3. Shape the meat mixture into a loaf. Place in loaf pan and bake for 40 minutes. Let cool to room temperature. Cover and refrigerate to use later.

4. When ready to make pita pockets, cut 2 slices of meat loaf. Open a pita pocket at one end and slide the meat loaf into the pocket. Add a slice of avocado and tomato.

Mushroom Burgers

You don't need a bun to enjoy these hearty burgers.

1. Preheat broiler or toaster oven.

2. Combine all ingredients except cooking spray and lightly toss together. Shape mixture into 6 patties about 1½" thick.

3. Place patties on rack. Broil 3–5 inches from heat for 6 or 7 minutes on each side.

Cookin' on the Grill

If you're having a barbeque, these mushroom burgers are even better cooked outside on the grill. If you're having a group, just double the recipe and if there are leftovers you can pop one in the microwave the next day for a quick snack or light lunch.

Serves 6

Calories: 254.51
Fat: 14.95 grams
Saturated Fat: 5.68 grams
Carbohydrates: 1.02 grams
Calcium: 20.98 mg
Lactose: 0.0 grams

1½ pounds ground chuck
1 2-ounce can mushroom stems and pieces, drained and finely chopped
1 tablespoon minced onion
1 tablespoon soy sauce
¼ teaspoon pepper
Nonstick cooking spray

Broccoli Cheese Stuffed Potatoes

Not only is this a great stuffing for baked potatoes but it's great stuffed into a pita pocket and warmed up the next day for lunch!

1. Prepare broccoli according to package directions. Drain. Squeeze out excess liquid and chop finely.

2. In a medium bowl, whisk yogurt cheese, Parmesan cheese, lemon juice, and mustard together until smooth. Fold in broccoli, egg whites, and seasonings. Cover and chill until ready to use.

3. Slice each baked potato in half lengthwise. Fluff up the insides with a fork. Top each half with about one-fourth cup of broccoli-cheese mixture. Warm a bit in microwave if desired.

Serves 6

Calories: 194.14
Fat: 1.94 grams
Saturated Fat: 1.01 grams
Carbohydrates: 35.80 grams
Calcium: 133.33 mg
Lactose: 0.02 grams

1 10-ounce package frozen chopped broccoli
⅓ cup yogurt cheese
3 tablespoons grated Parmesan cheese
1 tablespoon fresh lemon juice
1 tablespoon Dijon mustard
3 hard-boiled egg whites, finely chopped
Salt and pepper to taste
3 baked potatoes

Herb Cheesecake

Serves 16

Calories: 54.74
Fat: 1.83 grams
Saturated Fat: 1.15 grams
Carbohydrates: 3.63 grams
Calcium: 123.67 mg
Lactose: 0.02 grams

Nonstick cooking spray
2 cups yogurt cheese
*¼ cup grated Parmesan
    cheese*
3 cloves garlic, minced
1½ tablespoons dried basil
⅛ teaspoon black pepper
4 egg whites, slightly beaten

This herb cheesecake is a great entrée for a light lunch and is also good left over to pack for lunch the next day. Cut in small wedges, it also makes a great snack and only contains a small trace of lactose.

1. Preheat oven to 325°F. Spray a 7" springform pan with nonstick cooking spray.

2. Whisk together yogurt cheese with Parmesan cheese, garlic, basil, and pepper in a medium bowl. Make sure mixture is well blended.

3. Fold in egg whites, mixing well. Pour into the pan, smoothing top with a spatula. Bake about 55 minutes or until center is set.

4. Cool slightly on a wire rack. Chill thoroughly. Serve with fruit and crackers.

Herbs and Health

Herbs are not just for flavoring! Herbal remedies today are gaining popularity; some people prefer them over drugs made of chemicals. Experiment with a variety of herbs in your cooking. Your palate will wonder what you're up to, and you'll be amazed to learn how you're adding tasty health benefits to your diet!

Tofu Lasagna

Tofu is the chameleon of the food world. It absorbs the flavors it's cooked with, and you may not even notice it in a dish with as many ingredients as this one. This recipe is enjoyable for everyone, whether or not they adhere to an LI lifestyle!

1. Preheat oven to 350°F.

2. Heat oil in large, heavy saucepan. Add onion, green pepper, and garlic. Cook over medium-high heat for about 5 minutes or until onion is translucent. Add zucchini and mushrooms and cook 5 minutes longer. Cut tofu in ½" cubes and stir in tofu, tomatoes, tomato paste, 1 teaspoon oregano, 1 teaspoon basil, salt, red pepper, and bay leaf. Reduce heat and partially cover with lid. Simmer 15 minutes, stirring occasionally.

3. Remove bay leaf and cool slightly. Stir in half the mozzarella. Prepare lasagna noodles according to package directions. Prepare a 13" × 9" × 2" baking dish with nonstick cooking spray.

4. Spread half the tofu mixture in bottom of baking dish. Arrange half the noodles on top of the tofu mixture, overlapping each noodle slightly. Repeat with remaining tofu mixture and noodles. Top with tomato sauce, remaining herbs, and mozzarella.

5. Bake about 30 minutes until lasagna is bubbling and lightly browned. Let stand about 15 minutes before serving.

Serves 8

Calories: 317.74
Fat: 9.97 grams
Saturated Fat: 4.23 grams
Carbohydrates: 41.42 grams
Calcium: 261.21 mg
Lactose: 0.0 grams

1 tablespoon plus 1 teaspoon olive oil
1 cup chopped onion
1 cup sliced green bell pepper
5 garlic cloves, minced
2 cups sliced zucchini
1 cup sliced mushrooms
12 ounces firm tofu
2 cups canned crushed tomatoes
½ cup tomato paste
1½ teaspoons dried oregano
1½ teaspoons dried basil
½ teaspoon salt
¼ teaspoon ground red pepper
1 bay leaf
8 ounces shredded mozzarella cheese
9 ounces lasagna noodles
1 cup tomato sauce
Nonstick cooking spray

Shepherd's Pie

This is a great "make ahead" dish made with soy milk, so it's very LI friendly. Make it on a Sunday afternoon so it's ready to pop in the oven when you get home after the usual Monday maze.

⚜

Serves 6–8

Calories: 216.46
Fat: 10.33 grams
Saturated Fat: 1.09 grams
Carbohydrates: 28.13 grams
Calcium: 53.94 mg
Lactose: 0.0 grams

5 cups coarsely chopped baking potatoes
2½ tablespoons olive oil
1½ cups chopped onion
1 medium-sized eggplant, peeled and diced
2 cups diced zucchini
1 cup sliced mushrooms
1 cup frozen baby peas
2 cloves garlic, chopped
2 tablespoons tomato paste
1 14.5-ounce can Italian style tomatoes
¼ cup chopped fresh basil
1½ tablespoons balsamic vinegar
1 teaspoon chopped fresh thyme
Salt and pepper to taste
1 cup warm soy milk
3 tablespoons canola oil

1. Preheat oven to 375°F. Grease a medium-sized casserole dish.

2. Put potatoes in medium saucepan. Add enough salted water to cover potatoes; water line should rest 1" above potatoes. Bring to a boil. Reduce heat and simmer about 15 minutes or until potatoes are fork tender.

3. Warm olive oil in large, deep skillet over medium heat. Add onion. Cook for 5 minutes, stirring constantly. Add eggplant and zucchini to skillet. Cook, partially covered, for 4 minutes, stirring often. Add mushrooms, peas, and garlic. Cook, partially covered, for 3 more minutes, stirring often.

4. Add tomato paste, cooking about 2 minutes longer. Add tomatoes, basil, vinegar, and thyme. Salt and pepper to taste. Bring to a slow simmer. Cook for about 3 minutes, partially covered.

5. Transfer mixture to prepared casserole dish. Drain potatoes and mash them, gradually adding soymilk and canola oil. Spread evenly over filling. Bake 20 to 25 minutes or until bubbling hot. Cool at least 5 minutes before serving.

Basil Basics

Basil has a spicy aroma with a warm flavor reminiscent of clove. It's a bit peppery. To bring out the best in basil leaves, be sure to tear rather than chop the leaves. Basil is fragile and needs to be handled with care. It's best when used fresh!

Easy Taco Salad

Taco salad is an easy and light lunch. This recipe comes together quickly whether you're cooking for one or several. If the mozzarella cheese isn't on your personal LI list, then just skip it or choose a cheese that likes your tummy.

1. Cook onion and garlic in oil in a heavy skillet until tender. Add ground beef and brown. Drain.

2. Add tomato sauce, chili powder, water, and salt to beef. Cook over low heat for 10 minutes. Cool at room temperature.

3. Place shredded lettuce in a bowl. Add chili meat mixture, corn chips, green onions, tomato, and cheese. Toss and serve with salsa.

Serves 6

Calories: 294.64
Fat: 14.08 grams
Saturated Fat: 4.14 grams
Carbohydrates: 18.00 grams
Calcium: 122.67 mg
Lactose: 0.0 grams

⅔ cup onion, chopped
1 clove garlic, minced
1 tablespoon oil
1 pound lean ground beef
1 8-ounce can tomato sauce
1 teaspoon chili powder
2 tablespoons water
1 teaspoon salt
4 cups lettuce, shredded
2 cups baked corn chips
2 tablespoons green onions, chopped
1 tomato, chopped
½ cup shredded mozzarella cheese
1 cup salsa

Tofu Chalupas

If you love Mexican food, you're going to love this recipe. Depending on where you are on the LI Richter scale, exercise your option on the shredded Cheddar!

─◈─

1. Preheat oven to 350°F.

2. Coat a large skillet with cooking spray. Heat over medium-high heat. Add onion and sauté until tender. Add tofu and garlic. Cook for 3 minutes, stirring constantly.

3. Stir in tomatoes, pepper, chili powder, cumin, oregano, and cilantro. Continue cooking over medium heat heat, stirring frequently.

4. Wrap tortillas in aluminum foil. Bake for 10 minutes.

5. Evenly divide lettuce, tofu mixture, avocado, and cheese and top each tortilla. Serve immediately.

Serves 4

Calories: 192.78
Fat: 9.43 grams
Saturated Fat: 2.68 grams
Carbohydrates: 19.97 grams
Calcium: 255.64 mg
Lactose: 0.02 grams

Nonstick cooking spray
⅓ cup finely chopped onion
1 10-ounce package firm tofu, drained and crumbled
2 cloves garlic, crushed
2 tomatoes, seeded and chopped
1 jalapeño pepper, seeded and chopped
¼ teaspoon chili powder
¼ teaspoon ground cumin
½ teaspoon dried whole oregano
2 tablespoons chopped fresh cilantro
4 6" corn tortillas
½ cup shredded iceberg lettuce
½ medium avocado, peeled and chopped
¼ cup shredded Cheddar cheese (optional)

Ginger Garlic Stir Fry

Garlic lovers delight! Don't be shy—if you want to add another teaspoon or two of garlic, just do it.

1. Cut tofu into ½" cubes.

2. Heat ⅔ teaspoon oil in a nonstick skillet. Add Worcestershire sauce, celery salt, and tofu. Stir-fry until tofu is browned and crusted on all sides.

3. Heat remaining oil in a separate nonstick skillet. Stir in broccoli, asparagus, onion, celery, green onions, water chestnuts, garlic, vinegar, five-spice powder, gingerroot, soy sauce, and salt and pepper. Stir-fry about 5 minutes or until vegetables are crisp-tender.

4. Place vegetables on serving plate and top with tofu.

Ginger Trivia

Flavoring food with ginger dates way back to very early civilization. Ginger was brought to the New World in the early 1500s by Spanish settlers. Ginger is also looked to as a soother for nausea and in the prevention of motion sickness. Some studies suggest that ginger may even help reduce the inflammation of arthritis.

Serves 3

Calories: 190.60
Fat: 8.99 grams
Saturated Fat: 0.97 grams
Carbohydrates: 17.59 grams
Calcium: 272.80 grams
Lactose: 0.0 grams

12 ounces extra-firm tofu, ½" cubes
2 cups broccoli florets
½ cup asparagus spears
½ cup red onion, thinly sliced
⅓ cup green onions, sliced
1 cup celery, sliced
⅓ cup water chestnuts, sliced
1⅓ teaspoons olive oil, divided
2 teaspoons garlic, minced
1 tablespoon cider vinegar
½ teaspoon Chinese five-spice powder
½ teaspoon Worcestershire sauce
⅛ teaspoon celery salt
2 teaspoons fresh gingerroot, minced
1 tablespoon soy sauce
Salt and pepper to taste

Broccoli Walnut Stir Fry

*The walnuts in this stir fry are what sets it apart from ho-hum stir fry.
If you like pecans more than walnuts, simply substitute them. The finished
dish can be served with your choice of rice but it is delicious just as is!*

Serves 6

Calories: 255.98
Fat: 20.97 grams
Saturated Fat: 2.64 grams
Carbohydrates: 10.76 grams
Calcium: 192.69 mg
Lactose: 0.0 grams

1 pound firm tofu
2 tablespoons olive oil
1 cup water
½ teaspoon salt
2 carrots, sliced thinly
2 cups fresh broccoli florets
1 tablespoon olive oil
1 medium onion, thinly sliced
1 cup fresh mushrooms, sliced
1 cup walnut halves
1 tablespoon cornstarch
3 tablespoons soy sauce
½ teaspoon pepper

1. Cut tofu into 1" cubes. Heat 2 tablespoons of oil in wok or heavy skillet. Lightly brown tofu. Set aside.

2. Bring salted water to a boil. Add the sliced carrots and the broccoli florets. Boil for 1 minute. Drain and reserve the vegetable stock.

3. Temporarily remove tofu from skillet. Add 1 tablespoon oil to skillet. Sauté onion over medium heat until soft and transparent. Add mushrooms and walnut halves. Turn heat to high and add carrots and broccoli, stirring constantly. Add tofu cubes and stir.

4. In a medium pan, bring reserved vegetable stock to a bare boil. Add the cornstarch, soy sauce, and pepper, stirring constantly until it begins to thicken. Pour over the vegetables and tofu mixture in skillet.

5. Stir everything together until bubbling. Serve with rice if desired.

Chapter 7
Savory Soups

Quick Veggie Soup

You can cook healthfully and quickly at the same time. Use this recipe as a base and add your favorite veggies along with your favorite seasonings.

Serves 4

Calories: 195.03
Fat: 7.98 grams
Saturated Fat: 2.96 grams
Carbohydrates: 16.31 grams
Calcium: 41.29 mg
Lactose: 0.0 grams

½ pound ground chuck
¼ cup chopped green pepper
¼ cup chopped onion
1 14-ounce can stewed tomatoes, undrained
1 cup frozen mixed vegetables
1 cup water
¼ teaspoon dried whole basil
⅛ teaspoon garlic powder
½ teaspoon freshly ground pepper

1. In a microwave-safe 2-quart casserole dish, combine ground chuck, green pepper, and chopped onion. Cover with plastic wrap. Microwave for 4 minutes on high. Stir after 2 minutes. Make sure the meat is no longer pink.

2. Drain well in a colander, patting dry with paper towels. Wipe casserole dish dry with a paper towel, returning drained meat mixture to casserole.

3. Add remaining ingredients to meat mixture. Cover with plastic wrap. Microwave for 9–10 minutes on high, stirring every 3 minutes. Serve hot.

Can You Boil Water?

If the answer is "yes," you have an unlimited world of soups to explore. Homemade soups don't have all that sodium and preservatives! Don't be afraid to change recipe ingredients—just stick with the basics and add your favorites. No worries on lactose when it comes to veggies— you've got the entire rainbow to choose from!

Zucchini Spaghetti Soup

*When you're buying zucchini, look for firm, heavy fruit.
For this recipe and others with zucchini, scrub the outside and slice
thinly. When you peel them, you peel away a lot of nutrients!*

1. In a large saucepan, sauté onion and garlic in olive oil. Add zucchini, tomato, seasonings, and broth. Cover and simmer over low heat 1½ hours.

2. Add short lengths of uncooked spaghetti. Continue simmering another 10 minutes or until spaghetti is tender.

Serves 4

Calories: 372.65
Fat: 14.96 grams
Saturated Fat: 2.08 grams
Carbohydrates: 47.78 grams
Calcium: 50.80 mg
Lactose: 0.0 grams

1 medium onion, minced
1 clove garlic, minced
¼ cup olive oil
4 medium zucchini, thinly
*   sliced*
1 tomato, peeled and
*   chopped*
½ teaspoon basil
Salt and pepper to taste
1 cup chicken broth
½ pound uncooked spaghetti

Cauliflower Soup

*This creamy, smooth soup is perfect for cauliflower lovers.
Who would have thought that something this "creamy" would be
totally lactose free? Serve it with a nice side salad and you're set.*

1. Cut off cauliflower leaves, rinse, and cut into small pieces. Place cauliflower in a large soup pot with water, margarine, and bouillon cubes.

2. Simmer until cauliflower is tender and soft. Blend in blender until smooth. Season to taste.

3. Sprinkle with fresh parsley and serve hot.

Serves 4

Calories: 113.94
Fat: 6.81 grams
Saturated Fat: 1.18 grams
Carbohydrates: 11.35 grams
Calcium: 54.37 mg
Lactose: 0.0 grams

1 large cauliflower
6 cups water
2 tablespoons margarine
6 cubes bouillon
Salt and pepper to taste
Fresh parsley, minced
*   (optional)*

Creamy Broccoli Soup

Soy milk may not be your choice of milk for this recipe. If you prefer, substitute with the same amount of rice milk, which will give you the same delicious results. This recipe is packed full of great flavor and healthy ingredients!

❧

Serves 6

Calories: 165.62
Fat: 1.23 grams
Saturated Fat: 0.15 grams
Carbohydrates: 31.24 grams
Calcium: 82.53 mg
Lactose: 0.24 grams

1¼ pounds russet potatoes
1½ pounds broccoli, cut into small florets
1 large yellow onion, coarsely chopped
3 cups chicken stock
½ cup dry white wine
¼ teaspoon freshly squeezed lemon juice
2 whole bay leaves
½ teaspoon salt
⅛ teaspoon pepper
¾ cup soy milk
Grated lemon zest for garnish (optional)

1. Peel potatoes and cut into 2" pieces. In a large soup pot, combine potatoes, broccoli, onion, chicken stock, wine, lemon juice, bay leaves, salt, and pepper. Bring to a boil. Reduce heat to low, cover, and simmer until vegetables are fork-tender, about 25 minutes.

2. Remove the soup from the heat. Discard bay leaves.

3. Pour half of soup mixture in blender. Add ½ cup of the soy milk. Purée until smooth. Empty soup mixture into a large bowl. Repeat with the remaining soup, adding ¼ cup soy milk.

4. Place puréed soup back in soup pot. If necessary, thin the soup by adding more soy milk, a little at a time, until desired consistency. Reheat soup over low heat, stirring occasionally. Take care not to boil soup. Serve hot with lemon zest for garnish if desired.

And the Award Goes to . . . Broccoli!

The deeper the color, the higher nutritional value. Broccoli is packed with essential vitamins and minerals. There isn't enough space here to tout all of the fine traits of broccoli. One cup of cooked broccoli contains 74 mg of calcium and 123 mg of vitamin C.

Split Pea Soup

Lots of people love split pea soup but have a notion that it's difficult to create. The creamy texture of this soup is sure to satisfy your yearning for "creamy stuff," and it's totally lactose free!

1. Sort and wash dried peas. Place peas in a large heavy saucepan.

2. Add remaining ingredients. Bring to a boil. Reduce heat, cover and simmer until peas are tender, about 1 hour.

3. Process half the mixture at a time in a blender until smooth. Serve hot.

Serves 4; Serving size 1¼ cup

Calories: 240.86
Fat: 2.19 grams
Saturated Fat: 0.58 grams
Carbohydrates: 39.19 grams
Calcium: 44.29 mg
Lactose: 0.0 grams

½ pound dried split peas
4 cups water
¾ cup chopped onion
½ cup chopped carrots
½ cup chopped lean ham
½ teaspoon ground celery seeds
¼ teaspoon salt
¼ teaspoon freshly ground pepper
¼ teaspoon dried whole marjoram, crushed
⅛ teaspoon dried whole thyme

Chinese Chicken Soup

Use this flavorful twist on chicken noodle soup to help get over a cold.

1. Cut chicken into strips. Coat a heavy medium saucepan with cooking spray. Add oil and place over medium-high heat.

2. Add chicken strips and mushrooms. Sauté, stirring occasionally. Be sure chicken is no longer pink. Add chicken broth and bring to a boil.

3. In a small bowl, combine cornstarch, water, and soy sauce. Stir until well-blended, then stir into mixture in saucepan. Reduce heat and simmer for 5 minutes.

4. Remove from heat. Stir in lemon juice. Serve while hot. Garnish each bowl with a lemon slice.

Serves 4

Calories: 177.70
Fat: 4.81 grams
Saturated Fat: 1.17 grams
Carbohydrates: 5.21 grams
Calcium: 21.59 mg
Lactose: 0.0 grams

3 boneless, skinless chicken breasts
Nonstick cooking spray
1 teaspoon olive oil
8 large fresh mushrooms, sliced
4 cups chicken broth
1 tablespoon cornstarch
2 tablespoons water
1 tablespoon soy sauce
2 tablespoons lemon juice
Lemon slices for garnish (optional)

Bean, Barley, and Mushroom Soup

This easy-to-make recipe warms your house and fills it with
tantalizing aromas for hours leading up to dinner time.

Serves 6

Calories: 171.26
Fat: 0.68 grams
Saturated Fat: 0.18 grams
Carbohydrates: 33.89 grams
Calcium: 80.89 mg
Lactose: 0.01 grams

1 cup dried lima beans
4 tablespoons pearl barley
2 large onions, chopped
2 ribs celery, chopped
1 medium carrot, chopped
2 tablespoons fresh parsley,
*   chopped*
8 cups water
½ pound fresh mushrooms,
*   sliced*
1½ teaspoons salt
½ teaspoon freshly ground
*   black pepper*

1. Soak dried lima beans and barley overnight. Rinse and drain.

2. In a large soup pot, combine beans, barley, onions, celery, carrot, parsley, and water. Cover and cook over low heat until beans are tender, approximately 2½ hours.

3. Add mushrooms. Salt and pepper to taste. Cook for an additional 10 minutes.

Ruby Red Borscht

Borscht is usually served cold; however, some people prefer it hot.
Try it both ways and see which gets your vote!

Serves 4

Calories: 190.61
Fat: 4.84 grams
Saturated Fat: 1.41 grams
Carbohydrates: 23.70 grams
Calcium: 68.48 mg
Lactose: 0.04 grams

5 large beets, peeled and
*   grated*
2 medium onions, finely
*   chopped*
6 cups chicken broth
1 tablespoon lemon juice
¼ teaspoon sugar
¼ teaspoon pepper
2 eggs, slightly beaten
Fresh dill (optional)

1. In a large soup pot, combine beets, onion, and broth. Cover and bring to a boil.

2. Reduce heat and simmer for 45 minutes. Add lemon juice, sugar, and pepper. Simmer an additional 15 minutes.

3. Remove from heat. Gradually stir about one-fourth of hot mixture into beaten eggs. Add to remaining hot mixture, stirring constantly.

4. Chill thoroughly. Garnish with fresh dill, if desired.

Potato Leek Soup

*The white and pale green sections of the leeks are the most
tender and flavorful parts on this onion-like veggie.*

1. Using the white and pale green part of the leek only, slice in 1" thick pieces. Peel potatoes and cut into 2" pieces.

2. Melt margarine over medium-high heat in a large soup pot. Add the pieces of leek. Sauté until soft, not allowing to brown, about 3 minutes. Add chicken broth, potatoes, salt, and pepper. Bring to a boil. Reduce heat to low, cover, and simmer until the vegetables are fork-tender, about 20 minutes. Remove from heat.

3. Divide soup in half. Place in blender, adding ¾ cup of soy milk. Purée until smooth. Empty soup into a large bowl. Repeat with remaining soup, adding ½ cup soy milk.

4. Place puréed soup back in soup pot. If necessary, thin the soup by adding more soy milk, a little at a time, until desired consistency. Reheat soup over low heat, stirring occasionally. Take care not to boil soup. Serve hot with fresh chives for garnish if desired.

Serves 6

Calories: 226.95
Fat: 7.52 grams
Saturated Fat: 1.26 grams
Carbohydrates: 34.05 grams
Calcium: 69.59 mg
Lactose: 0.0 grams

4 medium leeks
*1½ pounds potatoes, peeled
    and cut into 2" pieces*
3 tablespoons margarine
2½ cups chicken both
½ teaspoon salt
*⅛ teaspoon ground white
    pepper*
1¼ cups soy milk
*Fresh chopped chives for
    garnish (optional)*

Pasta and Fava Bean Soup

*Dried fava beans require overnight soaking and longer
cooking than canned favas. The flavor and heartiness of this soup
can be attained whether you use dried fava beans or canned.*

Serves 6

Calories: 270.16
Fat: 13.46 grams
Saturated Fat: 2.11 grams
Carbohydrates: 27.02 grams
Calcium: 57.28 mg
Lactose: 0.0 grams

1 cup fava beans
5 tablespoons olive oil
2 cloves garlic, chopped
2 large carrots, peeled and
    diced
1 large onion, cubed
2 stalks celery, diced
1 14-ounce can chopped
    tomatoes
7 cups chicken stock
4 tablespoons freshly
    chopped parsley
1 tablespoon freshly chopped
    oregano
½ teaspoon rosemary
½ teaspoon thyme
1 bay leaf
1¼ cups macaroni or bow tie
    pasta
Salt and pepper to taste

1. Soak fava beans overnight unless using canned beans. Heat oil over medium heat in a stockpot. Add garlic, carrots, onion, and celery. Sauté for 5 minutes.

2. Add chopped tomatoes, chicken stock, beans, parsley, oregano, rosemary, thyme, and bay leaf. Bring to a boil. Allow to boil rapidly for 10 minutes.

3. Reduce heat, cover, and simmer until beans are tender, about 45 minutes.

4. Add pasta and continue cooking for another 10 minutes. Pasta should be soft but not mushy. Season to taste.

Fava Bean Facts

You may hear fava beans called by other names: broad bean, English bean, horse bean, Scotch bean, Silkworm bean, and Windsor bean. You may be surprised to learn that the fava bean can be used as a coffee extender when roasted and ground!

Tortilla Soup

Tortilla soup has become a favorite in restaurants.
Add more hot sauce to this easy recipe for added zing.

1. Coat a medium, heavy-bottom saucepan with cooking spray. Place over medium heat until hot. Add onion, chilies, and garlic. Cook until onion is tender, stirring frequently.

2. Add water, tomato juice, tomato, bouillon granules, cumin, chili powder, Worcestershire sauce, pepper, and hot sauce, stirring well. Bring to a boil. Reduce heat, cover, and simmer one hour.

3. Cut tortillas into ½" strips. Add to soup mixture. Cover and simmer 10 minutes.

4. Serve steaming hot. Sprinkle cheese over each. Garnish with a fresh cilantro sprig.

Serves 4

Calories: 133.69
Fat: 4.98 grams
Saturated Fat: 2.80 grams
Carbohydrates: 18.08 grams
Calcium: 169.03 mg
Lactose: 0.0 grams

Nonstick cooking spray
½ cup chopped onion
1 4-ounce can chopped green chilies, undrained
2 cloves garlic, crushed
3¾ cups water
1½ cups tomato juice
1 medium tomato, peeled and chopped
1 teaspoon beef-flavored bouillon granules
1 teaspoon ground cumin
1 teaspoon chili powder
1 teaspoon Worcestershire sauce
¼ teaspoon pepper
3 drops hot sauce or to taste
3 6" corn tortillas
½ cup shredded Monterey Jack cheese
Fresh cilantro sprigs

Cioppino

*Talk about yummy! This bouillabaisse fish stew known as cioppino
is truly a seafood lover's delight. You can add squid, other types
of fish, lobster—the bigger the pot, the better the stew!*

Yields 6 cups

Calories: 292.85
Fat: 3.17 grams
Saturated Fat: 0.38 grams
Carbohydrates: 17.34 grams
Calcium: 127.27 mg
Lactose: 0.0 grams

9 littleneck clams, cleaned
½ pound fresh cod fillets
½ pound scallops
*½ pound medium peeled
   shrimp*
4 crab legs
*1 medium-sized green
   pepper, seeded and diced*
1 small onion, diced
1 clove garlic, minced
*1 16-ounce can whole
   tomatoes, undrained and
   chopped*
*1 8-ounce can whole
   tomatoes, undrained and
   chopped*
½ cup clam juice
½ cup red wine
*2 tablespoons minced fresh
   parsley*
*1 tablespoon chopped fresh
   basil*
¼ teaspoon pepper
¼ teaspoon red pepper flakes
⅛ teaspoon rubbed sage
¼ teaspoon oregano
*Fresh Parmesan cheese
   (optional)*

1. Clean clams, cut cod fillets into 1" pieces, and cut scallops in half. Rinse shrimp and crab legs. Combine green pepper, onion, garlic, tomatoes, and clam juice in a large soup pot. Bring to a boil.

2. Add wine. Reduce heat, cover, and simmer until onion and pepper are tender, about 10 minutes. Stir in remaining ingredients. Bring to a boil. Reduce heat, cover, and simmer another 8 minutes. Fish will flake easily and clams will open when soup is done. Be sure not to overcook. Serve hot. Sprinkle with freshly grated Parmesan cheese, if desired.

More Than Just Fish Stew

The base of this delightful and fresh treat can be made ahead of time. Heat the prepared base and add the fresh seafood, which will cook in just a matter of minutes! Keep in mind that cioppino is another one of those dishes that is best when you eat the whole thing because it's not as good the next day!

Tofu Eggplant Gumbo

If you're not a tofu fan, this gumbo will ease you into it! There are so many flavors mingled in this stew that you won't even notice the tofu.

1. Cut tofu in 1" cubes. Heat ⅔ teaspoon oil in a medium nonstick sauté pan. Stir in ½ teaspoon Worcestershire sauce and celery salt. Add tofu and stir-fry until crusted and golden brown on all sides.

2. Heat remaining oil in another nonstick pan. Place onion, green onion, green peppers, celery, tomato, and eggplant in pan. Sprinkle with remaining Worcestershire sauce and spices.

3. Cook vegetables until fork tender. Add okra and beef stock. Continue cooking until liquid thickens. Top with tofu at serving time.

Serves 4

Calories: 155.20
Fat: 6.80 grams
Saturated Fat: 0.75 grams
Carbohydrates: 14.14 grams
Calcium: 210.05 mg
Lactose: 0.0 grams

12 ounces extra-firm tofu
1⅓ teaspoons olive oil, divided
2 teaspoons Worcestershire sauce, divided
⅛ teaspoon celery salt
½ cup onion, chopped
½ cup green onion, chopped
1¼ cups green pepper, chopped
1 cup celery, sliced
1¼ cups tomato, crushed
¾ cup eggplant, diced
2 teaspoons garlic, chopped
½ teaspoon dried thyme
⅛ teaspoon cayenne pepper
¼ cup fresh parsley, chopped
¾ cup okra, sliced
2 cups beef stock

Cold Blueberry Soup

Cold fruit soups are great for a summer brunch or a special occasion.

Serves 4

Calories: 94.90
Fat: 0.24 grams
Saturated Fat: 0.04 grams
Carbohydrates: 23.62 grams
Calcium: 10.44 mg
Lactose: 0.0 grams

1½ cups fresh blueberries
1¼ cups unsweetened grape
    juice
1 cup water
1 3" stick cinnamon
2 teaspoons sugar
1 tablespoon cornstarch
¼ cup water
¼ teaspoon ground
    cardamom
Extra blueberries for garnish
    (optional)

1. Combine blueberries, grape juice, 1 cup water, cinnamon, and sugar in a medium saucepan. Bring to a boil. Reduce heat, cover, and simmer 5 minutes.

2. Combine cornstarch and ¼ cup water. Stir until well blended. Add cardamom to cornstarch mixture. Stir mixture into soup, stirring constantly.

3. When mixture begins to thicken, remove from heat. Let cool to room temperature. Cover and refrigerate until thoroughly chilled. Remove cinnamon stick before serving. Garnish with a sprinkling of whole blueberries on top.

Cold Apricot Soup

Fresh is the word! Serve this in crystal stemmed glasses with a fresh apricot slice on the side, a shortbread cookie, and a cup of tea.

Serves 4

Calories: 240.03
Fat: 4.47 grams
Saturated Fat: 2.60 grams
Carbohydrates: 30.59 grams
Calcium: 174.28 mg
Lactose: 0.0 grams

3 cups fresh apricots, pitted
    and chopped
1½ cups fruity white wine
3 tablespoons apricot
    preserves
1 pint plain yogurt
Soy milk (optional)
Apricot slices for garnish

1. Combine chopped apricots, wine, and preserves in blender. Purée until smooth.

2. Place apricot mixture in a large bowl. Add yogurt and whisk until smooth. If necessary, add soy milk to thin.

3. Cover and refrigerate about an hour. Chill soup bowls or crystal stemmed glasses while soup is getting cold. Garnish with apricot slices.

Chapter 8
Slaws and Salads

Overnight Coleslaw

Serves 8

Calories: 34.14
Fat: 0.20 grams
Saturated Fat: 0.02 grams
Carbohydrates: 7.96 grams
Calcium: 34.21 mg
Lactose: 0.0 grams

4 cups shredded cabbage
2 cups shredded carrots
¾ cup thinly sliced green
   onions
¾ cup unsweetened apple
   juice
⅔ cup cider vinegar
1 tablespoon prepared
   mustard
1½ teaspoons paprika
1 teaspoon mustard seeds
½ teaspoon garlic salt
½ teaspoon celery seeds
½ teaspoon pepper

This is a perfect dish to take to a barbecue or party. Prepare it the night before and just grab it out of the fridge when you're ready to go!

1. In a large bowl, combine cabbage, carrots, and green onions.

2. In a jar with a secure lid, combine apple juice, vinegar, mustard, paprika, mustard seeds, garlic salt, celery seeds, and pepper. Tightly screw jar lid and shake vigorously.

3. Pour over coleslaw mixture. Toss lightly to coat.

4. Cover and refrigerate overnight. Toss well before serving.

Icing Cabbage

If you want really crispy coleslaw, immerse the head(s) of cabbage in ice water before shredding. After you've shredded the icy cabbage, refrigerate it. That way it's chilly and crisp when you serve it!

Chinese Coleslaw

With water chestnuts and sesame seeds, this coleslaw
has a crunch to it that will wake up your palate!

1. Toss veggies and sesame seeds together.

2. In a small bowl, whisk together oils, sugar, cilantro, pepper, vinegar, and soy sauce. Pour dressing over slaw. Toss until well mixed.

3. Refrigerate at least two 2 hours before serving. Toss at serving time.

Chinese Cabbage

Chinese cabbage, also known as bok choy, is very healthy! In fact, Chinese cabbage is higher in calcium than other cabbage. It looks different because it grows in white celery-like stalks with dark green leaves instead of a forming a head. It's yet another veggie to add to your ongoing list of ways to get your calcium requirements without lactose concerns.

Serves 12

Calories: 84.32
Fat: 5.60 grams
Saturated Fat: 0.78 grams
Carbohydrates: 8.03 grams
Calcium: 26.31 mg
Lactose: 0.0 grams

5 cups Chinese cabbage, coarsely chopped
1 cup carrots, shredded
½ cup chopped green onions
1 8-ounce can sliced water chestnuts
2 tablespoons toasted sesame seeds
¼ cup olive oil
1 teaspoon dark sesame oil
2 tablespoons sugar
1 tablespoon minced cilantro
½ teaspoon pepper
½ cup wine vinegar
1 tablespoon soy sauce

Black Bean Slaw

And you thought coleslaw was just shredded cabbage! There are hundreds of different kinds of cabbage, and adding different ingredients and dressings gives you a wide variety of tasty options!

Calories: 80.71
Fat: 1.11 grams
Saturated Fat: 0.41 grams
Carbohydrates: 13.95 grams
Calcium: 64.16 mg
Lactose: 0.0 grams

2½ cups finely shredded cabbage
1 15-ounce can black beans, rinsed and drained
½ cup shredded carrot
½ cup chopped purple onion
¼ cup chopped fresh cilantro
½ cup plain yogurt
½ cup salsa
2 tablespoons mayonnaise
2 teaspoons white wine vinegar
2 teaspoons lime juice
Fresh cilantro sprigs (optional)

1. In a large bowl, combine cabbage, beans, carrot, onion, and chopped cilantro. Toss well.

2. In a small bowl, combine yogurt, salsa, mayonnaise, vinegar, and lime juice. Stir well. Pour over cabbage mixture and gently toss.

3. Tightly cover. Refrigerate at least 2 hours. Garnish with fresh cilantro sprigs, if desired.

Veggie Slaw

A dish with fresh red cabbage always makes a pretty addition to a table setting, and it's a double win when it tastes great too!

1. In a large bowl, combine cabbage, carrot, yellow squash, zucchini, green pepper, and chopped onion.

2. In a small bowl, combine pineapple juice, sugar, vinegar, water, bouillon, paprika, celery seeds, garlic powder, and red pepper. Stir well.

3. Pour over vegetable mixture. Toss gently.

4. Cover tightly and refrigerate at least 4 hours before serving. Toss gently at serving time.

Red Cabbage Trivia

Some people call red cabbage by a slightly different name—purple cabbage. Its color does change according to the environment it's in; it will even turn blue if served with non-acidic food. All colors aside, red cabbage happens to be much higher in vitamin C than other types of cabbage.

Serves 4

Calories: 65.61
Fat: 0.29 grams
Saturated Fat: 0.06 grams
Carbohydrates: 15.19 grams
Calcium: 35.99 mg
Lactose: 0.0 grams

1½ cups shredded red cabbage
1 cup shredded carrot
¾ cup shredded yellow squash
¾ cup shredded zucchini
½ cup chopped green pepper
⅓ cup finely chopped onion
¼ cup unsweetened pineapple juice
1½ tablespoons sugar
3 tablespoons cider vinegar
2 tablespoons water
½ teaspoon chicken-flavored bouillon granules
¼ teaspoon paprika
¼ teaspoon celery seeds
⅛ teaspoon garlic powder
Dash of ground red pepper

Tangy Horseradish Coleslaw

No horsing around with this recipe! If you love horseradish,
feel free to add more than what's called for in this recipe.
The combinations of colors in the coleslaw are truly beautiful.

Serves 8

Calories: 84.70
Fat: 2.64 grams
Saturated Fat: 1.42 grams
Carbohydrates: 13.42 grams
Calcium: 92.47 mg
Lactose: 0.01 grams

4 cups coarsely shredded cabbage
2 cups chopped tomato
1½ cups frozen whole kernel corn, thawed
1 cup coarsely shredded red cabbage
1 cup chopped green pepper
1 cup plain yogurt
2 tablespoons Dijon mustard
1 tablespoon plus 1 teaspoon prepared horseradish
¼ teaspoon salt
¼ teaspoon hot sauce
¼ cup shredded Cheddar cheese (optional)

1. In a large bowl, combine cabbage, chopped tomato, corn, red cabbage, and green pepper. Gently toss.

2. In a small bowl, combine yogurt, mustard, horseradish, salt, and hot sauce, stirring well.

3. Add to cabbage mixture, tossing gently until cabbage mixture is well coated. Cover tightly and refrigerate for at least 1 hour before serving.

4. Just before serving, sprinkle Cheddar cheese over slaw, if desired.

Picnic Coleslaw

This coleslaw isn't made with mayonnaise so it keeps very well for about a week in the refrigerator and it also travels nicely for a picnic.

1. Combine cabbage, carrot, onion, bell pepper, and chopped olives in a large bowl.

2. Combine brown sugar, salt, celery seed, mustard, ground pepper, oil, and vinegar in a small saucepan. Bring to a boil over high heat. Reduce heat and simmer for 3 minutes.

3. Pour warm dressing over cabbage mixture. Toss gently, coating evenly.

4. Cover and refrigerate for at least 6 hours before serving. Toss the coleslaw a couple of times while it's chilling. Serve chilled.

Mayonnaise Maze

When a recipe calls for mayo, think about substituting yogurt. It's a healthy and comfy option for people with LI. In addition, you'll find that yogurt usually makes the dish you're preparing even creamier!

Serves 8

Calories: 100.58
Fat: 3.14 grams
Saturated Fat: 0.44 grams
Carbohydrates: 17.50 grams
Calcium: 59.01 mg
Lactose: 0.0 grams

8 cups shredded cabbage
1 cup finely grated carrot
1 cup chopped sweet onion
1 cup chopped green pepper
12 green olives, chopped
⅓ cup firmly packed brown sugar
½ teaspoon salt
1 teaspoon celery seed
1 teaspoon Dijon mustard
⅛ teaspoon coarsely ground black pepper
4 teaspoons olive oil
⅔ cup balsamic vinegar

Carrot and Cabbage Slaw

Serves 6

Calories: 92.61
Fat: 2.66 grams
Saturated Fat: 0.36 grams
Carbohydrates: 16.33 grams
Calcium: 69.13 mg
Lactose: 0.0 grams

2 cups shredded cabbage
1 cup shredded carrots
½ cup raisins
¼ cup toasted slivered
    almonds
½ cup vanilla yogurt
2 teaspoons lemon juice
⅛ teaspoon nutmeg

If you have toddlers or young children in your family, you might want to serve the toasted almonds on the side for the adults at the table as they could be a choking hazard for little ones. But watch those little fingers pick out the raisins first!

1. Combine cabbage, carrots, raisins, and almonds in a large bowl.

2. Combine yogurt, lemon juice, and nutmeg in a small bowl, stirring until mixed well.

3. Gently toss and chill.

Oriental Spinach Salad

Serves 8

Calories: 71.18
Fat: 5.18 grams
Saturated Fat: 0.71 grams
Carbohydrates: 4.65 grams
Calcium: 69.96 mg
Lactose: 0.0 grams

1 pound fresh spinach leaves,
    torn
2 cups shredded Chinese
    cabbage
½ pound fresh mushrooms,
    sliced
3 green onions, sliced
2 tablespoons toasted
    sesame seeds
2 tablespoons vinegar
2 tablespoons vegetable oil
1 tablespoon soy sauce
¼ teaspoon ground ginger

The mild flavor of Chinese cabbage combined with fresh spinach is enhanced by the ginger and soy sauce. If you have fresh ginger on hand, use it in place of the ground ginger. Its flavor is stronger and tastier.

1. In a large salad bowl, combine spinach, cabbage, mushrooms, onions, and sesame seeds. Lightly toss.

2. Combine vinegar, oil, soy sauce, and ginger in a jar with a lid; cover tightly and shake vigorously. Pour over salad.

3. Gently toss and serve immediately.

Spinach Radicchio Salad

Your taste buds will stand at attention for the radicchio in this salad. With its tender and firm texture, it has a slight bite when eaten alone; however, it adds flavor when mixed with other greens and veggies.

1. In a salad bowl, combine radicchio, spinach, mushrooms, red pepper, and olives. Chill until serving time.

2. Combine vinegar, lemon juice, olive oil, and pepper in a glass jar with lid. Make sure lid is secure and shake vigorously.

3. Pour mixture evenly over salad and toss. Distribute evenly in individual chilled salad bowls.

4. Garnish each salad with a sprinkling of one teaspoon Parmesan cheese before serving.

Serves 4

Calories: 100.58
Fat: 7.04 grams
Saturated Fat: 1.26 grams
Carbohydrates: 7.39 grams
Calcium: 96.98 mg
Lactose: 0.0 grams

¼ pound radicchio, washed
½ pound fresh spinach, washed and torn
½ cup thinly sliced fresh mushrooms
1 sweet red pepper, seeded and thinly sliced
8 pitted ripe olives, sliced
¼ cup red wine vinegar
2 tablespoons lemon juice
1 tablespoon plus 1½ teaspoons olive oil
¼ teaspoon freshly ground pepper
1 tablespoon plus 1 teaspoon grated Parmesan cheese

Tofu Tossed Salad

Serves 6

Calories: 183.94
Fat: 8.98 grams
Saturated Fat: 1.56 grams
Carbohydrates: 19.90 grams
Calcium: 202.91 mg
Lactose: 0.0 grams

1 bunch red leaf lettuce
1 5-ounce container alfalfa
    sprouts
1 small jicama, peeled and
    sliced into strips
½ dill pickle, chopped
1 tablespoon fresh chopped
    cilantro
1 6-ounce jar marinated
    artichoke hearts, drained
2 zucchini, sliced
2 green onions, minced
¼ pound fresh mushrooms,
    sliced
2 ripe tomatoes, sliced
1 14-ounce container firm
    tofu
½ cup Italian salad dressing

This salad is tossed with all kinds of tasty and healthy things. The tofu absorbs the flavors around it, and the alfalfa sprouts and jicama add crunch.

1. Tear red leaf lettuce into small pieces.

2. In a large bowl, combine lettuce, sprouts, jicama, pickle, cilantro, artichoke hearts, zucchini, green onions, mushrooms, and tomatoes.

3. Drain tofu and cut into small squares. Add to salad.

4. Pour your favorite Italian salad dressing over salad just before serving. Toss well.

Jicama Trivia

Jicama is sometimes referred to as the Mexican potato. It's key in stir-fry recipes in place of water chestnuts; it provides the same crunch! Peel jicama just before using it; like potatoes, it turns dark when exposed to the air. Jicama is an excellent source of vitamin C.

Fresh Greens and Red Pepper Dressing

Take a little extra time and go to a little extra trouble in roasting the red peppers—you won't be sorry! If you do it once, you'll do it for many other recipes.

1. Preheat oven to 425°F. Cut pepper in half lengthwise. Remove seeds and membrane. Place pepper, skin side up, on a foil-lined baking sheet. Bake for about 20 minutes or until skin is browned.

2. Cover with aluminum foil. Set aside and allow to cool. When pepper is cooled to room temperature, peel and discard skin.

3. Blend roasted pepper, vinegar, water, olive oil, salt, and red pepper until smooth. Place roasted pepper mixture in a small bowl. Stir in basil. Cover tightly and refrigerate for at least 60 minutes.

4. In a large bowl, combine lettuces, tomato, and cucumber. Toss gently.

5. Top with red pepper mixture over salads and serve immediately.

Serves 6

Calories: 36.03
Fat: 1.76 grams
Saturated Fat: 0.25 grams
Carbohydrates: 4.49 grams
Calcium: 22.29 mg
Lactose: 0.0 grams

1 large sweet red pepper
3 tablespoons white wine vinegar
2 tablespoons water
2 teaspoons olive oil
¼ teaspoon salt
⅛ teaspoon ground red pepper
1 tablespoon minced fresh basil
2 cups torn red leaf lettuce
2 cups torn green leaf lettuce
2 cups torn romaine lettuce
1 cup chopped tomato
1 cup chopped cucumber

Tofu Garden Salad with Sesame Dressing

This salad is packed with all kinds of wonderful garden veggies!
If you're fortunate enough to shop farmers' markets you'll have
super fresh ingredients for this gardener's delight of a salad!

1. Prepare dressing first by combining sugar, vinegar, soy sauce, sesame oil, salt, and pepper to taste. Blend well.

2. Seed and cut the tomato into ½" pieces; wash and slice the mushrooms; blanch the bean sprouts and drain well; trim the ends of the snow peas; cut tofu into ½" cubes.

3. In a heavy skillet, heat oil until hot. Sauté tofu pieces until they turn light brown at the edges (about 5 minutes). Drain well on paper towels.

4. Add tofu to vegetables. Pour dressing over all and toss lightly to coat. Serve immediately.

Papaya Salad

This is a very refreshing salad—not to mention a very pretty presentation—served in a scooped out papaya!

Serves 4

Calories: 254.31
Fat: 4.12 grams
Saturated Fat: 1.51 grams
Carbohydrates: 30.13 grams
Calcium: 191.70 mg
Lactose: 0.0 grams

1. Halve the papaya and scoop out seeds. Leave about ¼" of flesh in the shell of the papaya. Remove the rest of the flesh and dice into ½" cubes.

2. Combine the green pepper, celery, green onion, and crab meat with the papaya. Place in refrigerator while making dressing.

3. In a small bowl, combine the yogurt, honey, orange zest, and cinnamon. Stir well to blend ingredients. Set aside.

4. Fill the papaya shells and garnish with the orange sections and sliced kiwi. Top with honey dressing. Chill before serving.

1 fresh papaya
1 small fresh bell pepper, chopped
2 stalks celery, diced
2 green onions, thinly sliced
1 pound fresh crab meat
1 cup plain yogurt
2 tablespoons honey
2 teaspoons orange zest
1 teaspoon cinnamon
1 orange, peeled and sectioned
1 kiwi fruit, peeled and sliced
Salt to taste (optional)

Papaya Trivia

This yellow-orange fruit contains papain, which is an enzyme similar to pepsin, the digestive juice. The seeds of papayas are usually thrown away; however, they can be dried and used like peppercorns. Papaya is very high in vitamin C and beta carotene.

Cool-As-a-Cucumber Salad

This is a great summer supper salad. It needs to chill in the refrigerator for at least 8 hours so the flavors can mingle.

Serves 4

Calories: 73.79
Fat: 2.16 grams
Saturated Fat: 1.34 grams
Carbohydrates: 11.61 grams
Calcium: 100.39 mg
Lactose: 0.0 grams

2 cucumbers, thinly sliced
1½ tablespoons balsamic vinegar
½ teaspoon salt
1 tablespoon sugar
1 cup plain yogurt
1 green onion, snipped
½ teaspoon celery seed
¼ teaspoon dry mustard

1. Slice cucumbers and place in refrigerator.

2. Combine remaining ingredients in blender. Mix well until smooth.

3. Pour dressing over cucumbers.

4. Cover and refrigerate for several hours or overnight.

Marinated Avocado and Mushroom Salad

Be sure to let this salad happily marinate in the fridge for about 3 hours before serving so the flavors can mingle.

Serves 4

Calories: 234.86
Fat: 18.76 grams
Saturated Fat: 3.23 grams
Carbohydrates: 14.07 grams
Calcium: 19.04 mg
Lactose: 0.0 grams

2 medium avocados
1 cup sliced fresh mushrooms
2 thin slices onion, separated in rings
2 teaspoons lemon juice
¼ cup salad oil
¼ cup dry white wine
2 tablespoons vinegar
½ teaspoon sugar
¼ teaspoon salt
¼ teaspoon dried basil, crumbled
Bibb lettuce leaves for serving

1. Cut avocados in half and remove seeds. Peel and slice.

2. In a large bowl, combine avocado, mushrooms, and onion rings. Sprinkle lemon juice over avocado mixture to prevent avocado from turning dark.

3. In a screw-top jar, combine oil, wine, vinegar, sugar, salt, and basil. Shake well and pour over vegetables.

4. Cover salad tightly and chill for at least 3 hours, stirring occasionally.

5. Drain avocado mixture. Serve on chilled salad plates on Bibb lettuce leaves.

Zucchini Macaroni Salad

A little twist on other recipes for macaroni salad, this one is made with yogurt instead of mayonnaise.

1. Wash summer squash and dice but don't peel.

2. Combine all ingredients except dill seed and leaf lettuce in a large bowl. Toss to mix well.

3. Sprinkle with dill seed. Chill well.

4. Arrange leaf lettuce on salad plates and spoon salad on top of lettuce. Serve immediately.

Zukes!

Zucchini has a mild and unobtrusive flavor and therefore is a complement to other ingredients in many recipes. It is low in calories and a good source of vitamins A and C and folate.

Serves 6

Calories: 169.80
Fat: 2.19 grams
Saturated Fat: 1.03 grams
Carbohydrates: 31.52 grams
Calcium: 85.29 mg
Lactose: 0.0 grams

2 cups small summer squash
3 cups shell macaroni, cooked
2 cups cabbage, shredded
1 cup carrots, shredded
½ cup green pepper, chopped
½ cup red radishes, sliced
3 tablespoons onion, minced
1 cup plain yogurt
2 tablespoons lemon juice
1½ teaspoons sugar
1½ teaspoons dry mustard
1 teaspoon salt
Dill seed
Leaf lettuce

New Potato Salad

Off for a summer picnic? This is a great potato salad to tote along because it doesn't contain any mayonnaise. Try chilling it prior to taking it on a picnic and packing it in a cooler.

Serves 10

Calories: 210.87
Fat: 5.69 grams
Saturated Fat: 0.45 grams
Carbohydrates: 37.73 grams
Calcium: 18.22 mg
Lactose: 0.0 grams

4 pounds new potatoes
½ cup chopped red bell pepper
½ cup chopped green bell pepper
¼ cup chopped celery
¼ cup chopped red onion
¼ cup chopped chives
2 tablespoons minced parsley
¼ cup oil
2 tablespoons red wine vinegar
1 teaspoon dried thyme
Salt and pepper to taste

1. Scrub potatoes. Cook in salted water for 20 minutes until potatoes are tender yet still firm. Drain and cool at room temperature. Cut into bite-sized pieces.

2. In a large bowl combine potatoes, peppers, celery, onion, and herbs.

3. Combine oil, vinegar, thyme, salt, and pepper in a jar with screw top. Shake until blended. Pour over potato mixture.

4. Toss gently until all the vegetables are thoroughly coated. Serve at room temperature.

Keep the Skins on Potatoes!

When you peel potatoes, you peel away most of the nutrients! Rather than peeling them, keep the skins on. Scrub them really well with a vegetable brush. The flavor of the potatoes is even better with their jackets left on!

Strawberry Spinach Salad

The flavor of fresh dill and fresh strawberries mingled together is quite an adventure for your taste buds! This salad spells summer and is great served for a special summer luncheon or supper. You can serve it as a side salad or an entrée.

Serves 6

Calories: 118.50
Fat: 9.54 grams
Saturated Fat: 1.31 grams
Carbohydrates: 8.16 grams
Calcium: 38.50 mg
Lactose: 0.0 grams

6 cups fresh spinach
1 teaspoon toasted sesame seeds
2 cups fresh strawberries
¼ cup light olive oil
2 tablespoons red wine vinegar
1½ tablespoons sugar
1½ teaspoons minced fresh dill
⅛ teaspoon onion powder
⅛ teaspoon garlic powder
⅛ teaspoon dry mustard
⅛ teaspoon salt (optional)

1. Wash the spinach carefully. Remove stems and heavy veins. Tear into bite-sized pieces.

2. Place spinach in a large bowl. Sprinkle with the toasted sesame seeds.

3. Cut strawberries into halves or quarters. Add strawberries to the spinach.

4. In a screw top jar, combine the remaining ingredients. Shake until well mixed. Chill.

5. Shake dressing again and pour over spinach mixture. Toss gently. Garnish with a whole strawberry, if desired.

Sweet Strawberries

Did you know that more than seventy varieties of strawberries are grown in the United States? Even though strawberry seeds may get stuck in your teeth from time to time, those seeds provide you with insoluble fiber. Strawberries are a great source of pectin and soluble fibers that research shows may help lower cholesterol.

Cauliflower Salad

You can use store-bought Italian dressing in this recipe or make your own. If you do use store-bought, don't forget to read the label and look for hidden lactose.

Serves 6

Calories: 48.28
Fat: 2.55 grams
Saturated Fat: 0.57 grams
Carbohydrates: 5.40 grams
Calcium: 35.91 mg
Lactose: 0.0 grams

3½ cups cauliflower florets
¼ cup sweet red pepper
¼ cup celery
1 tablespoon green onion
¼ cup plain yogurt
3 tablespoons Italian salad
    dressing
6 leaves red leaf lettuce
Paprika for garnish (optional)

1. Thinly slice cauliflower; chop red pepper, and dice the celery and green onion. Combine all in a medium bowl.

2. Combine yogurt and salad dressing in a small bowl. Pour over cauliflower mixture. Toss to coat evenly.

3. Cover tightly. Refrigerate until thoroughly chilled.

4. Arrange lettuce leaves on individual salad plates. Spoon chilled vegetable mixture evenly over lettuce. Garnish with a dash of paprika, if desired.

Wild Rice Cranberry Salad

The vividness of this salad is second only to its incredible tastiness! Serve chilled or at room temperature.

Serves 4

Calories: 224.98
Fat: 2.83 grams
Saturated Fat: 0.46 grams
Carbohydrates: 45.20 grams
Calcium: 33.08 mg
Lactose: 0.0 grams

6 ounces wild rice, uncooked
6 ounces fresh cranberries
¼ cup cranberry juice cocktail
1 tablespoon sugar
½ cup carrots cut in strips
1 cup minced green onions
1 tablespoon apple cider
    vinegar
2 teaspoons peanut oil
Dash freshly ground pepper

1. Prepare rice according to package directions. Set aside.

2. Combine cranberries, juice, and sugar in a medium saucepan. Cook over medium heat. Stir occasionally until cranberries pop, about 5 minutes.

3. Remove from heat and cool slightly.

4. Transfer cranberry mixture to a large mixing bowl. Add remaining ingredients. Toss gently until combined well.

5. Cover and refrigerate until serving time.

Chapter 9
Easy Homemade Salad Dressings

Tofu Mayonnaise

This mayonnaise recipe gives you a very light alternative to store-bought mayo. A touch of Dijon adds a rich and enjoyable flavor twist.

Yields 2 cups

Calories: 36.84
Fat: 2.88 grams
Saturated Fat: 0.50 grams
Carbohydrates: 1.12 grams
Calcium: 37.48 mg
Lactose: 0.0 grams

15 ounces soft tofu
6 tablespoons plain yogurt
3 tablespoons vinegar
2 teaspoons Dijon mustard
1 garlic clove
1 teaspoon sugar
½ teaspoon salt
2 tablespoons olive oil

1. Combine all ingredients except oil in a food processor and blend until smooth.

2. Slowly drizzle oil through feed tube until mixture becomes creamy. Mixture will thicken when chilled.

3. Refrigerate in covered container.

Mustard and Tarragon Dressing

Tarragon takes mustard into another realm! If you're into specialty vinegars, substitute the cider vinegar for the vinegar of your choice. This recipe can also be used as a marinade for grilled fish or meat.

Yields 1 quart

Calories: 126.78
Fat: 10.37 grams
Saturated Fat: 1.41 grams
Carbohydrates: 7.22 grams
Calcium: 7.32 mg
Lactose: 0.0 grams

1 cup sugar
1 cup cider vinegar
2 teaspoons Worcestershire sauce
1 cup dry sherry
2 teaspoons salt
1 cup Dijon mustard
1½ cups olive oil
2 teaspoons dry tarragon leaves, crushed

1. Combine all ingredients in blender and mix until smooth. Refrigerate until serving time.

Tarragon Trivia

Tarragon has a warm aroma with a peppery taste and a light touch of anise. It's easy for tarragon to overwhelm other flavors, yet with a light hand it will enhance other herbs and bring out the best in them. If you want to make homemade herb vinegars, try tarragon vinegar.

Creamy Caesar Dressing

Don't miss out on creamy dressings just because you're lactose intolerant. Make them fresh; they don't take much time and the taste is worth it!

1. Mash garlic. Add salt and form a paste. Place paste in a medium bowl.

2. Add remaining ingredients. Combine well, stirring with a wire whisk.

3. Cover tightly and chill. Serve with salad greens.

Caesar Dressing

Classic Caesar dressings include anchovies and raw eggs. These ingredients make some people turn up their noses to a favorite recipe. By leaving the lactose out of Caesar dressing, you can enjoy a truly delicious dressing with no objectionable flavors or ingredients.

Yields ¾ cup

Calories: 32.83
Fat: 2.29 grams
Saturated Fat: 0.65 grams
Carbohydrates: 2.42 grams
Calcium: 31.62 mg
Lactose: 0.0 grams

¼ teaspoon salt
1 large clove garlic
½ cup yogurt
2 tablespoons lemon juice
2 tablespoons soy milk
1 tablespoon Worcestershire
    sauce
2 teaspoons olive oil
1 teaspoon Dijon mustard
½ teaspoon freshly ground
    pepper

Fresh Basil Dressing

This dressing is sure to please basil lovers. A little tip on basil: If you want to retain its wonderful flavor and aroma, always tear it rather than cutting or chopping it.

1. Soften gelatin in cold water; stir in ½ cup boiling water until gelatin dissolves. Set aside.

2. Combine remaining ingredients in blender and process until smooth.

3. Add gelatin mixture and process until well combined, about 1 minute.

4. Cover and chill thoroughly. Stir well before serving.

Yields 1 cup

Calories: 14.60
Fat: 0.36 grams
Saturated Fat: 0.22 grams
Carbohydrates: 0.34 grams
Calcium: 16.24 mg
Lactose: 0.0 grams

¾ teaspoon unflavored gelatin
2 tablespoons cold water
½ cup boiling water
¼ cup red wine vinegar
2 tablespoons grated
    Parmesan cheese
2 tablespoons torn fresh basil
1 tablespoon chopped fresh
    parsley
1 tablespoon lemon juice
1 clove garlic, crushed
⅛ teaspoon pepper

Creamy Avocado Dressing

Combining the freshly squeezed lemon juice with the avocado in this recipe serves two purposes. One is for the flavor; the other is to prevent the dressing from turning dark.

Calories: 78.37
Fat: 7.25 grams
Saturated Fat: 1.06 grams
Carbohydrates: 3.53 grams
Calcium: 7.18 mg
Lactose: 0.0 grams

1 ripe avocado
⅓ cup soy milk
2 tablespoons freshly squeezed lemon juice
1 tablespoon extra virgin olive oil
2 tablespoons mayonnaise
½ teaspoon fresh dill
¼ teaspoon salt
⅛ teaspoon ground white pepper

1. Halve the avocado and remove the pit; peel the avocado.

2. Combine the avocado, soy milk, lemon juice, olive oil, mayonnaise, dill, salt, and pepper in a blender. Blend until smooth, scraping the sides with a rubber spatula.

3. Pour dressing into a jar with a tight-fitting lid. Cover and refrigerate for at least 4 hours or overnight.

4. Before serving, shake to blend. This dressing will keep for 5 days in the refrigerator, tightly covered.

Recipe Variation

Instead of store-bought mayonnaise, you may want to substitute your newly found Tofu Mayonnaise (page 114). Loosen up in the kitchen and be flexible—try substituting new LI-friendly ingredients. You'll find you'll enjoy your cooking a lot more, and you'll more than likely eat healthier.

Orange Yogurt Dressing

This tangy dressing is quick and tasty. It's a great dressing to keep in the fridge for summer fruit snacks. You can pour it over fresh fruit or dip it!

1. Combine all ingredients in blender.

2. Process until mixture reaches a smooth consistency.

3. Chill for at least 2 hours before serving. Serve over fresh fruit.

Serves 2 cups

Calories: 44.90
Fat: 2.06 grams
Saturated Fat: 1.29 grams
Carbohydrates: 4.62 grams
Calcium: 85.02 mg
Lactose: 0.0 grams

1½ cups plain yogurt
½ cup finely chopped parsley
⅓ cup chopped mandarin
*   orange sections*

Yogurt Dill Dressing

Use this refreshing dressing for a variety of purposes—dressing fresh salad greens, dipping fresh veggies, and serving with fish.

1. Combine all ingredients in blender. Process until smooth.

2. Cover tightly. Refrigerate for at least 60 minutes.

3. Serve over fresh salad greens.

Dill Trivia

Fresh dill is the best! The aroma is very fragrant, and the taste has a warm flavor with a bit of a bite. When you're preparing fresh dill, it's best if you snip it rather than chopping it. Dill is a bit fragile and likes to be handled with care!

Yields 1 cup

Calories: 18.30
Fat: 0.79 grams
Saturated Fat: 0.36 grams
Carbohydrates: 1.76 grams
Calcium: 24.76 mg
Lactose: 0.0 grams

½ cup plain yogurt
½ cup soy milk
1 tablespoon lemon juice
2 teaspoons grated onion
1 teaspoon fresh dill weed,
*   snipped*
½ teaspoon garlic salt
⅛ teaspoon dried whole
*   oregano*
⅛ teaspoon freshly ground
*   pepper*

Cucumber Yogurt Dressing

The colder this dressing, the better! It is a delightful lunch or dinner on a hot day when served over crispy cold greens on a chilled plate.

Yields 1½ cups

Calories: 12.18
Fat: 0.46 grams
Saturated Fat: 0.29 grams
Carbohydrates: 1.55 grams
Calcium: 19.31 mg
Lactose: 0.0 grams

1 cup peeled and diced cucumber
2 tablespoons freshly squeezed lemon juice
¼ cup diced white onion
¼ cup diced celery
⅔ cup plain yogurt

1. Combine cucumber, lemon juice, onion, and celery in blender. Purée to a slightly chunky consistency.

2. Transfer to a medium-sized bowl. Whisk in yogurt.

3. Cover and chill for at least 2 hours. Serve chilled.

Yogurt Honey Poppy Seed Dressing

This dressing makes a unique fruit dip or a delicious dressing for a salad.

Yields 1½ cups

Calories: 34.68
Fat: 0.72 grams
Saturated Fat: 0.41 grams
Carbohydrates: 6.90 grams
Calcium: 26.81 mg
Lactose: 0.0 grams

1 8-ounce carton plain yogurt
¼ cup honey
1 tablespoon plus 1 teaspoon lemon juice
1 teaspoon poppy seeds

1. Combine all ingredients in a small, deep bowl. Mix well.

2. Chill and serve dressing over fresh fruit.

Poppy Seed Trivia

These tiny little black seeds may surprise you. They are packed with an oil that's rich in two essential fatty acids—linoleic and linolenic—which are unsaturated fats. Just a tablespoon of these little black roly-poly seeds contain more than 10 percent of your daily value for calcium.

Mango Chili Lime Dressing

*This dressing has something for every taste bud—
a little sweet, a little sour, and a little spicy.*

1. Combine all ingredients in blender. Process until smooth.

2. Transfer to a medium bowl. Cover tightly and chill thoroughly.

3. Serve with salad greens or try it over your favorite chicken salad served on a bed of greens.

Mango Munching

Mangoes are notoriously messy to eat. Slice the mango vertically on each side of the seed. Grab your sharpest paring knife and remove half the mango from the oversized seed. Now you can actually slice the fruit and peel it slice by slice.

Yields 1¼ cups

Calories: 24.35
Fat: 1.40 grams
Saturated Fat: 0.20 grams
Carbohydrates: 3.19 grams
Calcium: 2.49 mg
Lactose: 0.0 grams

1 cup peeled, diced ripe mango
3 tablespoons lime juice
2 tablespoons white wine vinegar
1 tablespoon olive oil
2 teaspoons grated fresh gingerroot
1 teaspoon chili powder
½ teaspoon ground cumin
¼ teaspoon garlic powder
⅛ teaspoon salt

Honey Curry Dressing 🌑

*If you're a curry lover, then up the amount of curry in this recipe!
There's an abundant amount of flavor in this sweet-hot dressing.*

1. In a medium saucepan, combine water, honey, flour, curry powder, dry mustard, and salt.

2. Add egg and stir well. Add orange juice and vinegar until smooth.

3. Cook over low heat, stirring constantly until thickened.

4. Cover tightly and chill. Serve over fresh fruit or fresh greens.

Yields 1 cup

Calories: 29.56
Fat: 0.64 grams
Saturated Fat: 0.20 grams
Carbohydrates: 5.26 grams
Calcium: 4.23 mg
Lactose: 0.01 grams

½ cup water
2 tablespoons honey
2 teaspoons all-purpose flour
1 teaspoon curry powder
¼ teaspoon dry mustard
⅛ teaspoon salt
1 egg, beaten
2 tablespoons unsweetened orange juice
1 tablespoon vinegar

Red Wine Vinegar Dressing

If you're looking for a great standard and simple vinegar dressing recipe, look no further. It's right here.

Yields ¾ cup

Calories: 7.37
Fat: 0.08 grams
Saturated Fat: 0.01 grams
Carbohydrates: 0.70 grams
Calcium: 4.83 mg
Lactose: 0.0 grams

1 tablespoon Dijon mustard
3 tablespoons water
½ cup red wine vinegar
1 large clove garlic, crushed
1½ tablespoons finely chopped white onion
¼ teaspoon freshly ground black pepper
⅛ teaspoon dried oregano

1. Whisk together mustard and water in a small, deep bowl.

2. Whisk in vinegar. Add remaining ingredients and mix thoroughly.

3. Serve over fresh salad greens or fresh veggies.

Dijon Vinaigrette Dressing

It's up to you how much or how little hot sauce you add to this recipe.

Yields ¼ cup

Calories: 67.89
Fat: 6.91 grams
Saturated Fat: 0.94 grams
Carbohydrates: 0.89 grams
Calcium: 7.68 mg
Lactose: 0.0 grams

1 tablespoon water
2 tablespoons white wine vinegar
1 tablespoon olive oil
2 teaspoons Dijon mustard
1 clove garlic, crushed
2 drops of hot sauce (optional)

1. In a glass jar with a tight fitting lid, combine water, vinegar, oil, mustard, garlic, and hot sauce.

2. Cover tightly and shake vigorously.

3. Serve immediately over salad greens.

Recipe Variation

Experiment with different mustards for this recipe. Different regions of the world have their own distinct mustards, so be adventurous and go beyond Dijon. You can also mix and match the salads and vegetables you pair this vinaigrette with. Your own imagination is the limit.

Papaya Dream Vinaigrette

*Make sure the papaya you choose is not green but definitely ripe.
Otherwise, your mouth might pucker instead of smile! The sweet
taste of the vanilla soy milk blends well with the papaya flavor,
giving you a refreshing creamy delight that's lactose free!*

Yields 1½ cups

Calories: 27.81
Fat: 1.27 grams
Saturated Fat: 0.20 grams
Carbohydrates: 4.08 grams
Calcium: 10.25 mg
Lactose: 0.0 grams

1 ripe papaya
¼ cup vanilla soy milk
3 tablespoons freshly
*   squeezed lime juice*
2 tablespoons mayonnaise
2 tablespoons apple cider
*   vinegar*
¼ teaspoon salt

1. Peel papaya and scoop out seeds. Cut into quarters.

2. Combine papaya, soy milk, lime juice, mayonnaise, vinegar, and salt in a blender. Process on high for one minute.

3. Pour dressing into a container with a tight-fitting lid. Cover and refrigerate for at least 3 hours or overnight.

4. Before serving, whisk the dressing to blend.

Store-Bought Mayo Trivia

It's all about the oil and fillers used in the mayo that you buy at the grocery store! Be sure to check the labels of commercial mayonnaise and see what type of oil you're buying. The oils in store-bought mayonnaise range from olive oil to sunflower oil to safflower oil and some less desirable oils!

Raspberry Mango Vinaigrette

What a blend of flavors and a beautiful color to pour over fresh salad greens! This recipe is bound to bring rave reviews from guests that don't have a clue that you created this recipe to fit your LI lifestyle!

Yields 2½ cups

Calories: 86.22
Fat: 8.15 grams
Saturated Fat: 1.12 grams
Carbohydrates: 3.70 grams
Calcium: 2.34 mg
Lactose: 0.0 grams

¾ cup fresh, chopped mango
¾ cup fresh red raspberries
3 tablespoons white wine
  vinegar
2 tablespoons honey
¾ cup extra virgin olive oil
Salt and pepper to taste

1. Peel and chop mango. Combine raspberries and mango together in a blender and process until smooth.

2. Add vinegar and honey. Continue blending into a smooth purée. Slowly add the oil in a thin stream with blender running.

3. Salt and pepper to taste.

4. Strain entire liquid through a fine strainer to remove any seeds or pulp. Store in the refrigerator and use within two days.

Raspberry Seeds

Even the seeds in raspberries are good for you! Those little rascals contain an insoluble fiber that helps prevent constipation. This delectable fruit itself is high in pectin, which helps control blood cholesterol levels.

Chapter 10
Dips and Salsas

Hot Crab Dip

Serves 12

Calories: 89.01
Fat: 2.34 grams
Saturated Fat: 1.21 grams
Carbohydrates: 5.38 grams
Calcium: 161.57 mg
Lactose: 0.0 grams

1 cup yogurt cheese
1 small clove garlic, minced
1 tablespoon lemon juice
1 tablespoon Dijon mustard
2 teaspoons white wine
*   Worcestershire sauce*
Pinch cayenne pepper
6 ounces cooked crab meat,
*   flaked*

Hot crab dip is decadent for crab lovers! This dip can also be used as a spread on a slice of whole wheat bread with some trimmings for a hearty snack.

1. In a medium-sized bowl, combine the yogurt cheese, garlic, lemon juice, mustard, Worcestershire sauce, and cayenne pepper. Whisk until smooth. Fold in crab meat.

2. Transfer to a saucepan. Heat on medium-low and warm slowly. Do not allow mixture to boil.

3. Serve at once with crackers or small cubes of French bread on tooth-picks.

Crabby Trivia

Fresh crab is an excellent source of selenium, an essential trace mineral that enhances the antioxidant effect of vitamin E. It's also a good source of magnesium, which is an essential mineral to the human body. Magnesium is responsible for making new cells, relaxing muscles, clotting blood, and activating B vitamins. The secretion and action of insulin also requires magnesium.

Spicy Tuna Dip

*Get healthy corn chips. This dip is a great healthy snack
so don't mess it up with chips that are full of preservatives and
hidden sugars! It can be used as a spread for a quick snack.*

1. Drain tuna. In a small bowl, mix tuna, chili sauce, and lemon juice.

2. Add Tabasco sauce. Chill thoroughly.

3. Serve with corn chips.

Serves 12

Calories: 138.95
Fat: 4.98 grams
Saturated Fat: 0.67 grams
Carbohydrates: 14.47 grams
Calcium: 34.22 mg
Lactose: 0.0 grams

*1 12-ounce can tuna, packed
    in water
1 8-ounce bottle chili sauce
3 tablespoons lemon juice
Dash Tabasco sauce
1 7-ounce bag corn chips*

Festive Spinach Dip

*Even people who don't like spinach like spinach dip! Serve spinach
dip with a platter of fresh vegetables or whole wheat crackers.*

1. Finely chop spinach.

2. In a medium-sized bowl, combine all ingredients and mix well.

3. Cover tightly and chill several hours before serving.

Serves 12

Calories: 66.25
Fat: 5.89 grams
Saturated Fat: 1.32 grams
Carbohydrates: 2.37 grams
Calcium: 64.00 mg
Lactose: 0.0 grams

*10 ounces frozen chopped
    spinach, thawed and
    drained
1 cup plain yogurt
⅓ cup margarine
¼ cup onion, chopped
2 tablespoons parsley flakes
½ teaspoon pepper
½ teaspoon rosemary leaves*

Hummus Dip

Calories: 142.21
Fat: 4.83 grams
Saturated Fat: 0.63 grams
Carbohydrates: 17.47 grams
Calcium: 63.50 mg
Lactose: 0.0 grams

12 ounces drained, cooked
   chickpeas
6 ounces soft tofu
¼ cup chopped onion
¼ cup chicken broth
2 tablespoons soy sauce
2 tablespoons dry white wine
1 tablespoon olive oil
1 garlic clove, minced
¼ teaspoon ground cumin
¼ teaspoon ground red
   pepper
3 cups assorted raw
   vegetables; carrot sticks,
   cucumber rounds, sliced
   yellow squash

There isn't a vegetable in the "veggie rainbow" that isn't good dipped in hummus! Carrots, cucumbers, and squash work particularly well, but be sure to include your favorites in this tasty and bold display of natural color and goodness! Best of all, the entire "veggie rainbow" is lactose free!

1. Combine all ingredients except assorted vegetables in blender. Purée until smooth.

2. Transfer to serving bowl and surround with a rainbow of vegetables.

Recipe Variation

You can easily make this into a salad dressing by adding ¼ cup of liquid. Water is usually the liquid of choice; however, you could also use ¼ cup of your favorite wine! Hummus is also good used as a spread on whole wheat bread with some sliced turkey and trimmings.

Lemon Chive Dip

When you're preparing lemon zest, be sure to scrub the peel before zesting. Lemon trees are sometimes sprayed with fungicides and pesticides to prevent the growth of mold and to kill insects.

1. In a deep, small mixing bowl, combine yogurt, chives, lemon juice, lemon zest, salt, and freshly ground pepper.

2. Stir until well blended.

3. Chill well. Use as a dip for fresh veggies or as accompaniment to grilled fish or chicken.

Chive Chat

Chives are of the onion clan. They are the babies of the group, being the smallest and mildest member of the family. Fresh chives are a bit on the fragile side and will wilt quickly. Use chives to enhance salads, soups, yogurt, and tofu.

Serves 8

Calories: 19.50
Fat: 1.00 grams
Saturated Fat: 0.64 grams
Carbohydrates: 1.64 grams
Calcium: 38.22 mg
Lactose: 0.0 grams

1 cup plain yogurt
3 tablespoons chopped fresh chives
1 tablespoon fresh lemon juice
½ teaspoon finely grated lemon zest
¼ teaspoon salt
¼ teaspoon freshly ground pepper

Strawberry Yogurt Dip

This is a cooling and delightful dessert in the summer. If you're in a hurry to serve, pop the dip in the freezer for about 10 minutes!

Serves 6

Calories: 76.58
Fat: 1.51 grams
Saturated Fat: 0.87 grams
Carbohydrates: 14.85 grams
Calcium: 59.07 mg
Lactose: 0.0 grams

1 cup vanilla yogurt
1 teaspoon finely grated
    lemon peel
1 teaspoon lemon juice
½ cup powdered sugar
2 cups fresh strawberries with
    stems

1. In a medium-sized mixing bowl, combine yogurt, lemon peel, lemon juice, and powdered sugar. Beat until blended well and light and fluffy.

2. Chill well.

3. Place in small serving bowls and surround with large, fresh strawberries.

Banana Peanut Butter Dip

What's better than peanut butter and bananas? Elvis had a peanut butter and banana sandwich almost every day when he was growing up! This creamy dip is bound to become a favorite for serving guests and for everyday snacking!

Serves 3

Calories: 108.57
Fat: 5.25 grams
Saturated Fat: 0.93 grams
Carbohydrates: 11.62 grams
Calcium: 197.21 mg
Lactose: 0.0 grams

3 ounces firm tofu
1 tablespoon peanut butter
½ medium, ripe banana,
    mashed
1 teaspoon lemon juice
1 teaspoon honey
1 teaspoon vanilla extract
2 teaspoons sugar
Ground cinnamon to taste

1. Drain tofu. Rinse and slice.

2. Place tofu between layers of paper towels to soak up excess water.

3. In a small bowl, mash tofu with a fork. Add remaining ingredients, mixing well.

4. Chill. Sprinkle with cinnamon before serving.

Peanutty Prattle!

Peanut butter made its public debut alongside ice cream cones, hot dogs, and hamburgers at the 1904 World's Fair in St. Louis. The original patent was held by Dr. John Harvey Kellogg—the same Kellogg whose name adorns cereal boxes in today's supermarkets.

Tofu Guacamole Dip

If you like hot, then add hot salsa to this dip. If your mouth says no, then skip the pepper sauce and add a mild salsa for a smooth and mild guacamole dip.

1. Drain and rinse tofu. Pat dry with paper towels. Place tofu in blender and blend until smooth.

2. Halve avocados; pit and peel. Mash avocados with a fork in a small bowl.

3. Add tofu and other ingredients to mashed avocados. Mix well.

4. Press a piece of plastic wrap on the surface of the dip to prevent darkening. Chill.

5. Serve as a dip for fresh vegetables, chips, or as a topping for taco salad.

Serves 8

Calories: 95.03
Fat: 8.03 grams
Saturated Fat: 1.21 grams
Carbohydrates: 5.48 grams
Calcium: 40.36 mg
Lactose: 0.0 grams

½ cup firm tofu
2 ripe avocados
½ small onion, minced
1 clove garlic, minced
1 tablespoon lemon juice
1 teaspoon Worcestershire sauce
3 drops hot pepper sauce (optional)
1 teaspoon salt
½ teaspoon salsa

Tomato Pesto

Serve this fresh tomato pesto over pasta or fresh vegetables.

Serves 8

Calories: 16.81
Fat: 0.26 grams
Saturated Fat: 0.11 grams
Carbohydrates: 3.23 grams
Calcium: 10.34 mg
Lactose: 0.0 grams

2 medium tomatoes
1 sweet red pepper
2 tablespoons minced fresh parsley
2 cloves garlic
¼ cup chopped fresh basil leaves
1 tablespoon plus 1½ teaspoons all-purpose flour
¼ teaspoon salt
⅛ teaspoon pepper
2 teaspoons grated fresh Parmesan cheese (optional)

1. Coarsely chop tomatoes. Seed and coarsely chop red pepper.

2. Combine tomato, red pepper, parsley, garlic, and basil in blender. Process until finely puréed.

3. Add flour, salt, and pepper to mixture. Process in blender until thoroughly combined.

4. Transfer mixture to a heavy saucepan. Bring to a boil over medium-high heat. Reduce heat and simmer for 15 minutes.

5. Add Parmesan cheese if desired and stir well.

Storing Pesto

Most pesto freezes very well. Instead of freezing the whole batch of pesto, freeze it in portion-sized amounts in individual containers with tight-fitting lids. Skip the cheese when freezing; add it right before serving.

Basil Pesto

This pesto is best when it is used fresh. Don't plan to store it in the refrigerator for more than three days!

1. Wash basil leaves and blot dry using paper towels. Remove any long stems and discard.

2. Add the Parmesan, garlic, and pine nuts to a food processor or blender and process until the mixture is coarsely ground.

3. Add basil and process until entire mixture is coarsely ground. While blender is running, slowly add the oil in a thin stream.

4. When entire mixture is evenly blended to a coarse, chopped consistency, add salt and pepper to taste.

5. Store in the refrigerator or freeze in small amounts.

Serves 16

Calories: 111.08
Fat: 11.04 grams
Saturated Fat: 2.01 grams
Carbohydrates: 1.14 grams
Calcium: 72.57 mg
Lactose: 0.0 grams

2 cups fresh basil leaves
1 cup shredded Parmesan cheese
3 cloves garlic, peeled
½ cup pine nuts
½ cup extra virgin olive oil
Salt and pepper to taste

Black Bean Salsa

This black bean salsa is tasty rolled in a tortilla with some fresh greens and some grilled chicken.

1. Drain black beans and rinse under cold water. Coarsely chop the onion.

2. In a small bowl, mix black beans and onion.

3. Add remaining ingredients and thoroughly mix.

4. Let stand at least 60 minutes before serving to allow the flavors to mingle.

5. Serve at room temperature or chilled. If refrigerating, be sure to cover tightly.

Serves 10

Calories: 23.65
Fat: 0.08 grams
Saturated Fat: 0.02 grams
Carbohydrates: 4.40 grams
Calcium: 9.97 mg
Lactose: 0.0 grams

1 cup canned black beans
2 tablespoons white onion
2 cloves minced garlic
⅛ teaspoon dried oregano
¼ teaspoon ground cumin
2 teaspoons chopped fresh cilantro
¾ teaspoon freshly squeezed lime juice

Tomatillo Salsa

*The fresh, tart, crisp flavor and green color of this salsa will blow
you away! You will find yourself dipping it like guacamole.*

Serves 12

Calories: 13.26
Fat: 0.14 grams
Saturated Fat: 0.02 grams
Carbohydrates: 2.99 grams
Calcium: 2.88 mg
Lactose: 0.0 grams

1 cup diced tomatillos
¼ cup diced sweet red pepper
*¼ cup diced sweet yellow
    pepper*
¼ cup diced onion
*2 tablespoons white wine
    vinegar*
1 tablespoon sugar
*1 tablespoon unsweetened
    orange juice*
1 tablespoon lime juice
1 tablespoon lemon juice
*2 teaspoons chopped fresh
    cilantro*
½ teaspoon ground cumin
*¼ teaspoon ground red
    pepper*

1. In a large glass bowl, combine diced tomatillos, sweet red pepper, sweet yellow pepper, and onion. Mix well.

2. Fold in vinegar, sugar, orange juice, lime juice, and lemon juice. Stir well to combine. Add cilantro, cumin, and ground red pepper, stirring well to combine.

3. Cover and refrigerate at least 2 hours.

4. Serve salsa with unsalted tortilla chips. This salsa also brings out the best in cooked chicken, pork, and beef and makes for a beautiful presentation for a meal.

I Say Tomato, You Say Tomatillo!

If you're not familiar with tomatillos, they are sometimes called the Mexican tomato or husk tomato. The fruit of the tomatillo is firm and bright green in color. Tomatillos have a papery outer skin. The flavor is tart and not like the commonly known red tomato.

Blueberry, Blackberry, and Orange Salsa

The fruity aroma of this salsa will have your mouth watering.
Serve it with your favorite grilled meat, chicken, or fish.

1. In a large mixing bowl, combine all ingredients. Mix well to combine.

2. Refrigerate and chill well before serving.

Fruit Salsas

There are many ways to get enough servings of fresh fruits, and fruit salsas are a great option! The antioxidants in the fresh blueberries and blackberries are healthy, and this recipe presents them in a unique way—a salsa!

Serves 8

Calories: 11.56
Fat: 0.09 grams
Saturated Fat: 0.01 grams
Carbohydrates: 2.75 grams
Calcium: 3.99 mg
Lactose: 0.0 grams

½ cup fresh blueberries, finely chopped
½ cup blackberries, finely chopped
½ jalapeño, cored, seeded, and finely chopped (optional)
1 tablespoon red onion, finely chopped
1 tablespoon chives, finely chopped
1 tablespoon cilantro, finely chopped
1 tablespoon fresh parsley, finely chopped
1 teaspoon orange zest, finely grated
1 teaspoon lemon zest, finely grated
2 tablespoons freshly squeezed orange juice
Salt and freshly ground black pepper to taste

Cranberry and Pineapple Salsa

This is a beautiful—not to mention palate-pleasing—addition to freshly baked turkey breast. It also makes a great spread for a fantastic sandwich made with leftover turkey.

Serves 6

Calories: 46.86
Fat: 0.07 grams
Saturated Fat: 0.0 grams
Carbohydrates: 12.48 grams
Calcium: 8.85 mg
Lactose: 0.0 grams

¾ cup finely chopped fresh pineapple
½ cup finely chopped fresh cranberries
¼ cup thinly sliced green onions
¼ cup finely chopped dried dates
1 tablespoon honey
1 teaspoon lemon juice
1 teaspoon grated fresh ginger
¼ teaspoon ground red pepper

1. Combine pineapple, cranberries, green onions, dates, honey, lemon juice, fresh ginger, and ground red pepper in a small bowl. Stir well.

2. Cover and chill salsa for at least 60 minutes before serving.

Beet and Raspberry Salsa

Beautiful is the word for this bright red salsa! This blend uniquely brings together the sweet and sour flavors of fresh beets and raspberries.

Serves 10

Calories: 20.04
Fat: 0.11 grams
Saturated Fat: 0.01 grams
Carbohydrates: 4.64 grams
Calcium: 7.35 mg
Lactose: 0.0 grams

1 medium red beet
½ pint fresh raspberries
1 tablespoon finely chopped red onion
1 tablespoon light brown sugar
1 tablespoon raspberry vinegar
1 tablespoon freshly squeezed orange juice
Salt and pepper to taste

1. Trim off the ends of the beet; coarsely chop the raspberries.

2. Place the beet in the microwave. Cook on high for about 4 minutes or until fork tender. Cool. Grate beet finely when cool.

3. Combine the grated beet, the raspberries, onion, sugar, vinegar, and orange juice in a medium-sized bowl.

4. Season to taste with salt and freshly ground pepper. Refrigerate until chilled through.

Chapter 11
Spreads

Basic Yogurt Cheese Recipe

Yields 8 servings

Calories: 343.00
Fat: 10.95 grams
Saturated Fat: 7.01 grams
Carbohydrates: 26.55 grams
Calcium: 838.08 mg
Lactose: 0.0 grams

3 cups plain yogurt (made without gelatin)

Yogurt cheese is sometimes fondly referred to as "yogo-cheese." Choose yogurt that isn't made with gelatin. The gelatin acts as a binder and will not allow the whey to separate.

1. Line a strainer with a coffee filter, using it as a sieve. (If you don't have a paper coffee filter, you can line a colander with paper towels.)

2. Spoon yogurt into coffee filter. Place strainer over a bowl so yogurt can drain. Make sure there is at least an inch between the bottom of the strainer and the bottom of the bowl.

3. Cover with plastic wrap. Refrigerate for 24 hours. Discard liquid.

4. Carefully remove homemade yogurt cheese from paper. Please note that the longer the yogurt drains, the thicker it becomes.

Garlic Cheese Spread

Yields 24 servings

Calories: 64.03
Fat: 3.10 grams
Saturated Fat: 1.39 grams
Carbohydrates: 3.90 grams
Calcium: 130.58 mg
Lactose: 0.0 grams

6 large cloves garlic, minced
½ teaspoon dried Italian herbs
¼ teaspoon freshly ground black pepper
1 tablespoon olive oil
1½ cups yogurt cheese
¼ cup grated Parmesan cheese
1 tablespoon snipped chives

You'll find all kinds of uses for spreading this tasty recipe around! In addition to spreading it on crackers and bagels, you can use it to fill celery sticks for a great snack that more than fits with your LI lifestyle.

1. Heat olive oil in a heavy skillet over medium-high heat. Sauté garlic, herbs, and pepper until the garlic is lightly browned. Pour off any excess oil.

2. Combine all ingredients in a medium-sized bowl. Whisk together until well blended.

3. Chill until ready to serve.

Onion Spinach Spread

This spinach spread can double as a dip! If you're serving it at a party or a barbecue, you can place both unsalted tortilla chips and wheat crackers with it and let your guests decide.

1. Heat margarine in a small skillet. Sauté onion until softened.

2. Cook spinach according to package directions and squeeze out excess liquid. Chop finely.

3. Combine yogurt cheese, garlic, lemon juice, salt, and pepper in a blender. Process until well blended and smooth.

4. Transfer to a bowl. Fold in the onion and spinach.

5. Cover and chill until ready to serve.

Yields 12 servings

Calories: 44.86
Fat: 2.55 grams
Saturated Fat: 0.67 grams
Carbohydrates: 3.68 grams
Calcium: 75.69 mg
Lactose: 0.0 grams

1 medium onion, minced
2 tablespoons light
    margarine
1 10-ounce package frozen
    chopped spinach
½ cup yogurt cheese
1 clove garlic, minced
1 tablespoon lemon juice
⅛ teaspoon salt
Freshly ground black pepper
    to taste

English Sage Derby Cheese

This spread makes a great appetizer or snack when served with your favorite crackers. It tastes like it should be expensive!

1. Combine all ingredients in a medium-sized bowl.

2. Whisk together until well blended.

3. Cover tightly. Chill until ready to serve.

Yogurt Cheese Pick-Ups

Yogurt cheese picks up whatever flavors, herbs, and spices you decide to blend it with. You can add a few slices of ripe tomato and some lettuce to this English Sage Cheese spread on your favorite whole wheat bread and have a quick and tasty lactose-free snack or sandwich in no time!

Yields 8 servings

Calories: 54.98
Fat: 2.35 grams
Saturated Fat: 0.98 grams
Carbohydrates: 3.92 grams
Calcium: 137.52 mg
Lactose: 0.0 grams

1 cup yogurt cheese
2 tablespoons minced green
    onion
1 tablespoon dried sage
2 tablespoons poppy seeds

Herb Cheese

A burst of herbs combined with yogurt cheese makes this cheese smell like a little herb garden—and it tastes even better! How does your little herb garden grow? Full of calcium and void of lactose weeds!

Yields 8 servings

Calories: 43.43
Fat: 1.37 grams
Saturated Fat: 0.88 grams
Carbohydrates: 3.44 grams
Calcium: 105.43 mg
Lactose: 0.0 grams

1 cup yogurt cheese
1 clove garlic, minced
1 teaspoon caraway seed
1 teaspoon dried basil
1 teaspoon dried dill weed
1 teaspoon snipped fresh
* chives*

1. Combine all ingredients in medium-sized bowl.

2. Whisk together until well blended.

3. Cover tightly. Chill until ready to serve.

Tropical Cream Cheese

When choosing canned fruits, make the healthy choice for those packed in their own juices with no extra sugar added!

Yields 12 servings

Calories: 74.71
Fat: 5.28 grams
Saturated Fat: 0.96 grams
Carbohydrates: 4.17 grams
Calcium: 75.07 mg
Lactose: 0.0 grams

1 cup yogurt cheese
1 teaspoon grated fresh
* gingerroot*
⅓ cup well-drained crushed
* pineapple*
½ cup finely chopped pecans

1. Combine yogurt cheese and ginger in a medium-sized bowl. Whisk until smooth.

2. Fold in nuts and pineapple.

3. Cover tightly. Chill until ready to serve.

Sweet Yogurt Cheese Spread

This is a real zero-lactose treat on bagels, English muffins, and toast! It resembles a fancy real cream cheese spread made with LI-friendly yogurt cheese!

1. Combine yogurt, dried fruit bits, honey, and cinnamon in a small bowl.

2. Chill mixture thoroughly before serving.

Dried Fruit Trivia

Dried fruits tend to be a more concentrated source of calories than fresh fruit. The drying process removes most of the moisture, which prevents the growth of bacteria. Naturally, some vitamins and beta carotene may be lost in dried fruits. Freeze drying maintains the highest amounts of nutrients in dried fruits.

Yields 16 servings

Calories: 67.03
Fat: 1.84 grams
Saturated Fat: 1.17 grams
Carbohydrates: 7.04 grams
Calcium: 140.97 mg
Lactose: 0.0 grams

2 cups yogurt cheese
3 tablespoons mixed dried fruit bits
1 teaspoon honey
½ teaspoon ground cinnamon

Apple Honey Spread

This simple spread is packed full of flavor.

1. Combine all ingredients in blender.

2. Process until smooth and well blended.

3. Cover tightly and chill until ready to serve.

Yields 8 servings

Calories: 53.46
Fat: 1.38 grams
Saturated Fat: 0.88 grams
Carbohydrates: 6.05 grams
Calcium: 105.53 mg
Lactose: 0.0 grams

1 cup yogurt cheese
2 tablespoons frozen apple juice concentrate, thawed
2 teaspoons honey

Blueberry Fruit Spread

A natural fruit spread can, of course, be spread around. Think about using a dollop of this blueberry fruit spread on top of a bowl of fresh fruit or melon balls.

Yields 16 servings

Calories: 16.95
Fat: 0.06 grams
Saturated Fat: 0.01 grams
Carbohydrates: 4.22 grams
Calcium: 1.21 mg
Lactose: 0.0 grams

1 teaspoon unflavored gelatin
¼ cup water
2 cups fresh blueberries
½ cup water
2 tablespoons sugar
1 teaspoon lemon juice

1. Combine gelatin and ¼ cup water in a small bowl. Stir well and set aside.

2. In a medium saucepan, combine blueberries, ½ cup water, sugar, and lemon juice.

3. Heat over medium-high heat and bring to a boil. Reduce heat and simmer uncovered for about 8 minutes, stirring frequently.

4. Remove saucepan from heat. Add gelatin. Stir until gelatin is completely dissolved.

5. Cool to room temperature. Pour into a pint glass jar or 2 half pints. Cover tightly. Keep refrigerated.

Fresh Fruit Spreads

You may be amazed to learn that a lot of homemade natural fruit spreads have fewer calories than butter! You may find you can make the switch to fresh fruit spreads from butter rather easily.

Strawberry Orange Spread

*Mingling orange rind and orange juice with fresh strawberries
makes a refreshing spread on crackers or small rounds of bread.
This spread would be great served at an afternoon tea!*

Yields 10 servings

Calories: 10.21
Fat: 0.07 grams
Saturated Fat: 0.0 grams
Carbohydrates: 2.24 grams
Calcium: 4.13 mg
Lactose: 0.0 grams

*1 teaspoon unflavored
    gelatin*
*¼ cup unsweetened orange
    juice*
*1 cup mashed, fresh
    strawberries*
1 tablespoon sugar
*1 teaspoon grated orange
    rind*
¼ teaspoon ground coriander

1. In a small, aluminum-free saucepan, soften gelatin in orange juice.

2. Cook over low heat, stirring constantly, until gelatin dissolves.

3. Remove from heat. Stir in mashed strawberries, sugar, orange rind, and ground coriander.

4. Cover and refrigerate until spread is firm.

Orange Peel Trivia

The orange peel, sometimes called zest, is an ingredient totally separate from the fruit inside! Orange peel contains an aromatic oil. Use a zester to get the zest, and don't get into the bitter white pith just under the orange peel. Be careful when purchasing your citrus for zesting; you need to make sure the fruit hasn't been waxed.

Banana Spread

This spread is best when it's made fresh. Spread on warm whole wheat toast or a toasted English muffin.

1. In a small, deep bowl, mash ripe bananas with a fork.

2. Blend lemon juice with mashed banana.

3. Add lemon zest, cinnamon, yogurt, and honey. Blend well.

Banana Trivia

Bananas are high in potassium, which is a necessary mineral for muscle function. Bananas are a great on-the-move snack because they come with their own packaging and can go just about anywhere with you!

Pineapple Peanut Butter Spread

Sweet and luscious pineapple combined with a favorite old stand-by makes for a delightful spread on warm toast or a dip for fresh fruit. You can also stuff celery with this spread for a snack that is beyond de-lish!

1. Drain pineapple, reserving juice.

2. Combine pineapple with peanut butter.

3. Add pineapple juice and cinnamon. Mix all ingredients until well blended.

Stove-Top Apple Butter

Apple butter is a great replacement for butter or margarine on toast.

Yields 56 servings

Calories: 44.59
Fat: 0.09 grams
Saturated Fat: 0.01 grams
Carbohydrates: 11.62 grams
Calcium: 6.87 mg
Lactose: 0.0 grams

12 large Granny Smith apples
1 cup frozen apple juice
* concentrate*
2 tablespoons lemon juice
1 cup brown sugar
1½ teaspoons cinnamon
¼ teaspoon salt
¼ teaspoon allspice
Pinch ground cloves

1. Peel, core, and slice the apples. Place in a large, heavy kettle. Add apple juice concentrate to apples.

2. Place over medium heat and bring the mixture to a boil. Reduce the heat and simmer until apples are tender, about 20 minutes.

3. Place the hot mixture in a blender. Purée briefly; there should still be small chunks of apples in the mixture. Return the mixture to the kettle. Add lemon juice, brown sugar, cinnamon, salt, allspice, and ground cloves.

4. Cook over low heat until mixture thickens, about 30 minutes. Be sure to stir often so mixture doesn't stick; apple butter scorches easily!

5. Allow to cool to room temperature and store in glass jars.

Granny Smith

One of the world's most famous apple varieties, Granny Smiths are bright green and shiny. They are very juicy and have a slightly tangy flavor. Granny Smiths were first cultivated in Australia in 1865 by Marie Ana Smith. They slowly made their way around the world, reaching the United States more than one hundred years after they were first cultivated.

Plum Pineapple Butter

Plum delicious! Plums contain lutein, which is good for your eyes!

Yields 12 servings

Calories: 42.98
Fat: 0.18 grams
Saturated Fat: 0.01 grams
Carbohydrates: 11.00 grams
Calcium: 6.51 mg
Lactose: 0.0 grams

1½ pounds plums
1 8-ounce can crushed
*   pineapple in juice,*
*   undrained*
2 tablespoons honey
2 teaspoons lemon juice
½ teaspoon ground
*   cardamom*
¼ teaspoon ground ginger

1. Pit and quarter plums. Combine all ingredients in a large, heavy saucepan.

2. Bring to a boil over medium heat. Reduce heat and simmer until plums are tender, about 10 minutes.

3. Pour hot mixture into blender. Process until smooth.

4. Return mixture to saucepan. Cook over medium heat until thickened, about 15–20 minutes. Stir frequently to prevent scorching.

5. Serve warm or chilled.

Fruit Medley Butter

This is a rich and fruity spread for toast, bagels, toasted
English muffins, or the specialty bread of the day!

Yields 18 servings

Calories: 56.51
Fat: 0.07 grams
Saturated Fat: 0.01 grams
Carbohydrates: 14.67 grams
Calcium: 5.35 mg
Lactose: 0.0 grams

8 ounces mixed dried fruit
1 cup apple juice
½ cup sugar
½ cup water
¼ teaspoon salt
¼ teaspoon ground
*   cinnamon*
⅛ teaspoon ground nutmeg

1. Combine all ingredients in a heavy, medium-sized saucepan. Bring to a boil over medium heat.

2. Reduce heat to medium-low. Cover and cook for 30 minutes.

3. Let stand uncovered for 10 minutes.

4. Transfer to a blender. Purée until smooth. Cool.

5. Cover tightly and refrigerate.

Chapter 12
Sauces

Mango Sauce

*This sauce is a tasty complement to fish or chicken.
It also makes the presentation very pretty!*

Serves 10

Calories: 28.90
Fat: 0.09 grams
Saturated Fat: 0.02 grams
Carbohydrates: 5.81 grams
Calcium: 3.02 mg
Lactose: 0.0 grams

*1 cup cubed mango
2 tablespoons orange-
   flavored liqueur
3 tablespoons unsweetened
   orange juice*

1. Combine all the ingredients in blender.

2. Process until smooth.

Mango Tango

Mangoes are very messy to eat! With recipes like this one, you get the full, fresh flavor of this awesome fruit without the mess. Pick plump, fragrant mangoes that are heavy for their size. To tell if a mango is ripe, push the skin. If it gives, it's ripe—but avoid fruit that feels mushy.

Strawberry Yogurt Sauce

*Top a bowl of fresh fruit with this sauce or make a beautiful
presentation of a fresh fruit platter and serve it as a fruit dip.*

Serves 6

Calories: 43.34
Fat: 1.40 grams
Saturated Fat: 0.86 grams
Carbohydrates: 6.52 grams
Calcium: 53.28 mg
Lactose: 0.0 grams

*1 cup plain yogurt
1 cup fresh strawberries,
   stemmed
1 teaspoon vanilla extract
4 teaspoons sugar*

1. Combine all ingredients in blender. Process until smooth and creamy.

2. Chill thoroughly.

Raspberry Sauce

This sauce is so tempting it's hard not to lick it right out of the pan!

1. Place raspberries in blender. Process until smooth purée.

2. In a small, heavy saucepan, combine raspberry liquid and cornstarch. Stir until well blended.

3. Over medium-high heat, bring to a boil. Reduce heat and cover. Stir constantly until mixture becomes smooth and thickened.

4. Remove from heat. Stir in orange juice.

5. Cover and chill thoroughly.

Serves 6

Calories: 60.81
Fat: 0.11 grams
Saturated Fat: 0.01 grams
Carbohydrates: 15.21 grams
Calcium: 8.83 mg
Lactose: 0.0 grams

1 10-ounce package frozen raspberries in light syrup, thawed
1 tablespoon cornstarch
¼ cup plus 2 tablespoons unsweetened orange juice

Horseradish Apple Sauce

Bye-bye, mayo! You're gonna love this on your sandwiches instead!

1. Cut celery into 1" pieces. Pare, core, and cube apples.

2. Place celery, apples, onions, orange juice, and horseradish in blender. Process until smooth.

3. Scrape into bowl. Stir in crushed fennel seeds.

4. Chill thoroughly.

Serves 16

Calories: 25.84
Fat: 0.19 grams
Saturated Fat: 0.03 grams
Carbohydrates: 6.60 grams
Calcium: 3.64 mg
Lactose: 0.0 grams

½ stalk celery
1½ pounds tart apples
¼ small onion, finely chopped
2 tablespoons unsweetened orange juice
1 tablespoon freshly grated horseradish
¼ teaspoon crushed fennel seeds

Yogurt Mint Sauce

Fresh mint in almost anything is so refreshing! This sauce can be a complement to an entrée or a great sauce or dip for fresh fruits or veggies.

1. Combine all ingredients in a medium-sized bowl.

2. Stir until well blended.

3. Cover tightly and chill thoroughly. Serve chilled.

Ah, Mint!

Can you smell it? Just reading the word conjures up the aroma and fresh smell of mint! Although the taste of mint is somewhat warm, its aftertaste is cool and refreshing. Its flavor is used in breath fresheners and candies, but fresh mint has its own strong, unique flavor.

Almond Apricot Sauce

Try this delicious sauce over a bowl of fresh fruit for a great summer dessert!

1. Purée apricots with syrup in blender until smooth.

2. In a medium saucepan, combine apricot purée, pineapple juice, sugar, and almond extract over medium-high heat, stirring constantly. Bring to a boil.

3. Reduce heat. Continue stirring constantly until mixture begins to thicken. Add cornstarch and water.

4. Remove from heat. Cool at room temperature.

Serves 8

Calories: 20.89
Fat: 1.02 grams
Saturated Fat: 0.65 grams
Carbohydrates: 2.00 grams
Calcium: 42.99 mg
Lactose: 0.0 grams

1 cup plain yogurt
¼ cup chopped fresh mint
2 tablespoons freshly squeezed lemon juice

Serves 10

Calories: 17.79
Fat: 0.02 grams
Saturated Fat: 0.0 grams
Carbohydrates: 4.41 grams
Calcium: 4.06 mg
Lactose: 0.0 grams

1 16-ounce can apricot halves, undrained
¼ cup unsweetened pineapple juice
2 teaspoons sugar
¼ teaspoon almond extract
1 tablespoon cornstarch
2 tablespoons water

Fruit Fondue Sauce

Fondue is back! This light fondue sauce is just waiting for you to dip in with angel food cake squares and fresh fruit!

1. In a small bowl, combine all ingredients.

2. Whisk until smooth and well blended.

3. Cover tightly. Chill until serving time.

Fondue Trivia

Fondue is a Swiss tradition and became extremely popular in the United States in the 1960s. The novelty of fondue has faded somewhat but has made a comeback in recent years. You can dip everything from fruit to meat in different fondue recipes.

Serves 4

Calories: 68.89
Fat: 1.37 grams
Saturated Fat: 0.88 grams
Carbohydrates: 10.03 grams
Calcium: 110.62 mg
Lactose: 0.0 grams

½ cup yogurt cheese
2 tablespoons light brown sugar
¾ teaspoon grated orange peel

Banana Fondue Sauce

Combining banana with yogurt cheese in this recipe gives a subtle taste of banana—a tasty complement to almost any fruit you want to dip in this fondue!

1. Cut banana into pieces.

2. Combine all ingredients in blender. Process until smooth.

3. Cover and chill for at least one hour.

4. Serve with fresh fruit chunks or angel food cake cubes.

Serves 8

Calories: 39.19
Fat: 0.74 grams
Saturated Fat: 0.46 grams
Carbohydrates: 6.17 grams
Calcium: 53.75 mg
Lactose: 0.0 grams

1 ripe banana
½ cup yogurt cheese
1 tablespoon frozen orange juice concentrate, thawed
⅛ teaspoon cinnamon

Nutty Raisin Sauce

*This recipe is almost addictive! Serve as a dipping sauce for fresh
fruit or drizzle over the top of single servings of fresh fruit.*

Serves 6

Calories: 56.72
Fat: 0.61 grams
Saturated Fat: 0.06 grams
Carbohydrates: 13.06 grams
Calcium: 9.96 mg
Lactose: 0.0 grams

*¼ cup plus 2 tablespoons
 unsweetened apple juice*
1½ teaspoons cornstarch
3 tablespoons cider vinegar
*1 tablespoon plus 1 teaspoon
 honey*
2 teaspoons Dijon mustard
*½ vanilla bean, split
 lengthwise*
⅓ cup golden raisins
*1 tablespoon chopped
 toasted almonds*

1. In a small saucepan, combine 2 tablespoons of the apple juice and cornstarch. Stir well and make sure cornstarch lumps are dissolved.

2. Add remaining ¼ cup apple juice, stirring constantly.

3. Cook over medium heat until mixture is bubbly and begins to thicken.

4. Remove from heat. Stir in vinegar, honey, and mustard.

5. Split vanilla bean and scrape out the seeds. Stir seeds, raisins, and almonds into cooked mixture. Chill thoroughly.

Dilled Mustard Sauce

*Want to wake up your freshly steamed veggies?
This homemade dilled mustard sauce will do it!*

Serves 8

Calories: 20.42
Fat: 1.04 grams
Saturated Fat: 0.60 grams
Carbohydrates: 1.81 grams
Calcium: 38.14 mg
Lactose: 0.0 grams

1 8-ounce carton plain yogurt
2 tablespoons Dijon mustard
*1 teaspoon chopped fresh
 chives*
*1 teaspoon Worcestershire
 sauce*
1 teaspoon lemon juice
*½ teaspoon dried whole dill
 weed*
Fresh dill sprig (optional)

1. In a small bowl, combine yogurt, mustard, chives, Worcestershire sauce, lemon juice, and dill weed. Mix well.

2. Cover tightly and chill.

3. Transfer to a serving container, and garnish with dill sprig, if desired.

4. Serve chilled mustard sauce over chicken, fish, or vegetables.

Tomato Fresca Sauce

Try this incredibly fresh sauce over spaghetti squash.

1. In a medium-sized bowl, combine tomatoes, garlic, salt, oregano, and basil. Mix well.

2. Add oil, mixing thoroughly.

3. Serve at room temperature. Store any extra sauce in the refrigerator for one day.

Serves 8

Calories: 12.98
Fat: 0.52 grams
Saturated Fat: 0.05 grams
Carbohydrates: 2.01 grams
Calcium: 5.86 mg
Lactose: 0.0 grams

2 cups diced fresh tomato
2 cloves minced garlic
⅛ teaspoon salt
¼ teaspoon dried oregano
1 tablespoon finely chopped fresh basil
¾ teaspoon canola oil

Easy Chocolate Sauce

Everyone's gotta have a little chocolate now and then in some form. Drizzle some chocolate sauce over a slice of pound cake and top with fresh strawberries.

1. Mix sugar, cocoa powder, and cornstarch in a microwave-safe measuring cup until well blended. Gradually add ⅓ cup water, stirring until lumps are dissolved.

2. Microwave on high for one minute and stir. Microwave for another minute, and stir again. Mixture will thicken.

3. If not thickened after 2 minutes, continue to microwave at 15 second intervals.

4. Stir in one teaspoon vanilla. This is best when served warm!

Serves 4

Calories: 85.20
Fat: 0.56 grams
Saturated Fat: 0.33 grams
Carbohydrates: 21.60 grams
Calcium: 5.41 mg
Lactose: 0.0 grams

⅓ cup sugar
3 tablespoons cocoa powder
1½ tablespoons cornstarch
⅓ cup water
1 teaspoon vanilla

Mustard Cream Sauce

Serves 10

Calories: 50.27
Fat: 2.67 grams
Saturated Fat: 0.44 grams
Carbohydrates: 4.60 grams
Calcium: 8.27 mg
Lactose: 0.0 grams

¾ cup beer
2 tablespoons minced green
    onion
2 tablespoons margarine
2 tablespoons flour
⅔ cup chicken stock
1 teaspoon dried tarragon
1½ tablespoons white wine
    vinegar
¼ cup Dijon mustard
2 teaspoons whole mustard
    seeds
1 tablespoon honey

This is a very versatile sauce that can be spooned over meats and fish before you cook or grill them. It makes a great topper for cooked entrées as well. If you're a tofu fan, stir-fry a little tofu and use this smooth and tangy sauce as a dipping sauce or a drizzle for a very low lactose delight!

1. In a small saucepan, combine beer and minced green onion. Place over high heat and bring to a boil. Boil for about 10 minutes. Liquid should be reduced to ¼ cup. Set aside.

2. Place a second saucepan over low heat, and melt margarine.

3. Whisking constantly, add flour and cook until it is smoothly combined and bubbling (about one minute).

4. Gradually whisk in the chicken stock, tarragon, vinegar, mustard, mustard seeds, honey, and beer mixture. Simmer for three minutes, allowing flavors to fully blend.

5. Serve hot if not using as a basting sauce before cooking the entrée.

What's Shakin' with Sodium?

Sodium makes its way into more foods than you may realize. It's in the baking soda used to leaven baked goods, preservatives used to keep food fresh, and mustard to enhance flavor. For the lowest salt content, choose foods with labels that clearly state "no added salt" or "unsalted." Sodium-free and salt-free options are also good.

Mushroom Sauce

As smooth as velvet with a slightly sweet flavor, this sauce can be spooned over steak, chicken, or freshly steamed veggies.

1. In a large saucepan, melt margarine over low heat. Whisking constantly, add flour and cook until it is smoothly combined and bubbling (about one minute).

2. Gradually whisk in the soy milk, ½ cup at a time. Continue whisking constantly for about 5 minutes or until sauce begins to thicken. Don't allow sauce to boil.

3. Blend in mushrooms. Cover and continue simmering, stirring occasionally. Allow to cook for 7 minutes or until the mixture is reduced by half.

4. Remove saucepan from heat. Stir in sherry, salt, and pepper, blending until smooth. Serve hot.

Serves 8

Calories: 31.62
Fat: 2.01 grams
Saturated Fat: 0.32 grams
Carbohydrates: 2.39 grams
Calcium: 6.10 mg
Lactose: 0.0 grams

3 tablespoons margarine
¼ cup flour
1 cup warm soy milk
¾ pound fresh button mushrooms, thinly sliced
1 tablespoon cream sherry
¼ teaspoon salt
⅛ teaspoon ground white pepper

Spicy Tofu Sauce

Calories: 87.53
Fat: 7.61 grams
Saturated Fat: 1.07 grams
Carbohydrates: 1.56 grams
Calcium: 174.83 mg
Lactose: 0.0 grams

2 cloves garlic
1 small Serrano chili
⅛ cup olive oil
½ cup firm tofu
⅛ cup white wine vinegar
1 tablespoon dried basil
½ teaspoon vegetable salt
1 teaspoon freshly grated
*   ginger*
⅛ cup water

*Depending on your level of tolerance for spiciness,
you may want to start out with half a Serrano chili.*

1. Place garlic and chili in blender and chop.

2. Add olive oil and blend flavors.

3. Rinse tofu and blot with paper towel. Break into pieces and add to spiced oil in blender.

4. Add vinegar, basil, salt, and fresh ginger. Blend all ingredients well.

5. If mixture is too thick, slowly add water until desired consistency is reached.

Hot, Hot, Hot!

Cooking with chiles can give your food incredible flavor, but you must be careful! Make sure to thoroughly wash your hands after seeding or cutting chiles; use rubber gloves if you're worried about your skin coming into contact with the oils from the chiles. Definitely avoid rubbing your eyes or nose before washing your hands—the oil can burn!

Bordelaise Sauce

*A complementary sauce to Herbed Lamb Chops (page 192)
and anything else you might decide to team it with!*

1. In a small saucepan, melt margarine over low heat.

2. Gradually add flour, stirring constantly until smooth (about one minute). Slowly add water and wine. Stir constantly until sauce reaches a smooth consistency.

3. Stir in onion, parsley, bay leaf, bouillon granules, thyme, and pepper. Cook over medium-high heat, stirring constantly, until thickened and bubbly.

4. Remove bay leaf.

5. Serve sauce warm over lamb chops or other entrée.

Serves 4

Calories: 37.36
Fat: 2.86 grams
Saturated Fat: 0.47 grams
Carbohydrates: 1.71 grams
Calcium: 2.27 mg
Lactose: 0.0 grams

1 tablespoon margarine
1 tablespoon all-purpose flour
½ cup water
1 tablespoon plus 1½ teaspoons dry red wine
1½ teaspoons minced green onion
1½ teaspoons minced fresh parsley
1 bay leaf
½ teaspoon beef-flavored bouillon granules
⅛ teaspoon dried whole thyme
Freshly ground black pepper to taste

Mustard Sauce

This mustard sauce is good with Salmon Cakes (page 196),
but try it with other entrées and veggies too!

Serves 4

Calories: 46.76
Fat: 3.44 grams
Saturated Fat: 0.54 grams
Carbohydrates: 2.71 grams
Calcium: 12.96 mg
Lactose: 0.0 grams

2 tablespoons margarine
1½ tablespoons all-purpose
flour
1 cup soy milk
1 teaspoon dry mustard
1 teaspoon lemon juice
¼ teaspoon salt

1. In a small skillet or sauté pan, melt margarine over low heat.

2. Add flour and cook for 1 minute, stirring constantly until smooth.

3. Gradually add soy milk. Cook over medium heat, stirring constantly until thickened and bubbly.

4. Remove from heat. Stir in dry mustard, lemon juice, and salt.

Yogurt Dill Sauce

Try this yogurt dill sauce with fish or veggies. This lactose-free and very creamy
dill sauce is a welcome addition for variety in your LI lifestyle!

Serves 4

Calories: 20.11
Fat: 1.05 grams
Saturated Fat: 0.65 grams
Carbohydrates: 1.63 grams
Calcium: 38.62 mg
Lactose: 0.0 grams

1 cup plain yogurt
1 tablespoon chopped fresh
dill
1 tablespoon Dijon mustard
1 teaspoon fresh lemon juice
½ teaspoon Tabasco sauce

1. In a small bowl stir together yogurt, fresh dill, Dijon mustard, fresh lemon juice, and Tabasco sauce.

2. Mix ingredients together thoroughly. Enjoy with fish or veggies.

Chapter 13
Beans and Lentils

Five-Bean Salad

Serves 10

Calories: 151.37
Fat: 3.29 grams
Saturated Fat: 0.45 grams
Carbohydrates: 25.08 grams
Calcium: 53.52 mg
Lactose: 0.0 grams

1 16-ounce can green beans
1 16-ounce can yellow wax
   beans
1 15-ounce can red kidney
   beans
1 16-ounce can garbanzo
   beans
1 16-ounce can pinto beans
½ cup chopped green pepper
½ cup chopped celery
½ cup finely chopped onion
⅓ cup sugar
⅔ cup tarragon vinegar
2 tablespoons olive oil
½ teaspoon salt
½ teaspoon garlic salt

Be sure to allow this salad to refrigerate for several hours and let the flavors mingle. This is one of those recipes that is always better the next day!

1. Combine all the beans, green pepper, celery, and onion in a large bowl.

2. Mix the sugar, vinegar, oil, salt, and garlic salt in a small bowl.

3. Pour the dressing mixture over the vegetables and stir gently.

4. Refrigerate for at least 6 hours. Stir several times while chilling so flavors mingle evenly.

Bean and Lentil Trivia

Beans and lentils have been found in 5,000-year-old settlements in the Eastern Mediterranean, in Egyptian pyramids, Hungarian caves, Britain, and Switzerland, and in even earlier civilizations such as those in Peru, the Middle East, and eastern India. Beans and lentils are thought to have originated from the wild lentils that still grow in India, Turkey, and other Middle Eastern countries.

Rice and Bean Salad

*A variety of beans coupled with rice, this salad is easy to prepare
and chock full of great nutrients. It's another overnighter; keep this
salad in the fridge to allow the flavors to penetrate. It's worth the wait!*

1. Drain both cans of beans.

2. Combine beans, rice, peas, celery, onion, and green chilies in a large bowl.

3. Pour salad dressing over the ingredients in the bowl. Toss, coating evenly.

4. Cover and refrigerate for 24 hours before serving.

Serves 12

Calories: 202.22
Fat: 6.02 grams
Saturated Fat: 0.99 grams
Carbohydrates: 30.93 grams
Calcium: 47.59 mg
Lactose: 0.0 grams

1 16-ounce can pinto beans
1 15-ounce can black beans
3 cups cooked rice of choice
*1 10-ounce package frozen
    green peas, thawed*
1 cup sliced celery
1 cup chopped onion
*2 4-ounce cans chopped
    green chilies*
*1 8-ounce bottle Italian salad
    dressing*

Tex-Mex Black Bean Dip

Serve this tangy dip with tortilla chips.

1. Place black beans in a bowl. Partially mash beans until chunky. Set aside.

2. Heat oil over medium-high heat in a nonstick skillet. Add onion and garlic. Sauté until tender, about 4 minutes.

3. Add beans, tomatoes, salsa, ground cumin, and chili powder. Stirring constantly, cook until mixture thickens, about 5 minutes.

4. Remove from heat. Add cheese if desired.

5. Stir in fresh cilantro and lime juice. Serve warm or at room temperature.

Serves 6

Calories: 199.38
Fat: 4.20 grams
Saturated Fat: 2.03 grams
Carbohydrates: 29.88 grams
Calcium: 137.70 mg
Lactose: 0.0 grams

*2 15-ounce cans black beans,
    drained*
1 teaspoon olive oil
1 cup onion, chopped
4 cloves garlic, minced
1 cup fresh tomato, chopped
⅔ cup salsa
1 teaspoon ground cumin
1 teaspoon chili powder
*½ cup shredded Monterey
    jack cheese (optional)*
½ cup cilantro, chopped
2 tablespoons fresh lime juice

Layered Four-Bean Salad

Serves 24

Calories: 313.84
Fat: 5.46 grams
Saturated Fat: 0.80 grams
Carbohydrates: 51.13 grams
Calcium: 88.08 mg
Lactose: 0.0 grams

1 pound black beans
1 pound navy beans
1 pound pinto beans
1 pound lima beans
½ cup sugar
½ cup red wine vinegar
½ cup light olive oil
2 tablespoons fresh parsley,
    chopped
½ teaspoon dry mustard
2 teaspoons fresh basil
½ teaspoon oregano
Salt and freshly ground black
    pepper to taste
Romaine lettuce leaves
1 medium red onion, sliced
    and separated into rings

This is a crowd-pleasing picnic dish! If you prepare it for a picnic, skip the glass dish and use a large plastic bowl with a top that seals.

1. Cook all dry beans according to package directions. Drain and chill beans.

2. Mix sugar, vinegar, oil, parsley, mustard, basil, oregano, salt, and pepper in a small bowl. Set aside.

3. Line a large glass bowl with romaine lettuce leaves.

4. Place a layer of black beans on bottom of bowl. Drizzle with one-fourth of the dressing.

5. Add the navy beans and drizzle with more dressing. Continue until you have four layers.

6. Garnish top with red onion rings. Chill thoroughly.

Bean Cooking Hints

Cooking beans is kind of like a treasure hunt. Before you cook them, be sure to pick through the beans and remove any stones, broken beans, or other foreign objects. It isn't surprising to find a bit of the bean field in the bag with your dried beans.

Old-Fashioned Pot 'O Beans Made New

Old-fashioned beans usually called for fat ham hocks for flavor and lots of greasy goop. This updated recipe calls for smoked pork chops in place of the ham hocks, and if you want to skip the pork chops, please do!

Serves 8

Calories: 281.37
Fat: 4.82 grams
Saturated Fat: 1.73 grams
Carbohydrates: 40.04 grams
Calcium: 120.83 mg
Lactose: 0.0 grams

1 pound great northern dried beans
2 quarts water
1 medium onion, minced
2 cloves garlic, minced
2 carrots, sliced
½ cup chopped celery
½ teaspoon black pepper
3 4-ounce smoked pork chops
2 teaspoons salt
1 teaspoon brown sugar
1 tablespoon prepared mustard

1. Wash and drain the beans. Place in large kettle with 2 quarts water. Let soak overnight.

2. Drain beans and cover with fresh water.

3. Add onion, garlic, carrots, and celery. Cover and simmer slowly for 2 hours. Stir occasionally. Add more water as needed, checking the level often.

4. Trim and cube pork chops. Add pepper, smoked pork chops, salt, brown sugar, and mustard. Simmer another 45–60 minutes until flavors blend.

Now We're Really Cooking . . .

Beans, that is. When you cook beans, be sure to use a large stock pot. You can even use a big slow cooker! After culling and rinsing them, cover beans with cold water. Read your package directions to be sure. Skim away any foam that surfaces while the beans are cooking. It's not the prettiest of culinary sights!

Cherry Tomatoes with Bean Stuffing

Stuffing cherry tomatoes with this flavorful and tasty bean stuffing is well worth it the time it takes. They are great at a party or a barbecue!

Yields 24

Calories: 214.85
Fat: 7.39 grams
Saturated Fat: 1.08 grams
Carbohydrates: 30.19 grams
Calcium: 101.21 mg
Lactose: 0.0 grams

36 cherry tomatoes, divided
1 bunch fresh basil plus 24 leaves
1 15-ounce can cannellini beans, drained
2 tablespoons garlic-flavored olive oil
2 tablespoons freshly squeezed lemon juice

1. Rinse tomatoes and set aside. Wash all basil. Set aside 24 small basil leaves. Chop remaining basil.

2. Cut 12 tomatoes in half. Squeeze out all the seeds and juice. Dice tomatoes and set aside.

3. In a blender purée beans, basil leaves, garlic oil, and lemon juice until finely chopped. Transfer bean mixture to a medium bowl. Stir in chopped tomatoes and chopped basil, mixing well.

4. Cut off top quarter of remaining 24 tomatoes. Gently squeeze out the seeds, liquid, and pulp using a small spoon to create a cavity in the tomato.

5. Fill tomatoes with the bean mixture, again using a small spoon. Garnish each tomato with a fresh basil leaf.

Cannellini Beans

Cannellini beans are very popular in Italy, especially in Tuscany, where the people living there have been affectionately nicknamed mangiafagiole—"beaneaters"! *Cannellini beans are sometimes referred to as white kidney beans and are related to navy and great northern beans. They have a very mellow flavor. Feel free to use them interchangeably with other white beans.*

Many-Bean Soup

This is an awesome winter soup to simmer on the stove for hours. It fills the house with warm, cozy aromas and will warm tummies when it's done!

1. Soak, rinse, and drain legumes. Place in large soup pot and cover with water.

2. Bring to a boil over medium-high heat. Reduce heat and simmer for about 1½ hours.

3. Add water chestnuts, celery, onion, carrot, tomatoes, garlic, and fennel.

4. Continue simmering for another 1½–2 hours over low heat until all legumes are tender.

5. Ladle soup into soup bowls. Top with seasoned croutons if desired. Serve immediately.

Serves 8

Calories: 317.70
Fat: 1.91 grams
Saturated Fat: 0.27 grams
Carbohydrates: 56.50 grams
Calcium: 101.04 mg
Lactose: 0.0 grams

¼ pound dried white kidney beans, soaked and rinsed
½ pound dried fava beans, soaked and rinsed
¼ pound dried garbanzos (chickpeas)
¼ pound dried lentils, any color
¼ pound dried split yellow peas
9–10 cups water
1 5-ounce can water chestnuts, drained and sliced
3 ribs celery, chopped
1 medium onion, diced
1 medium carrot, chopped
6 dry sun-dried tomatoes, finely chopped
2 garlic cloves, mashed
3 teaspoons ground fennel seeds
Salt and pepper to taste
Seasoned croutons (optional)

Turkey Black Bean Chili

*Black beans are a great staple in any pantry. Not only do they have a great flavor,
but it's hard to imagine anything that tastes this good is also good for you!*

Serves 6

Calories: 240.58
Fat: 5.31 grams
Saturated Fat: 1.29 grams
Carbohydrates: 31.26 grams
Calcium: 88.77 mg
Lactose: 0.0 grams

Nonstick cooking spray
1 tablespoon olive oil
1 cup coarsely chopped onion
½ cup sliced celery
2 15-ounce cans black beans
*1 10-ounce can diced
    tomatoes and green
    chilies, undrained*
*6 ounces cooked turkey
    breast, diced*
*1 tablespoon chili seasoning
    mix*
*¼ cup plus 1 tablespoon plain
    yogurt*
*Sweet red pepper strips
    (optional)*

1. Coat a small Dutch oven with cooking spray. Add olive oil. Heat over medium-high heat.

2. Add onion and celery. Sauté until tender. Allow to cool slightly.

3. Place mixture in blender. Drain beans, reserving liquid. Add half the beans with all the liquid to blender. Process until smooth. Stop once and scrape down sides.

4. Return mixture to Dutch oven. Add remaining beans, tomato, chilies, turkey, and chili seasoning. Cook over medium heat until heated thoroughly.

5. Ladle into bowls. Top evenly with yogurt. Garnish with pepper strips, if desired.

Black Bean Trivia

Black beans are commonly referred to as turtle beans, probably because of their shiny, dark, shell-like appearance. Black beans have rich flavor and a velvety texture. In addition to their high fiber and protein content, a new study finds that beans, particularly black ones, are a rich but overlooked source of antioxidants.

Black Bean Pancakes

*These black bean pancakes are very versatile; they can be served as a side dish
as a replacement for potatoes or rice and are excellent as an appetizer.*

1. Drain and rinse beans. Mash with a fork. Place beans, water, and sherry in blender. Process until smooth.

2. Scrape bean mixture in a medium bowl. Add eggs, flour, olive oil, green onions, garlic, parsley, salt, and pepper to taste. Stir until well blended.

3. Lightly spray a heavy frying pan or griddle with cooking spray. Heat until hot.

4. Pour 3 tablespoons of batter onto pan for each pancake. Cook over medium-high heat until edges begin to brown, about 45 seconds. Flip pancake. Cook other side for about 30 seconds.

5. Keep cooked pancakes warm and covered until all are cooked.

Serves 6

Calories: 133.54
Fat: 6.39 grams
Saturated Fat: 1.19 grams
Carbohydrates: 12.82 grams
Calcium: 22.01 mg
Lactose: 0.02 grams

1 cup cooked black beans
¼ cup water
2 tablespoons dry sherry
2 eggs, well beaten
⅓ cup all-purpose flour
2 tablespoons light olive oil
¼ cup green onions, finely minced
1 clove garlic, minced
1 tablespoon fresh chopped parsley
½ teaspoon salt
Pepper to taste
Nonstick cooking spray

Garbanzos and Rice

*Choose your favorite rice for this recipe. Serve it warm
as a dessert with honey, brown sugar, and cinnamon.*

1. Preheat oven to 350°F.

2. Combine all ingredients except cinnamon in a medium-sized bowl, blending thoroughly.

3. Pour mixture into a casserole dish. Dust with cinnamon.

4. Bake for 25 minutes.

Serves 4

Calories: 373.24
Fat: 2.19 grams
Saturated Fat: 0.32 grams
Carbohydrates: 83.74 grams
Calcium: 54.33 mg
Lactose: 0.0 grams

1½ cups canned garbanzo beans
2 cups cooked rice
1 teaspoon salt
1 teaspoon margarine
⅓ cup honey
⅓ cup brown sugar
¼ teaspoon cinnamon

Mediterranean Eggplant and Garbanzos

If you have an electric skillet, heat it to 300°F and cook all ingredients together for about 30 minutes instead of using the heavy skillet.

Serves 6

Calories: 221.91
Fat: 6.56 grams
Saturated Fat: 0.89 grams
Carbohydrates: 36.47 grams
Calcium: 74.35 mg
Lactose: 0.0 grams

1 large eggplant
1 large red bell pepper
2 tablespoons olive oil
2 medium onions, sliced
2 garlic cloves, mashed
2 medium zucchini, sliced
2 cups cooked garbanzos, drained
2 medium tomatoes, cut into eighths
1 16-ounce can tomatoes, drained and chopped
½ teaspoon dried turmeric
½ teaspoon oregano
½ teaspoon thyme
1 teaspoon ground cinnamon

1. Wash whole eggplant and prick skin in several places with a fork. Place on paper towel in microwave oven. Pre-cook in microwave on high for 8 minutes.

2. Set eggplant aside to cool. When cool to touch, cut in thick slices. Cover with damp paper towel. Seed and slice red bell pepper.

3. Put olive oil in a heavy skillet over medium-high heat. When oil is hot, add onions, garlic, and bell pepper. Sauté until soft.

4. Add eggplant slices, zucchini, beans, tomatoes, canned tomatoes, and spices. Cook until eggplant and zucchini are tender, about 45 minutes.

Garbanzo Bean Trivia

Garbanzo beans are also referred to as chickpeas. Like most beans, garbanzo beans are rich in soluble fiber, the best sort of fiber. Soluble fiber helps eliminate cholesterol from the body. Garbanzos are a good source of folate, vitamin E, potassium, iron, manganese, copper, zinc, and calcium. As a high-potassium, low-sodium food, they can help reduce blood pressure.

Bean and Potato Hash

What a great Sunday breakfast or brunch treat! Serve this dish with whole grain toast and you'll be the star of the weekend!

Serves 4

Calories: 318.93
Fat: 9.94 grams
Saturated Fat: 3.09 grams
Carbohydrates: 41.77 grams
Calcium: 131.49 mg
Lactose: 0.06 grams

1 pound red potatoes
1 15-ounce can red kidney
    beans
1 tablespoon margarine
1 small red onion, slivered
1 teaspoon chili powder
¼ cup plus 2 tablespoons
    water
1 large tomato, chopped
¾ teaspoon chopped fresh
    sage
4 large eggs
⅓ cup lightly packed cilantro
    leaves
¾ cup plain yogurt

1. Wash potatoes and leave skins on; cut into ¼" cubes. Drain and wash kidney beans.

2. Melt margarine in a large nonstick skillet or wok over medium-high heat. Add potatoes, onion, chili powder, and ¼ cup water.

3. Stir-fry until potatoes begin to brown and are fork tender, about 15 minutes. Watch heat level carefully so as not to burn the potatoes. If pan begins to get dry, add water, one tablespoon at a time.

4. Add beans, tomato, sage, and 2 tablespoons water to skillet. Stir-fry gently until heated thoroughly.

5. With the back of a tablespoon, make four depressions in potato mixture. Carefully break an egg into each depression. Reduce heat to low, cover, and cook until egg yolks are firm but moist. Sprinkle with cilantro and top with a dollop of yogurt.

Kidney Bean Shapes

True to their name, these popular beans are kidney shaped and are especially good in dishes that are simmered, where they absorb the flavors of seasonings of the other foods with which they are cooked.

Edamame and Veggie Salad

*Give edamame a try. Boil some frozen edamame beans, add
a little Himalayan sea salt for flavor, and eat it as a snack.*

Calories: 386.22
Fat: 31.07 grams
Saturated Fat: 4.22 grams
Carbohydrates: 20.76 grams
Calcium: 142.93 mg
Lactose: 0.05 grams

½ pound frozen edamame
1 cucumber, sliced thinly
1 medium onion, diced
1 green pepper, diced
3 carrots, shredded
1 cup cabbage, shredded
1 cup broccoli, chopped
¼ cup apple cider vinegar
2 cloves garlic
½ cup olive oil
Salt to taste
Pinch of oregano

1. Cook edamame according to package directions; drain and chill.

2. In a large bowl, combine edamame, cucumber, onion, green pepper, carrots, cabbage, and broccoli. Toss until veggies are well mixed. Set aside.

3. Combine vinegar, garlic, olive oil, salt, and oregano in a blender. Process at high speed until well blended. Pour dressing over veggies.

4. Toss until veggies are well coated. Chill for at least two hours before serving.

Edamame

Edamame is a green vegetable soy bean, harvested at the peak of ripening just before it dries and hardens. It can be eaten as a snack, a side dish, or added to your favorite recipes. Edamame scores high on phytochemicals, which are special compounds produced by plants that may help prevent disease.

New Potatoes and Beans

The flavor of new, small red potatoes just can't be beat. This is a good barbeque dish that makes a very colorful presentation and brings folks back for a second helping!

1. Bring water to boil in 3-quart saucepan over high heat.

2. Add potatoes, onion, bouillon, and garlic to boiling water. Return to boil.

3. Reduce heat to low and cover. Cook for about 10 minutes until potatoes are crisp-tender. Drain.

4. Rinse and drain red kidney beans. Cut green and red pepper into ¼-inch strips. Add kidney beans, pepper strips, olive oil, vinegar, parsley flakes, and rosemary leaves to potato mixture. Stir well to combine all ingredients. Return to medium heat.

5. Cook, uncovered, about 3 minutes or until hot. Stir occasionally to prevent sticking. Remove from heat and cover. Let stand for 5 minutes before serving.

Serves 6

Calories: 145.65
Fat: 2.67 grams
Saturated Fat: 0.40 grams
Carbohydrates: 25.57 grams
Calcium: 30.64 mg
Lactose: 0.0 grams

2 cups water
3 cups sliced new red potatoes
¼ cup chopped onion
2 teaspoons instant chicken bouillon granules
1 clove garlic, minced
1 15-ounce can red kidney beans
¼ cup green pepper strips
¼ cup red pepper strips
1 tablespoon olive oil
1 tablespoon red wine vinegar
2 teaspoons dried parsley flakes
¼ teaspoon dried rosemary leaves, crushed

Tortillas and Black Beans

Serves 8

Calories: 379.75
Fat: 6.63 grams
Saturated Fat: 1.44 grams
Carbohydrates: 66.68 grams
Calcium: 120.53 mg
Lactose: 0.0 grams

1 cup basmati rice
2 15-ounce cans black beans
1 tablespoon olive oil
1 medium yellow onion, chopped
1 large clove garlic, minced
1 bell pepper, chopped
1 jalapeño pepper, chopped
1 Roma tomato, chopped
1 teaspoon cumin
1 package 8" flour tortillas
Chopped avocado, fresh cilantro, hot sauce, yogurt or sour cream, grated cheese (optional)

This is a very satisfying and filling dish with high calcium scores, low lactose scores, and great flavor and taste!

1. Cook rice according to package directions. While rice is cooking, prepare the rest of the recipe. Rinse black beans and set aside.

2. Heat olive oil in a large skillet or wok. Add onion and sauté for one minute.

3. Add garlic and sauté another 2 minutes. Add bell pepper to skillet and continue sautéing another 2 minutes. Add jalapeño pepper, chopped tomato, cumin, beans, and cooked rice. Keep mixture warm.

4. Heat tortillas in oven or microwave according to package directions. Fill your warm tortilla with mixture.

5. Garnish with condiments of your choice such as sour cream, chopped green onions, and salsa.

No-Guilt Refried Beans

*Just a little note on pinto beans: You can find them in the freezer
section and make an awesome bean soup with them.*

Serves 4

Calories: 125.17
Fat: 3.76 grams
Saturated Fat: 0.65 grams
Carbohydrates: 18.00 grams
Calcium: 51.07 mg
Lactose: 0.0 grams

1 15-ounce can pinto beans
¼ cup thick and chunky salsa
*2 tablespoons finely chopped
    onion*
⅛ teaspoon garlic powder
1 tablespoon margarine

1. Drain and rinse pinto beans.

2. Combine beans, salsa, onion and garlic powder in a heavy 2-quart sauce-
    pan over medium-high heat. Bring mixture to a boil, stirring occasionally.

3. Reduce heat to medium-low and simmer until onion is translucent,
    about 8 minutes. Stir occasionally to prevent sticking. Add margarine
    and stir until melted.

4. Remove from heat and allow mixture to cool slightly.

5. Pour mixture into blender. Process until smooth.

Triple Bean Bake

*If you like a little sweetness in your beans, then go for the addition
of the light molasses. If you opt out of the molasses, the dry mustard
combined with the apple juice concentrate will give the flavor a new twist!*

Serves 8

Calories: 185.46
Fat: 1.87 grams
Saturated Fat: 0.28 grams
Carbohydrates: 35.40 grams
Calcium: 70.60 mg
Lactose: 0.0 grams

1 cup thinly sliced onion
½ cup thinly sliced celery
1 teaspoon light olive oil
1 15-ounce can pinto beans
1 15-ounce can butter beans
*1 15-ounce can garbanzo
    beans*
1 8-ounce can tomato sauce
*¼ cup frozen apple juice
    concentrate, defrosted*
½ teaspoon dry mustard
*1 tablespoon light molasses
    (optional)*

1. Preheat oven to 375°F. Drain and rinse all beans.

2. Put oil in a 10-inch nonstick skillet over medium heat. Add onion and
    celery. Cook until tender, about 6 minutes, stirring occasionally.

3. Add pinto beans, butter beans, garbanzo beans, tomato sauce, apple
    juice, dry mustard, and molasses, if desired. Stir until combined.

4. Spoon mixture into 2-quart casserole. Bake covered until hot and bub-
    bly, about 30 minutes.

Lentil Stew

This stew will literally warm your very soul on a cold winter day!

Serves 8

Calories: 169.25
Fat: 1.56 grams
Saturated Fat: 0.36 grams
Carbohydrates: 28.63 grams
Calcium: 46.37 mg
Lactose: 0.0 grams

2 large onions, chopped
2 medium carrots, chopped
1 cup dry lentils
½ cup chopped fresh parsley
1 16-ounce can whole tomatoes, undrained and coarsely chopped
3 cups chicken broth
¼ cup dry sherry
½ teaspoon dried whole thyme
½ teaspoon dried whole marjoram
½ teaspoon pepper

1. Combine all ingredients in a large soup pot. Bring to a boil.

2. Reduce heat and cover.

3. Simmer over low heat until lentils are tender, about 45 minutes.

4. Serve piping hot!

Liturgy of Lentils

Lentils, also referred to as "dal," is the staple food in every home in India. Dal is India's comfort food! A variety of lentils exist with colors that range from yellow to red-orange to green, brown, and black.

Lentil Salad

The colors of the lentils in this salad make it very inviting. The combination of lentils with spinach torn in small pieces gets very high ratings on the healthy scale!

1. Cook the lentils according to package directions. Drain and chill the lentils.

2. In a small bowl, combine onion, salsa, chili powder, oregano, and lemon juice. Set aside.

3. Put chopped spinach and salsa mixture in a medium bowl. Toss until mixed well.

4. Fold in lentils.

5. Place whole spinach leaves on 4 salad plates. Mound salad on top.

Serves 4

Calories: 106.44
Fat: 0.34 grams
Saturated Fat: 0.04 grams
Carbohydrates: 24.28 grams
Calcium: 33.97 mg
Lactose: 0.0 grams

½ cup mild onion, finely chopped
½ cup mild salsa
2 teaspoons chili powder
½ teaspoon dried oregano
2 tablespoons lemon juice
1 cup fresh spinach, torn
½ cup red lentils, cooked, drained, and chilled
½ cup yellow lentils, drained and chilled
Whole spinach leaves (optional)

Lentils and Rice

If you're accustomed to using veggie broth in your cooking, use it in this recipe as well. Veggie broth enhances the flavor of this dish.

Calories: 282.65
Fat: 8.66 grams
Saturated Fat: 1.48 grams
Carbohydrates: 39.39 grams
Calcium: 30.22 mg
Lactose: 0.0 grams

1 tablespoon margarine
2 tablespoons olive oil
2 cups sliced onions
1 cup lentils, rinsed
5 cups water
3 cups chicken or vegetable broth
½ cup long grain rice
¾ teaspoon salt
1 teaspoon ground cumin
Freshly ground black pepper to taste

1. Heat margarine and oil together until margarine melts in a large, heavy skillet over low heat. Add onion slices. Cook slowly, stirring.

2. Place water and lentils in a large stockpot, and bring to a boil over medium-high heat. Reduce heat and simmer, covered, for 20 minutes.

3. Drain lentils and place in a large, heavy saucepan. Add broth, rice, salt, cumin, and pepper.

4. Set aside ⅓ cup of the onions. Add the remainder of the onions to the lentil mixture. Bring to a boil. Reduce heat and cook, covered, until rice is tender, about 25 minutes.

5. Sprinkle the reserved onions over the top and serve immediately.

Chapter 14
Chicken Entrées

Chicken with Blackberry Mustard

Blackberry mustard is tantalizing to your taste buds! Be sure to check the label on the prepared mustard that you choose to buy for any lurking lactose.

Serves 5

Calories: 498.81
Fat: 9.49 grams
Saturated Fat: 1.75 grams
Carbohydrates: 67.70 grams
Calcium: 52.54 mg
Lactose: 0.0 grams

5 4-ounce boneless, skinless chicken breasts
1 teaspoon paprika
1 teaspoon coarse salt
⅛ teaspoon ground sage
1 teaspoon pepper
1 tablespoon onion powder
2 tablespoons olive oil
1½ cups blackberry jam
6 tablespoons Dijon mustard
¼ cup chopped fresh parsley

1. Cut chicken breasts into small, 1" cubes. Set aside in refrigerator until ready to use.

2. In a small bowl, combine paprika, salt, sage, pepper, and onion powder to make spice mix. Stir well. Dust chicken cubes with the spice mixture and allow to stand for 15 minutes.

3. Heat the olive oil in a large, heavy skillet over medium heat. Sauté the chicken until done. Set aside and keep warm.

4. Combine blackberry jam and Dijon mustard in the skillet over medium heat. Stir until well combined and warm.

5. Sprinkle chicken with chopped fresh parsley. Serve with blackberry mustard.

Blackberry Bramble

Wild blackberries grow on bramble bushes. These sweet and juicy little berries are high in fiber and pack a powerful antioxidant punch in addition to being a good source of vitamins C and E, iron, and calcium. Add fresh blackberries to your choice of yogurt for a great LI snack!

Spicy Chicken with Mango Sauce

The mango sauce is the star of this dish, and the chile provides a trace of kick.

1. Peel the mango, cutting fruit away from the seed in wide strips. Drizzle mango strips with lemon juice.

2. In a blender, finely purée one-third of the mango pieces with the yogurt until well combined and smooth. Cover and place in refrigerator until serving time.

3. Tear lettuce leaves into large pieces. Slit open the chile. Trim and cut into thin rings. Rinse chicken and pat dry with paper towels. Cut into finger-width strips.

4. Heat oil in a nonstick skillet over medium-high heat. Add chicken strips and chile when oil is hot. Sauté on all sides for about 4 minutes until golden brown. Make sure chicken is cooked thoroughly. Season with salt to taste.

5. Arrange the chicken and chile mixture on the lettuce on plates. Garnish with the mango pieces and drizzle with the mango sauce.

Mango Madness

Mangoes are an extremely versatile fruit. You can eat them for breakfast, lunch, dinner, snacks, and desserts—and when they're in season, it may be difficult to resist doing just that! Blend them into a smoothie for breakfast, use them to flavor your salad dressing for lunch, top your dinner with mango salsa, and eat it with a sorbet for dessert.

Serves 2

Calories: 342.84
Fat: 16.22 grams
Saturated Fat: 2.91 grams
Carbohydrates: 22.48 grams
Calcium: 64.81 mg
Lactose: 0.0 grams

1 ripe mango
2 tablespoons fresh lemon juice
2 ounces plain yogurt
4 leaves leaf lettuce
2 tablespoons olive oil
1 red chile or to taste
8 ounces boneless, skinless chicken breasts
Salt to taste

Oven-Fried Sesame Chicken

Serves 4

Calories: 262.29
Fat: 11.15 grams
Saturated Fat: 2.00 grams
Carbohydrates: 4.44 grams
Calcium: 22.34 mg
Lactose: 0.0 grams

*3 tablespoons toasted
    sesame seeds*
*2 tablespoons all-purpose
    flour*
¼ teaspoon pepper
2 tablespoons soy sauce
*4 4-ounce chicken breast
    halves, skinned*
*2 tablespoons margarine,
    melted*

There are ways to satisfy your hunger for fried foods in a healthy way. This oven-fried sesame chicken is sure to please that hankerin' for fried chicken!

1. Preheat oven to 400°F.

2. In a small, flat bowl, combine sesame seeds, flour, and pepper.

3. Pour soy sauce in a saucer. Dip chicken into soy sauce, then dredge in sesame seed mixture.

4. Arrange chicken, bone side down, in a large, shallow baking dish. Melt margarine and drizzle over chicken.

5. Bake for 45 minutes or until chicken is tender.

Lemon Chicken with Broccoli

Serves 4

Calories: 243.11
Fat: 4.98 grams
Saturated Fat: 0.87 grams
Carbohydrates: 21.44 grams
Calcium: 40.37 mg
Lactose: 0.0 grams

*4 4-ounce boneless, skinless
    chicken breasts*
1 tablespoon olive oil
½ pound broccoli crowns
1 teaspoon salt
¼ cup sugar
*1½ tablespoons fresh lemon
    juice*
¾ cup water
3 tablespoons cornstarch
*2 cups prepared steamed rice
    (optional)*

You just can't beat combining fresh broccoli with freshly squeezed lemon juice. If you're watching your weight, this recipe is great without the rice.

1. Dice chicken into bite-sized pieces. Heat oil in a large heavy skillet or wok. Stir-fry until chicken is done and no longer pink.

2. Break broccoli into florets and steam until crisp-tender. Add broccoli to chicken.

3. In a small saucepan, stir together salt, sugar, lemon juice, water, and cornstarch. Heat over medium heat, stirring constantly until sauce thickens.

4. Pour sauce over chicken and broccoli. Heat through. Serve over steamed rice.

Grilled Balsamic Chicken

*Balsamic vinegar is sweet yet simultaneously tart.
It blends deliciously with chicken.*

Serves 8

Calories: 419.16
Fat: 23.27 grams
Saturated Fat: 6.46 grams
Carbohydrates: 2.80 grams
Calcium: 35.22 mg
Lactose: 0.0 grams

1 3-pound chicken, quartered
¼ cup chicken broth
½ cup balsamic vinegar
⅓ cup green onions, chopped
2 tablespoons Dijon mustard
1 tablespoon garlic, minced
1 tablespoon sugar
*2 teaspoons Worcestershire
    sauce*
1 teaspoon dry mustard
*1 teaspoon cracked black
    pepper*

1. Rinse chicken pieces and pat dry. Arrange chicken in shallow baking dish.

2. Combine remaining ingredients in a small bowl and whisk to blend well. Pour marinade over chicken. Cover and refrigerate for at least 24 hours, turning occasionally.

3. Preheat oven to 325°F or prepare grill for cooking.

4. Oven instructions: Bring chicken and marinade to room temperature. (Don't let it sit out longer than 1½ hours to 2 hours at the most.) Bake for 30 to 40 minutes or until chicken is done.

5. Grilling instructions: Remove chicken from marinade. Place on grill until chicken is done (this will vary according to size of chicken quarters). Turn chicken only once during grilling.

Vinegar Trivia

Vinegar was a byproduct of wine for many years. The word vinegar comes from the French word vinaigre, *which means sour wine. You can choose from a whole rainbow of vinegars at your local market—white wine vinegar, red wine vinegar, apple cider vinegar—the list goes on, but none is quite so pleasing as rich, dark balsamic vinegar with its mild flavor.*

Pecan Chicken Breasts

Pecans provide a subtle crunch to a naturally soft bird. The texture and the taste blend for a startlingly exciting dish.

Serves 4

Calories: 449.72
Fat: 18.54 grams
Saturated Fat: 2.79 grams
Carbohydrates: 33.64 grams
Calcium: 94.80 mg
Lactose: 0.0 grams

1 cup bread crumbs
¼ cup finely chopped pecans
½ cup flour
Salt to taste
¼ teaspoon black pepper
½ cup egg substitute
1 tablespoon water
2 dashes Tabasco sauce or to taste
4 4-ounce boneless, skinless chicken breasts
Nonstick cooking spray
2 tablespoons margarine

1. Mix bread crumbs and pecans in a flat dish. Sprinkle flour in a shallow dish or glass pie plate. Season with salt and pepper.

2. Beat the egg substitute, water, and Tabasco sauce in a medium bowl.

3. Dip chicken breasts first in the flour, then in the egg mixture, then in the bread crumb mixture. Place on a plate. Cover and refrigerate for at least 30 minutes.

4. Coat a large skillet with cooking spray. Melt margarine over medium heat.

5. Add chicken breasts. Cook for about 30 minutes, making sure to brown evenly on all sides.

Pecan Prattle

Pecans are delicious and nutritious! The fat found in pecans contains no cholesterol and is mostly monounsaturated fat (60 percent monounsaturated, 30 percent polyunsaturated). Pecans bless you with vitamins A, B, and C, plus potassium, phosphorous, iron, and calcium. They are also a good source of protein and fiber—hard to believe a little nut can hold all that nutrition!

Paprika Yogurt Chicken

This dish's unique blend of tastes will please your palate even as your brain struggles to identify all the different flavors. Cooking with yogurt allows you to enjoy "creamy" and low lactose all at the same time!

1. Heat olive oil in a heavy 10" skillet.

2. Cook onion, ginger, and garlic together.

3. Add paprika, salt, cayenne pepper, sugar, mushrooms, tomatoes, and yogurt. Cook for about 5 minutes.

4. Add chicken and cook until thoroughly done.

5. Serve immediately.

Serves 4

Calories: 231.26
Fat: 6.65 grams
Saturated Fat: 1.64 grams
Carbohydrates: 13.33 grams
Calcium: 77.68 mg
Lactose: 0.0 grams

1 tablespoon olive oil
1 onion, finely chopped
1 tablespoon minced fresh ginger
2 cloves garlic, minced
2 tablespoons paprika
Salt to taste
Cayenne pepper to taste
Pinch of sugar
½ pound sliced fresh mushrooms
2 tomatoes, coarsely chopped
½ cup plain yogurt
1 pound boneless, skinless chicken breasts

Baked Lemon Pepper Chicken

This is a super easy recipe that is absolutely yummy in your LI tummy! If your tummy doesn't like Parmesan cheese, please substitute with a cheese that does.

Serves 4

Calories: 205.39
Fat: 4.52 grams
Saturated Fat: 1.42 grams
Carbohydrates: 2.84 grams
Calcium: 40.39 mg
Lactose: 0.01 grams

Nonstick cooking spray
1 medium onion, thinly sliced
4 skinless, bone-in chicken breast halves
1 teaspoon lemon pepper
1 tablespoon grated Parmesan cheese
1 teaspoon dried basil

1. Preheat oven to 400°F.

2. Spray a casserole dish with nonstick cooking spray; spread onions all over bottom. Place chicken breasts on top, bone side down.

3. Sprinkle with lemon pepper, Parmesan cheese, and basil.

4. Bake, uncovered, about 60 minutes. Make sure chicken is cooked through with no "pink" liquid running when fork tested.

Pink Chicken

It's very important to make sure any chicken that you are preparing has no pink juices running from it before you serve it. The most reliable way to test for doneness of chicken is to use a meat thermometer; however, you can prick the chicken and let the juices flow. If they're clear, you're in the clear and it's time to eat!

Berried Chicken

Berry, berry good! This colorful recipe is a fun variation for chicken.

1. Heat oil over medium-high heat in a large skillet or wok. Add garlic and slightly cook, stirring to mingle with hot oil. Remove garlic from skillet. Add chicken, browning on all sides. Sprinkle with salt if desired.

2. Combine cranberry sauce, vinegar, orange zest, and orange juice in a small bowl. Whisk to blend well. Pour over chicken in skillet. Reduce heat to low. Cover and simmer about 35 minutes or until chicken is fork tender.

3. Seed and rinse green pepper. Cut in strips, crosswise. Add green pepper and onion to skillet combination.

4. Combine cornstarch, water, and soy sauce in a screw top jar. Shake until lumps disappear. Add cornstarch mixture to chicken, stirring constantly to combine smoothly.

5. Simmer until mixture is clear and thickened. Cook only until veggies are crisp-tender. Don't overcook! Serve over hot rice if desired.

Serves 8

Calories: 296.36
Fat: 6.77 grams
Saturated Fat: 1.15 grams
Carbohydrates: 27.20 grams
Calcium: 22.37 mg
Lactose: 0.0 grams

2 tablespoons oil
1 clove minced garlic
2 pounds boneless chicken breast strips
1 teaspoon salt
1 16-ounce can whole cranberry sauce
½ cup cider vinegar
Zest and juice of ½ orange
2 tablespoons cornstarch
¾ cup water
1½ tablespoons soy sauce
1 large green pepper
½ cup thinly sliced onion
Cooked rice (optional)

Basil Orange Chicken

Fresh basil and fresh ginger blended with the balsamic
vinegar produce a sweet yet slightly tart flavor in this recipe.

Serves 4

Calories: 263.69
Fat: 2.82 grams
Saturated Fat: 0.57 grams
Carbohydrates: 31.66 grams
Calcium: 60.92 mg
Lactose: 0.0 grams

*3 tablespoons fresh chopped
    basil*
*2 tablespoons balsamic
    vinegar*
⅓ cup orange marmalade
⅔ cup orange juice
1 teaspoon olive oil
*¼ teaspoon fresh ginger,
    minced*
½ teaspoon salt
*4 boneless, skinless chicken
    breasts*
2 oranges
1½ teaspoons cornstarch

1. In a medium bowl, combine chopped basil, vinegar, orange marmalade, ⅓ cup of orange juice, oil, ginger, and salt. Whisk until well blended. Pour two-thirds of the mixture into a medium-sized flat glass dish. Set aside remaining orange mixture in bowl.

2. Thoroughly coat chicken breasts in orange mixture by placing in dish and turning several times. Place chicken in dish in refrigerator for at least 30 minutes to marinate. Peel and section oranges. Set aside.

3. Preheat broiler. Place chicken on broiler rack. Spoon orange marinade on top of chicken. Broil about 6–8 inches from heat for 5 minutes. Turn chicken breasts over and spoon on the rest of the orange marinade. Return chicken to broiler and broil for another 5 minutes until chicken is golden. Make sure liquid running from chicken is clear and chicken is cooked completely through.

4. While chicken is broiling, pour basil-orange mixture from bowl into a small saucepan. Bring to a boil over medium heat. Add cornstarch and cook until mixture begins to thicken, stirring constantly. Add orange sections and gently stir to combine with basil-orange sauce.

5. Place each chicken breast on a warmed plate. Spoon sauce over chicken breasts and serve immediately.

Chapter 15
Beef and Lamb Entrées

Stuffed Steak with Red Gravy

Who says gravies have to be made with milk? This hearty recipe takes a little time to prepare but is so worth it!

⬥

Serves 8

Calories: 328.88
Fat: 8.05 grams
Saturated Fat: 2.78 grams
Carbohydrates: 21.11 grams
Calcium: 145.54 mg
Lactose: 0.01 grams

2 pounds round steak
Salt and cayenne pepper to taste
2 cups water
½ cup long-grain rice, uncooked
2 10-ounce packages frozen chopped spinach, thawed
Salt and freshly ground pepper to taste
1 teaspoon dried basil
1 egg, lightly beaten
4 large carrots, 3 shredded and 1 sliced
1 medium onion, sliced
1 stalk celery, sliced
1½ cups tomato juice
2 tablespoons cornstarch
¼ cup cold water

1. Place steak on large cutting board. Cover with plastic wrap. Pound with side of meat mallet into large rectangle. Season to taste with salt and cayenne pepper. Refrigerate until ready to stuff.

2. In a medium saucepan, bring water to a boil. Add rice. Reduce heat and cover. Allow to simmer for about 20 minutes or until tender. Drain well. Place rice in a medium bowl and set aside.

3. Squeeze thawed spinach dry. Season spinach with salt and pepper. Remove steak from refrigerator. Using spatula, spread spinach in a flat layer about 4" wide across center of steak.

4. Add ½ teaspoon basil and egg to rice, mixing well. Spoon rice mixture on top of spinach. Spread evenly with spatula. Add salt, pepper, and remaining basil to shredded carrots; mix well. Spoon carrot mixture over rice, patting evenly.

5. Bring both ends of steak over filling, overlapping slightly. Secure with wooden picks. Place onion slices, carrot slices, and celery slices in bottom of large Dutch oven. Place rolled steak in pot, seam side down. Pour tomato juice around the bottom of the pan. Bring to a boil.

6. Cover, reduce heat, and simmer about 2 hours or until meat is tender, basting occasionally with pan drippings. Place meat on a large serving platter. Mix cornstarch and cold water in a small screw top jar. Pour over pan drippings. Cook over medium heat until thickened, stirring frequently. Serve immediately.

Beef Teriyaki

A good beef teriyaki recipe can be used in a variety of ways and doesn't always have to be served over rice. Toss the beef with a variety of freshly steamed veggies.

1. Cut slightly frozen beef into ⅛" thick strips.

2. In a medium bowl, mix soy sauce, sherry, sugar, ginger, and garlic powder. Stir in meat. Allow to marinate for 15 minutes.

3. Thread beef on skewers. Preheat broiler or prepare grill.

4. Broil 4" from heat for 2 minutes on each side or until done as desired. Serve on hot cooked rice.

Rice Spells "Variety"!

There are so many different varieties of rice. Be experimental with your rice choices. Read the labels and familiarize yourself with the nutritional values of rice, then take them home and cook with them to see which ones you like the best.

Serves 4

Calories: 166.48
Fat: 4.27 grams
Saturated Fat: 1.49 grams
Carbohydrates: 1.39 grams
Calcium: 6.19 mg
Lactose: 0.0 grams

1 pound beef round steak
¼ cup soy sauce
1 tablespoon dry sherry
1 tablespoon sugar
½ teaspoon grated fresh ginger
¼ teaspoon garlic powder
Cooked rice (optional)

Beef Stroganoff

Serve this to guests and they'll think they're dining in a fine restaurant instead of your home! Be sure to use "unsweetened" soy milk for this recipe or substitute your favorite lactose-free milk.

Serves 4

Calories: 325.59
Fat: 17.53 grams
Saturated Fat: 3.73 grams
Carbohydrates: 12.10 grams
Calcium: 46.29 mg
Lactose: 0.0 grams

1 cup unsweetened soy milk
1 tablespoon white vinegar
1 pound boneless tender beef
   steak
3 tablespoons olive oil
1 small onion, thinly sliced
½ pound fresh mushrooms,
   sliced
2½ tablespoons all-purpose
   flour
¼ cup soy sauce
1 clove garlic, pressed
¼ cup water
⅓ cup minced fresh parsley
Wide egg noodles, cooked

1. In a small bowl, combine soy milk and vinegar. Allow to stand for 15 minutes. Meanwhile, cut beef across grain into thin slices.

2. In a large skillet, heat one tablespoon oil over high heat. Add beef. Stir-fry for one minute. Remove beef from skillet.

3. Add remaining 2 tablespoons oil to skillet and heat. Add onion and mushrooms. Stir-fry 4 minutes. Reduce heat to medium.

4. In a small bowl, blend flour, soy sauce, garlic, and ¼ cup water. Add to skillet, stirring constantly. Bring to a boil. Stir constantly and cook for one minute.

5. Gradually add soy milk mixture. Add beef and parsley, continuing to stir constantly. Cook until just heated through. Serve over cooked noodles.

Curry Slurry

Your hand is rockin' the curry measurement.
If you're a curry fan, go for it! Curry is lactose free!

Serves 6

Calories: 227.57
Fat: 11.38 grams
Saturated Fat: 3.43 grams
Carbohydrates: 8.16 grams
Calcium: 28.73 mg
Lactose: 0.0 grams

Nonstick cooking spray
3 tablespoons margarine
1 pound lean ground beef
1 large yellow onion, finely
*   chopped*
1 tablespoon curry powder
*   (or to taste)*
2 Roma tomatoes, cut in
*   chunks*
1 9-ounce can peas,
*   undrained*
½ teaspoon chili powder
1 teaspoon paprika
1 teaspoon salt
Cooked rice (optional)

1. Spray large skillet with cooking spray. Heat margarine in skillet over medium-high heat.

2. Sauté onion and push to one side of skillet.

3. Shape ground beef into a large patty. Brown about 5 minutes on each side. Break meat into chunks.

4. Add all remaining ingredients to meat and onion mixture. Reduce heat and simmer for 30 minutes.

5. Serve over cooked rice if desired.

Old-Fashioned Meatloaf Heart Smart

Meatloaf is good for a hot entrée, and it makes great sandwiches the next day. In fact, some say the true test of meatloaf is whether it makes good sandwiches! Just remember to read labels on your store-bought condiment ingredients to check for any nasty lactose lurkers that will make your tummy not like the meatloaf.

1. Preheat oven to 350°F.

2. Combine all ingredients except the tomato sauce. Thoroughly mix with your hands. Shape into a loaf.

3. Place in a 9" × 5" pan. Spoon tomato sauce over top of loaf.

4. Bake for 1 hour. Drain fat and juices.

5. Let stand for 5 minutes before slicing and serving.

Leaner Than Lean

Do you know what those "lean" labels on ground beef really mean? Let's say you need one pound of ground beef. If the label reads that the ground beef is 95 percent lean, it has 23 grams of fat (before cooking). Compare that to one pound of ground beef that is 80 percent lean, which has 91 grams of fat.

Meatballs and Sauerkraut

This easy recipe is sure to be a hit at your next party. Use your slow cooker instead of stovetop cooking, and set it on the table for serving.

Serves 6

Calories: 370.37
Fat: 11.65 grams
Saturated Fat: 4.67 grams
Carbohydrates: 16.95 grams
Calcium: 81.22 mg
Lactose: 0.0 grams

1½ pounds lean ground beef
Salt and pepper to taste
1 cup diced onions
4 cups tomato juice
2 1-pound cans sauerkraut
1 tablespoon fresh lemon juice
1 teaspoon sugar

1. Preheat oven to 350°F. Place ground beef in a medium bowl. Salt and pepper to taste.

2. Shape meat into balls about the size of large walnuts. Place in a shallow baking pan on middle rack in oven. Bake for 30 minutes, uncovered, until meatballs are nicely browned.

3. Sprinkle onions in the bottom of a large saucepan. Add ½ cup of tomato juice. Cook over low heat until onions are tender. Add more tomato juice if necessary.

4. Begin layering meatballs and sauerkraut on top of onion and tomato mixture, beginning with meatballs. Alternate layers.

5. Add lemon juice and sugar to tomato juice. Stir to blend. Pour over meatballs and sauerkraut. Reduce heat to low; cover and simmer for one hour.

Sauerkraut's in a Pickle!

Sauerkraut only has 20 calories per half-cup serving. It also provides iron, vitamins C and B, potassium, calcium, and fiber. But beware of the sodium content. Read the labels. To reduce the sodium content, drain, rinse, and drain sauerkraut again before using.

Herbed Lamb Chops

Turn this delightful entrée into an elegant dish. Serve it with
Bordelaise Sauce (page 155) and garnish with fresh mint.

Serves 2

Calories: 221.78
Fat: 8.86 grams
Saturated Fat: 3.58 grams
Carbohydrates: 1.30 grams
Calcium: 19.38 mg
Lactose: 0.0 grams

2 tablespoons red wine vinegar
1 tablespoon water
2 teaspoons minced onion
2 teaspoons soy sauce
1 clove garlic, minced
¼ teaspoon dried whole
*   rosemary, crushed*
⅛ teaspoon dried whole
*   thyme, crushed*
Pepper to taste
2 5-ounce lamb chops, 1"
*   thick*

1. In a shallow 1-quart casserole dish, combine vinegar, water, onion, soy sauce, garlic, rosemary, thyme, and pepper. Add lamb chops to marinade and turn until well coated. Cover and refrigerate for at least 4 hours.

2. Drain lamb chops. Reserve marinade.

3. Preheat broiler or prepare grill.

4. Broil 5 inches from heating element (or pop on the grill) for about 5 minutes on each side, depending on your choice of doneness. Baste frequently with marinade.

5. Serve warm.

Skillet Lemony Lamb Chops

No muss, no fuss—a skillet meal that is quick and easy that
tastes like you've been slaving over a hot stove for hours!

Serves 2

Calories: 288.55
Fat: 13.64 grams
Saturated Fat: 5.73 grams
Carbohydrates: 1.10 grams
Calcium: 28.73 mg
Lactose: 0.0 grams

2 6-ounce lamb chops ¾"
*   thick*
3 tablespoons water
⅛ teaspoon lemon zest
2 teaspoons Worcestershire
*   sauce*
¼ teaspoon salt
⅛ teaspoon dried oregano
⅛ teaspoon dried rosemary,
*   crushed*
Freshly ground pepper to
*   taste*

1. Preheat broiler. Place lamb chops on broiler rack under broiler. Broil until brown on both sides.

2. Place chops in a medium nonstick skillet.

3. In a small bowl, combine water, lemon zest, Worcestershire sauce, salt, oregano, rosemary, and freshly ground pepper. Whisk until well blended. Pour mixture over lamb chops in skillet.

4. Cover and cook over medium-low heat about 30 minutes or until chops are tender.

Grecian Shish Kabobs

These kebabs taste excellent grilled. Soak wooden kebab skewers in water to avoid any unwanted grill fires.

Serves 2

Calories: 253.38
Fat: 12.46 grams
Saturated Fat: 5.59 grams
Carbohydrates: 6.92 grams
Calcium: 30.46 mg
Lactose: 0.0 grams

½ pound lean boneless lamb
2 tablespoons white wine vinegar
2 tablespoons water
1 tablespoon dry sherry
2 teaspoons chopped fresh parsley
1 teaspoon sugar
¾ teaspoon dried whole rosemary, crushed
⅛ teaspoon garlic salt
⅛ teaspoon pepper
1 small green pepper
6 medium-sized fresh mushrooms
4 cherry tomatoes

1. Cut lamb into 1" cubes.

2. In a small bowl, combine vinegar, water, sherry, parsley, sugar, rosemary, garlic salt, and pepper in a small bowl. Stir until well blended. Add cubed lamb. Stir until lamb is well coated. Cover and refrigerate overnight.

3. Seed green pepper and cut into 8 pieces. Place green pepper on a microwave-safe plate. Cover and microwave on high for 2 minutes.

4. Drain lamb. Discard marinade.

5. Alternate lamb and vegetables on four 10" wooden skewers. Place skewers on a microwave-safe roasting rack. Cover with waxed paper. Microwave on 50 percent power for 5–6 minutes.

6. Rearrange kabobs and microwave another 5 minutes or until desired degree of doneness. Note: If you're a grill master, these are awesome prepared on the grill. Just watch them closely so they don't burn!

Score Points for Lamb!

When you're talking nutrition and red meat, lamb scores points in high nutritional values! An excellent source of protein and much easier to digest than other meats, lamb is also a rich source of iron, calcium, potassium, phosphorus, and B-complex vitamins. Buy lean lamb so your kebabs don't turn out greasy.

Lamb with Fruit and Nut Sauce

Serves 4

Calories: 318.98
Fat: 10.08 grams
Saturated Fat: 2.92 grams
Carbohydrates: 24.62 grams
Calcium: 31.13 mg
Lactose: 0.0 grams

8 dried apricots, cut into strips
½ cup beef broth
¼ cup currants
¼ cup brandy
4 4-ounce slices lean boneless leg of lamb
2 tablespoons flour
Nonstick cooking spray
2 teaspoons oil
1 tablespoon toasted chopped pecans

This is a beautiful entrée to serve for special occasions. Serve it for a holiday entrée and you'll probably start a tradition!

1. In a small bowl, combine apricots, beef broth, currants, and brandy, stirring well. Cover and refrigerate at least 8 hours.

2. Place lamb between two sheets of heavy-duty plastic wrap. Using a meat mallet, flatten to ½" thickness. Dredge in flour.

3. Coat a skillet with cooking spray. Add oil and place over medium-high heat until hot. Add lamb. Cook 5 minutes on each side until lightly browned.

4. Add apricot mixture and pecans. Cover, reduce heat, and simmer until lamb is tender, about 15 minutes.

5. Place lamb on 4 individual plates and spoon apricot mixture over lamb. Serve immediately.

Chapter 16
Fish and Seafood Entrées

Salmon Cakes and Mustard Sauce

Salmon cakes' nutritional value hasn't changed in years, nor has their satisfying texture and flavor. Enjoy this old recipe made new!

Serves 4

Calories: 220.81
Fat: 10.12 grams
Saturated Fat: 2.49 grams
Carbohydrates: 6.54 grams
Calcium: 273.07 mg
Lactose: 0.03 grams

1 14-ounce can salmon,
    drained and flaked
¼ cup fine, dry bread crumbs
2 eggs, slightly beaten
2 tablespoons lemon juice
¼ teaspoon pepper
Nonstick cooking spray
½ cup finely chopped celery
⅓ cup finely chopped green
    onions
Mustard Sauce (see page 156)

*Note: Mustard sauce not included in nutritional information.

1. In a small bowl, combine salmon, bread crumbs, eggs, lemon juice, and pepper, mixing well. Set aside.

2. Coat a large skillet with cooking spray. Heat skillet over medium heat. Add celery and green onions and sauté until tender. Add to salmon mixture in bowl, mixing well.

3. Recoat skillet with cooking spray and reheat over medium-high heat.

4. Spoon about ¼ cup mixture onto skillet for each salmon cake. Shape into a patty with a spatula.

5. Cook until browned, about 2 minutes per side. Serve immediately with Mustard Sauce.

Salmon Savvy

Salmon is an excellent source of omega-3 fatty acids, vitamin D, and selenium. It is also a very good source of protein, niacin, vitamin B12, phosphorous, magnesium, and vitamin B6. Canned salmon is great for the LI lifestyle because it contains the bones, which adds points to the calcium score.

Baked Salmon with Buttered Thyme Potatoes

*This dish certainly makes very different and attractive presentation—
it's almost as impressive as the flavor.*

1. Preheat oven to 375°F. Slice potatoes into ¼" slices.

2. Using 1½ tablespoons of the margarine, coat the bottom of a large, heavy oven-proof skillet. Place half the potato slices so they overlap, covering a 5" by 5" area. Arrange the remaining potato slices in another cluster following the same overlapping arrangement.

3. Sprinkle with salt, freshly ground pepper, and shallots. Top each cluster with remaining margarine and a fresh thyme sprig. Place a salmon fillet on top of each potato cluster with skin side up. Place skillet over medium-high heat. Cook for 5 minutes without disturbing.

4. Transfer skillet to preheated oven. Bake for about 14 minutes, watching closely so potatoes don't scorch. Remove from oven when potatoes are golden and salmon is pale pink.

5. At serving time, use a metal spatula to flip each salmon cluster over so potatoes are on top. Garnish with remaining thyme sprigs. Serve warm.

Serves 2

Calories: 565.19
Fat: 30.13 grams
Saturated Fat: 11.05 grams
Carbohydrates: 35.31 grams
Calcium: 35.31 mg
Lactose: 0.0 grams

2 baking potatoes, peeled
2 tablespoons margarine
    softened, divided
Salt and fresh ground pepper
2 tablespoons minced
    shallots
2 6-ounce salmon fillets
4 sprigs fresh thyme

Sesame Ginger Salmon

Grill this salmon dish instead of broiling it for an even richer flavor.

Serves 4

Calories: 355.31
Fat: 25.93 grams
Saturated Fat: 4.41 grams
Carbohydrates: 6.56 grams
Calcium: 20.33 mg
Lactose: 0.0 grams

2 8-ounce salmon fillets
½ cup sesame oil
3 tablespoons light brown
*   sugar*
¼ cup teriyaki sauce
1½ teaspoons grated fresh
*   ginger*
Nonstick cooking spray

1. Combine sesame oil, brown sugar, teriyaki sauce, and ginger in blender. Process until well blended.

2. Place salmon fillets in a plastic container. Pour half the marinade over them. Cover and refrigerate for 60 minutes. Reserve the other half of the marinade.

3. Remove salmon from refrigerator. Discard marinade.

4. Place fish in a shallow baking dish. Baste with reserved marinade.

5. Coat broiler pan with cooking spray. Place salmon on broiler pan. Broil approximately 5 minutes per side until the outside is crispy and the inside is pale pink.

Salmon: Pretty in Pink

There are endless ways to prepare the lovely pink-hued salmon, which is an all-time favorite among fresh fish lovers. Even folks who don't care for fish are open to ordering fresh salmon when it's on the menu! Eating this incredibly nutritious pinkish fish helps keep your health in the pink as well!

Poached Salmon and Yogurt Dill Sauce

Dill sauce with salmon isn't a new way to cook fish; however, this dill sauce is made with yogurt and a little bite of Dijon mustard so it comes up with zero lactose. You can decide for yourself if you prefer this recipe best hot or cold—it's a toss up!

1. In large skillet combine water, wine, lemon, onion, bay leaves, peppercorn, dill, Tabasco, and salt. Bring to a boil.

2. Reduce heat. Cover and simmer for 15 minutes.

3. Add salmon to skillet. Simmer covered until fish flakes easily when fork tested, about 15 minutes.

4. Serve warm or chilled with Yogurt Dill Sauce (page 156).

Grilled Salmon with Creamy Tarragon Sauce

Substitute fresh herbs for dried whenever possible. The fresh herbs add more flavor and punch than dried herbs ever could.

1. In a small glass bowl combine yogurt, mayonnaise, green onions, tarragon, lime juice, and hot pepper sauce. Cover and refrigerate at least 1½ hours.

2. Remove skin from salmon. Cut into four equal portions. Brush with olive oil.

3. Grill salmon over medium heat until fish flakes easily with fork, about 5 minutes on each side. If you prefer, broil salmon for about 4 minutes on each side, 5" from broiler.

4. Serve with fresh tarragon sauce.

Serves 8

Calories: 207.40
Fat: 12.30 grams
Saturated Fat: 2.47 grams
Carbohydrates: 0.0 grams
Calcium: 13.60 mg
Lactose: 0.0 grams

2 cups water
1 cup dry white wine
1 lemon, sliced
1 small onion, sliced, optional
2 bay leaves
8 black peppercorns
4 dill sprigs
1 teaspoon Tabasco sauce
¼ teaspoon salt
4 8-ounce salmon steaks
Yogurt Dill Sauce (page 156)

*Note: Yogurt Dill Sauce not included in the nutritional information.

Serves 4

Calories: 285.58
Fat: 18.40 grams
Saturated Fat: 4.35 grams
Carbohydrates: 4.02 grams
Calcium: 91.91 mg
Lactose: 0.0 grams

1 cup plain yogurt
1 tablespoon mayonnaise
¼ cup minced green onions
1 tablespoon minced fresh
    tarragon
2 teaspoons lime juice
1 teaspoon hot pepper sauce
16-ounce salmon fillet,
    1" thick, skinned
1 tablespoon olive oil

Snapper with Lemon Dill Spinach

Feel free to substitute the snapper with another type of similar fish in this recipe if snapper isn't your cup of tea or isn't readily available.

Serves 6

Calories: 171.01
Fat: 3.09 grams
Saturated Fat: 0.57 grams
Carbohydrates: 4.08 grams
Calcium: 140.92 mg
Lactose: 0.0 grams

Nonstick cooking spray
6 4-ounce skinless snapper fillets
1 tablespoon fresh lemon juice
4 teaspoons Dijon mustard
½ cup finely chopped fresh dill
1 teaspoon extra virgin olive oil
2 10-ounce bags fresh spinach leaves, stems removed, washed and drained
1 garlic clove, minced
1 lemon, quartered lengthwise

1. Preheat oven to 400°F. Spray glass baking dish with cooking spray.

2. Arrange snapper fillets in dish. Sprinkle with lemon juice. Spread Dijon mustard over each fillet.

3. Reserve one tablespoon of the fresh dill. Sprinkle remaining dill over snapper fillets. Bake until just cooked through, 18–20 minutes.

4. While fish is baking, heat olive oil in large skillet over medium heat. Add spinach and minced garlic. Stir together for about 4 minutes or until spinach is wilted.

5. Using tongs, divide spinach on plates without pan juices. Place hot fish fillets over spinach. Sprinkle remaining fresh dill on top. Garnish with lemon wedges. Serve immediately.

Snapper Surprises

There are seventeen different varieties of "snapper." The two most popular varieties are yellowtail snapper and red snapper. On the healthy side, snapper is low in calories and contains almost no saturated fat. It packs plenty of protein and calcium and iron too!

Herbed Flounder Pinwheels

Want to look like you've been slaving in the kitchen all day to produce a gourmet meal for guests? This recipe is a ticket to get you there!

1. Preheat oven at 375°F.

2. Steam spinach in vegetable steamer over boiling water until spinach is just wilted. Drain and chop spinach. In a small bowl, combine spinach, egg, bread crumbs, thyme, and pepper. Set aside.

3. Rinse flounder fillets with cold water and pat dry. Divide spinach mixture equally. Spoon mixture in center of each fillet. Beginning at narrow end, roll up in jellyroll fashion. Place seam side down in an 8" square baking dish. Cover and bake for 15–20 minutes.

4. Transfer rolls to a warmed serving platter. Keep rolls warm. Combine cornstarch and water in a small saucepan, stirring until lumps disappear and mixture is smooth. Gradually stir in cocktail juice. Cook over medium heat until thickened and bubbly.

5. Pour sauce over fish rolls. Garnish with fresh parsley sprigs. Serve immediately.

Serves 4

Calories: 180.31
Fat: 3.27 grams
Saturated Fat: 0.85 grams
Carbohydrates: 7.54 grams
Calcium: 62.31 mg
Lactose: 0.01 grams

3 cups fresh spinach leaves, chopped
1 egg, beaten
¼ cup soft bread crumbs
¼ teaspoon dried whole thyme
Dash of pepper
4 4-ounce flounder fillets
1½ teaspoons cornstarch
2 tablespoons water
1 6-ounce can vegetable cocktail juice
Fresh parsley sprigs (optional)

Baked Halibut with Artichoke Hearts

Serve this fish entrée with a fresh garden salad.

Serves 8

Calories: 259.98
Fat: 17.52 grams
Saturated Fat: 3.35 grams
Carbohydrates: 6.88 grams
Calcium: 53.68 mg
Lactose: 0.0 grams

Nonstick cooking spray
¼ cup chopped green onion
2 tablespoons chopped fresh parsley
1 14-ounce can artichoke hearts
3 tablespoons grated Parmesan cheese (optional)
3 tablespoons mayonnaise
1 tablespoon fresh lemon juice
½ teaspoon garlic powder
¼ teaspoon red pepper flakes
8 4-ounce halibut steaks

1. Preheat oven to 375°F.

2. Coat a medium skillet with cooking spray and heat skillet over medium heat. Add onion and parsley. Sauté until tender.

3. Drain and chop artichoke hearts. Stir in artichoke hearts, Parmesan cheese (if desired), mayonnaise, fresh lemon juice, garlic powder, and red pepper. Set aside.

4. Rinse halibut with cold water and pat dry. Place halibut steaks in a large aluminum foil-lined shallow roasting pan. Spoon artichoke mixture evenly over steaks.

5. Bake, uncovered, until steaks flake easily when fork tested, about 10 minutes. Serve on warmed plates.

Halibut Hailings

The colder the water, the better, if you ask a halibut! Halibut run in deep, deep waters and live sometimes for more than 40 years—unless, of course, they end up in the recipe above! Halibut have a white, lean, and firm flesh with a delightfully delicate flavor.

Oven-Fried Trout

*The distinctive flavor of trout really comes through
in the oven-fried method used in this recipe.*

1. Preheat oven to 500°F. Rinse trout with cold water and pat dry.

2. Brush fillets with oil. Sprinkle with salt, garlic powder, and pepper. Dredge in cornflake crumbs.

3. Coat a 12" × 8" × 2" baking dish with cooking spray. Arrange fillets in a single layer in baking dish.

4. Bake, uncovered, until fillets flake easily when tested with a fork, about 10 minutes.

5. Carefully transfer to a warmed serving platter. Garnish with lemon slices and parsley. Serve immediately.

Serves 4

Calories: 248.51
Fat: 6.69 grams
Saturated Fat: 2.03 grams
Carbohydrates: 4.05 grams
Calcium: 58.61 mg
Lactose: 0.0 grams

4 4-ounce trout fillets
1 tablespoon olive oil
¼ teaspoon salt
⅛ teaspoon garlic powder
⅛ teaspoon pepper
⅓ cup cornflake crumbs
Nonstick cooking spray
Lemon slices
Fresh parsley sprigs

Sole and Veggies En Papillote

A meal all wrapped up in a little packet makes for easy and mess-free cooking and easy serving.

Serves 12–16

Calories: 146.95
Fat: 4.30 grams
Saturated Fat: 0.80 grams
Carbohydrates: 5.89 grams
Calcium: 34.65 mg
Lactose: 0.0 grams

1 tablespoon margarine
1 sweet red pepper, seeded and sliced
2 medium carrots, cut into julienne strips
⅔ cup fresh broccoli flowerets
1 clove garlic, crushed
4 1-pound sole fillets
2 teaspoons fresh lemon juice
¼ teaspoon paprika
⅛ teaspoon pepper

1. Place margarine in a one-quart casserole dish. Microwave on high until melted, about 20 seconds.

2. Add red pepper, carrots, broccoli, and garlic to casserole. Stir to combine ingredients. Cover and microwave on high until just crisp-tender, 2–3 minutes. Set aside.

3. Cut four 16" × 12" pieces of parchment paper. Then cut each into a large heart shape. Fold heart in half and then open flat.

4. Place a fillet along center fold on each sheet of paper. Sprinkle fillets with lemon juice, paprika, and pepper. Top each fillet with equal amounts of vegetable mixture. Fold paper edges over to seal securely.

5. Place two pouches on a microwave-safe 12" platter. Microwave at high for 3–4 minutes; set aside and keep warm. Repeat process and serve.

En Papillote

Cooking en papillote *is fun and fancy. You can wrap up just about any ingredients that you like in parchment paper and cook them* en papillote*! It delivers crispy, crunchy veggies with freshness extraordinaire and seals in the natural juices of fish and meats.*

Blackened Bass

Bass is great eating (and fun to fish for, too)! If you like your fish blackened a bit, this recipe will suit your fancy!

1. Rinse fillets under cold water and leave damp. Place in a shallow dish.

2. Combine 2 tablespoons water and hot sauce in a small bowl. Spoon mixture over fillets. Cover and marinate in refrigerator for at least 2 hours, turning once.

3. Remove fillets from marinade. Discard marinade. In a small flat dish, combine onion powder, garlic powder, paprika, thyme, oregano, pepper, and red pepper. Dredge fillets in spices and coat well.

4. Coat a large cast-iron skillet with cooking spray. Add margarine. Place over medium-high heat until margarine melts. Add fillets. Cook 2–3 minutes on each side, turning carefully. If you prefer, cook the fillets on a grill. Keep in mind that you're cooking "blackened bass" and it will have a charred look.

Serves 4

Calories: 167.45
Fat: 6.02 grams
Saturated Fat: 1.24 grams
Carbohydrates: 2.02 grams
Calcium: 21.26 mg
Lactose: 0.0 grams

1 pound bass fillets, ½" thick
2 tablespoons water
1 tablespoon hot sauce
2 teaspoons onion powder
2 teaspoons garlic powder
2 tablespoons paprika
1 teaspoon dried whole thyme, crushed
1 teaspoon dried whole oregano, crushed
2 teaspoons pepper
1 teaspoon red pepper
Nonstick cooking spray
1 tablespoon margarine

Baked Sea Bass and Veggies

A complete meal all under one roof—well, under the lid of one skillet anyway!

Serves 6

Calories: 267.95
Fat: 8.30 grams
Saturated Fat: 1.65 grams
Carbohydrates: 19.15 grams
Calcium: 50.84 mg
Lactose: 0.0 grams

Nonstick cooking spray
2 tablespoons margarine
2 cups finely chopped red potato
1 cup chopped onion
¾ cup chopped carrot
2 teaspoons minced garlic
2 cups thinly sliced sweet red pepper
2 cups peeled, seeded, and chopped tomato
1 cup chicken broth
3 tablespoons sliced ripe olives
2 teaspoons capers, drained
½ teaspoon dried whole thyme
6 4-ounce sea bass fillets, 1" thick
2 tablespoons fresh lemon juice

1. Coat a large skillet with cooking spray. Melt margarine in skillet over medium heat.

2. Add potato, onion, carrot, and garlic. Cover and cook 3 minutes. Add red pepper, chopped tomato, chicken broth, ripe olives, capers, and thyme. Cover and cook until veggies are crisp-tender, about 15 minutes.

3. Place fillets over vegetable mixture in skillet. Cover and cook until fish flakes easily when fork tested, about 10 minutes.

4. Using a slotted spoon, transfer fillets and veggie mixture to a warmed serving platter.

5. Drizzle lemon juice evenly over dish and serve immediately.

Sea Bass Trivia

Sea bass are the largest family of fish in the world. Sea bass are valued for their firm, white flesh and versatility in cooking.

Orange Marinated Swordfish

Swordfish is a distinctively flavored fish on its own. Adding this marinade of mingled flavors makes for an entrée that will make your mouth sing!

1. Combine orange juice, fresh mint, grated gingerroot, orange rind, and bourbon (if desired) in a large, shallow dish.

2. Place swordfish steaks and orange slices in a single layer in the dish. Turn to coat evenly. Cover and place in refrigerator for at least 30 minutes. Turn once while swordfish is marinating.

3. Coat grill rack with cooking spray. Place swordfish steaks on medium-hot grill. Cover and cook until fish flakes easily when fork tested, about 5 minutes on each side.

4. Transfer steaks to a warm serving platter. Cut each steak in half.

5. Place orange slices on grill rack. Cover and cook two minutes on each side. Cut each orange slice into thirds. Arrange with fish on serving platter. Garnish with fresh mint sprigs, if desired.

Swordfish Trivia

Swordfish have long, round bodies. They have no teeth and no scales. They grow to a maximum size of 14 feet. Swordfish are rich in vitamin B12 and a good source of omega-3 fatty acids.

Serves 4

Calories: 181.31
Fat: 5.54 grams
Saturated Fat: 1.50 grams
Carbohydrates: 4.03 grams
Calcium: 15.70 mg
Lactose: 0.0 grams

¼ cup unsweetened orange juice
3 tablespoons minced fresh mint
1 tablespoon peeled, grated gingerroot
1 tablespoon grated orange rind
2 tablespoons bourbon (optional)
2 8-ounce swordfish steaks ¾" thick
4 orange slices, ¼" thick
Nonstick cooking spray
Fresh mint sprigs (optional)

Flaky Fish Tacos

Any firm-flesh white fish in fillet form can be used for this recipe. Haddock, cod, and whiting are usually easy to find and all taste delicious in this recipe.

Serves 6

Calories: 215.11
Fat: 6.81 grams
Saturated Fat: 1.01 grams
Carbohydrates: 18.83 grams
Calcium: 87.83 mg
Lactose: 0.0 grams

3 cups chicken broth
1 teaspoon fresh lime juice
1 tablespoon juice from a jar of pickled jalapeños
¼ teaspoon salt
1 pound fillet of any firm-fleshed white fish
2 cups shredded lettuce
3 green onions, including green part, thinly sliced
1 medium-sized tomato, diced
12 warmed taco shells
Shredded cheese (optional)
Salsa (optional)

1. In a large, heavy saucepan, combine chicken broth, lime juice, jalapeño juice, and salt. Bring to a boil.

2. Add the fish fillets and return to simmering point. Reduce heat, cover, and simmer until fish becomes opaque, about 7 minutes. Be careful not to overcook fish. Drain well.

3. Place fish in a bowl. Remove any skin or bones. Flake fish with a fork.

4. Warm taco shells. Put a layer of lettuce in each taco shell. Spoon the flaked fish on top. Add a layer of green onions and a layer of diced tomatoes.

5. Top with cheese and salsa, if desired. Serve at once.

Catfish Gumbo

Gumbo warms the cockles of your heart and your entire body!
You can use this gumbo recipe as a base recipe and
substitute whatever type of fish appeals to you.

1. In a large, heavy kettle, cook celery, onion, green pepper, and garlic in hot oil until tender.

2. Stir in beef broth, tomatoes, bay leaf, salt, thyme, red pepper, and oregano. Bring to a boil. Reduce heat and simmer, covered, for 15 minutes.

3. Add catfish and okra. Return to boiling.

4. Reduce heat, cover, and simmer until fish flakes easily, about 15 minutes.

5. Serve in soup bowls over hot cooked rice.

Catfish Trivia

Catfish are freshwater fish that have no scales! The flesh of this popular fish is pure white, and some varieties can easily reach 100 pounds. The texture of catfish is firm and has a sweet milk flavor. Catfish ranks number four in popularity of fish favorites in America!

Serves 8

Calories: 357.09
Fat: 14.44 grams
Saturated Fat: 2.96 grams
Carbohydrates: 33.48 grams
Calcium: 79.93 mg
Lactose: 0.0 grams

1 cup celery, chopped
1 cup onion, chopped
1 cup green pepper, chopped
2 cloves garlic, minced
3 tablespoons olive oil
4 cups beef broth
1 16-ounce can whole tomatoes, cut up
1 bay leaf
1 teaspoon salt
½ teaspoon dried thyme
½ teaspoon ground red pepper
½ teaspoon dried oregano, crushed
2 pounds catfish fillets, cut into bite-sized pieces
1 10-ounce package frozen sliced okra
4 cups hot cooked rice

Scallop Ceviche

*If this is your first time making ceviche you'll find it interesting
that the lime juice brings about a chemical change similar to that produced
by heat. The scallops will become opaque.*

Serves 6

Calories: 301.58
Fat: 18.20 grams
Saturated Fat: 2.79 grams
Carbohydrates: 15.39 grams
Calcium: 51.06 mg
Lactose: 0.0 grams

1½ pounds scallops
Juice of 6 limes or lemons
*2 green chilies, seeded and
finely sliced*
*3 large tomatoes, skinned,
deseeded and diced*
*1 small red onion, finely
chopped*
6 tablespoons chopped dill
⅓ cup olive oil
*1 avocado and a few sprigs of
dill to garnish*

1. Place scallops in a shallow dish. Add enough lime juice to cover. Turn scallops to coat all sides.

2. Cover dish with plastic wrap and refrigerate for at least 4 hours. Scallops will become opaque. Drain scallops and discard juice.

3. In a medium bowl combine marinated scallops, chilies, tomatoes, onion, chopped dill, and olive oil. Salt to taste. Cover and refrigerate until ready to serve.

4. At serving time, peel and slice avocado. Brush avocado with lime juice to prevent it from discoloring.

5. Garnish scallop ceviche with avocado and fresh dill. Serve with crackers.

Ceviche Trivia

Ceviche isn't considered safe to eat unless the fish has been frozen to 31°F for 15 hours or unless you use sushi grade scallops. The acid doesn't cook the fish; it just denatures the protein. Seviche is a Mediterranean method of preserving raw fish. The Latin American Spanish word seviche *comes from the Iberian Spanish* escabeche, *also called* chebbeci *in Sicily, a word that means "marinated fish."*

Oregano Scallop Medley

*Most seafood is versatile, and scallops are no exception.
Couple the rich taste of scallops with oregano and you have
a very different approach to serving bay scallops!*

1. Rinse scallops with cold water and pat dry.

2. Coat a large skillet with cooking spray; add olive oil and place over medium heat until hot. Add scallops. Sauté for 3 minutes.

3. Remove scallops from skillet, discarding liquid. Add mushrooms, green onions, and oregano to skillet. Sauté together for 3 minutes.

4. Add reserved scallops and tomatoes to skillet. Sauté until thoroughly heated, about 1 minute.

5. Sprinkle with cheese, if desired. Serve immediately.

Serves 4

Calories: 147.62
Fat: 4.17 grams
Saturated Fat: 0.97 grams
Carbohydrates: 5.71 grams
Calcium: 71.16 mg
Lactose: 0.0 grams

1 pound fresh bay scallops
Nonstick cooking spray
2 teaspoons olive oil
1 cup sliced fresh mushrooms
2 green onions with tops, sliced
1 tablespoon dried whole oregano
12 cherry tomatoes, cut in half
2 tablespoons grated Parmesan cheese (optional)

Scallops in Tangerine Sauce

If you're serving these scallops in tangerine sauce to guests, you might as well print out some recipe cards before they arrive!

Serves 4

Calories: 223.65
Fat: 1.60 grams
Saturated Fat: 0.24 grams
Carbohydrates: 28.47 grams
Calcium: 49.83 mg
Lactose: 0.0 grams

1 cup clam juice
2 tablespoons chopped fresh parsley
1 tablespoon lemon juice
1 teaspoon dried whole thyme
1 teaspoon dried whole basil
¼ teaspoon pepper
1 pound fresh bay scallops
4 ounces spinach fettuccine, uncooked
⅔ cup fresh squeezed tangerine juice
1 tablespoon lemon juice
1 tablespoon cornstarch
¼ cup water

1. In a small saucepan, combine clam juice, fresh parsley, lemon juice, thyme, basil, and pepper. Bring to a boil. Reduce heat and simmer for 10 minutes. Add scallops and cook until scallops are opaque, about 6 minutes.

2. Drain scallops and reserve ½ cup liquid. Set scallops aside, cover, and keep warm. Cook fettuccine according to package directions. Drain well and set aside, keeping warm.

3. In a small, heavy saucepan, combine reserved ½ cup liquid, tangerine juice, and 1 tablespoon lemon juice. Bring mixture to a boil over medium heat.

4. Combine cornstarch and water in a small screw top jar and shake until lumps are gone. Slowly add to juice mixture. Reduce heat and cook until mixture begins to bubble and is thickened, stirring constantly.

5. Transfer fettuccine to a warm serving platter. Place scallops on top and spoon tangerine sauce over scallops.

Scallop Tips

Bay scallops, sea scallops, and calico scallops are all mollusks that are full of nutrients, including those much sought after omega-3 fatty acids. Scallops are easy to cook. The only thing you need to look out for is overcooking them. Since scallops are of the mollusk family, they get very tough if they are overcooked, and that doesn't equal tasty!

Garlic Shrimp

A large helping of garlic can be good when preparing a shrimp dish like this. Use as much or as little garlic as you desire.

Serves 6

Calories: 170.70
Fat: 2.62 grams
Saturated Fat: 0.50 grams
Carbohydrates: 2.17 grams
Calcium: 83.59 mg
Lactose: 0.0 grams

6 cups water
2 pounds unpeeled large fresh shrimp
Nonstick cooking spray
¼ cup green onions
2 teaspoons minced garlic
¼ cup dry white wine
¼ cup water
1 teaspoon lemon juice
½ teaspoon salt
⅛ teaspoon coarsely ground black pepper
1 teaspoon dried whole dill weed
1 teaspoon chopped fresh parsley
3 cups hot cooked rice (optional)

1. In a large stockpot, bring 6 cups water to a boil. Add shrimp and return to a boil. Reduce heat and simmer for about 4 minutes.

2. Drain shrimp well and rinse with cold water. Peel and de-vein shrimp.

3. Coat a large skillet with cooking spray and heat over medium heat. Add green onions and garlic to skillet. Sauté until green onions are tender.

4. Add shrimp, white wine, water, lemon juice, salt, and pepper. Cook over medium heat about 5 minutes or until shrimp turns light pink, stirring occasionally. Note: Be careful not to overcook shrimp as it will be rubbery. Stir in dill weed and parsley.

5. Serve over rice, if desired.

Mandarin Shrimp and Veggie Stir Fry

*Orange marmalade combined with fresh ginger and garlic
with shrimp as the base of the recipe is bound to be a pleaser.
This is a great dish on its own, but add rice to complement it.*

Serves 6

Calories: 248.29
Fat: 5.38 grams
Saturated Fat: 0.79 grams
Carbohydrates: 43.98
grams
Calcium: 75.60 mg
Lactose: 0.0 grams

24 fresh jumbo shrimp
1 cup orange marmalade
3 tablespoons soy sauce
2 tablespoons white vinegar
2 teaspoons Tabasco sauce
1½ tablespoons cornstarch
2 tablespoons light olive oil
*1 tablespoon chopped fresh
    ginger*
*1 tablespoon chopped fresh
    garlic*
1 red bell pepper, chopped
1 green bell pepper, chopped
3 cups broccoli flowerets
½ cup water
1 cup chopped green onions

1. Peel and de-vein shrimp. In a small bowl, combine orange marmalade, soy sauce, vinegar, Tabasco, and cornstarch. Stir well to dissolve cornstarch. Set aside.

2. Place a large skillet or wok over high heat. Heat skillet for 1 minute and add olive oil. Heat oil for 30 seconds. Add ginger, garlic, and shrimp. Stir-fry shrimp until they begin to turn pink, about 3 minutes. Remove shrimp from skillet and set aside.

3. Add the peppers and broccoli to skillet. Cook on high heat for 1 minute. Reduce heat to medium. Add water and cover. Cook veggies until tender, about 5 minutes.

4. Remove cover. Return heat to high. Add shrimp and marmalade mixture. Cook shrimp for another 2 minutes until sauce is thickened and shrimp are completely cooked.

5. Stir in green onions. Serve with cooked rice if desired.

Shrimp Tips

When you're buying fresh shrimp, make sure the meat is firm. If you're buying frozen shrimp, purchase shrimp in a clear plastic bag so you can see any freezer burn. You can grill 'em, and they're great sautéed, roasted, stir-fried, baked, or in a shrimp cocktail. Shrimp are rich in vitamin B12, niacin, omega-3 fatty acids, iron, zinc, and copper.

Chapter 17
Rice and Couscous

Pistachio Basmati Rice

Pistachio nuts add a wonderful flavor and crunch to already delightful basmati rice.

Serves 6

Calories: 342.09
Fat: 14.31 grams
Saturated Fat: 1.86 grams
Carbohydrates: 46.38 grams
Calcium: 64.62 mg
Lactose: 0.0 grams

10 ounces basmati rice
2 bunches green onions
2 tablespoons olive oil
1 cup pistachio nuts, shelled, coarsely chopped
1 teaspoon crushed red pepper flakes

1. Cook rice in a large, covered pan according to package directions.

2. Rinse green onions and cut into ½" diagonal slices.

3. Heat one tablespoon of the olive oil in a small skillet. Add green onions and sauté over medium heat for a short minute.

4. Stir in pistachio nuts and cook for another minute, stirring constantly. Set aside.

5. At serving time, uncover rice and fold in red pepper flakes, green onions, and nuts with a fork. Drizzle remaining oil over rice. Serve immediately.

Basmati Rice Ramblings

Did you know that basmati rice has a delicate reputation? It is known for being the most aromatic, delicate, and delicious member of the rice family! To prepare the rice, rinse it several times in cold water and let it soak for about 30 minutes. This will help give the rice its characteristic fluffiness.

Wild Rice with Cranberries and Toasted Pine Nuts

*Talk about tasty! The pine nuts lend a little crunch, and the
dried cranberries add just the right touch of sweetness.*

1. Remove stems from green onions and rinse. Slice green onions into
   ¼" diagonal pieces.

2. Heat one tablespoon of the olive oil in a small skillet.

3. Add green onions and sauté over medium high heat for about 2 minutes, stirring constantly. Set skillet aside.

4. Prepare wild rice according to package instructions.

5. After rice has cooked, fold in green onions, dried cranberries, toasted
   pine nuts, and the remaining tablespoon of olive oil. Heat for 1 minute.
   Serve warm.

Serves 4

Calories: 329.18
Fat: 14.98 grams
Saturated Fat: 2.17 grams
Carbohydrates: 44.35 grams
Calcium: 54.22 mg
Lactose: 0.0 grams

2 bunches green onions
2 tablespoons olive oil
1 5-ounce package wild rice
2 ounces dried cranberries
1¾ ounces toasted pine nuts

Orange Rice

*Because of the citrus combo with the long grain rice,
this is a perfect complement to chicken and fish.*

1. In a medium saucepan, combine water, orange peel, orange juice, and
   salt. Bring to a boil.

2. Stir in rice and raisins. Return to boiling.

3. Reduce heat and cook, covered, over low heat until rice is tender and
   liquid is absorbed, about 25 minutes. Serve hot with orange slice garnish, if desired.

Serves 6

Calories: 157.80
Fat: 0.32 grams
Saturated Fat: 0.07 grams
Carbohydrates: 36.31 grams
Calcium: 16.75 mg
Lactose: 0.0 grams

2 cups water
*2 tablespoons grated orange
    peel*
½ cup orange juice
½ teaspoon salt
*1 cup uncooked, long grain
    rice*
½ cup raisins
*Orange slice for garnish
    (optional)*

Baked Wild Rice with Herbs

*This fine potpourri of a recipe fills the house with
warm, inviting aromas while it's cooking.*

Serves 8

Calories: 181.82
Fat: 7.56 grams
Saturated Fat: 1.41 grams
Carbohydrates: 22.35 grams
Calcium: 19.95 mg
Lactose: 0.0 grams

1 cup uncooked wild rice
¼ cup margarine
1 cup chopped celery
1 cup chopped onion
½ cup sliced mushrooms
4½ cups chicken broth
*1 tablespoon chopped fresh
    parsley*
¼ teaspoon thyme
¼ teaspoon dried basil
½ teaspoon salt
½ teaspoon black pepper

1. Preheat oven to 350°F.

2. Rinse the wild rice carefully. Let soak according to package directions if called for.

3. Melt margarine in a large skillet over medium heat. Add celery, onion, and mushrooms, cooking while stirring constantly until vegetables are translucent.

4. Drain wild rice. Add rice to skillet. Cook, stirring constantly for 2 minutes. Place wild rice mixture in a 2-quart baking dish. Stir in 4 cups of the chicken broth. Add herbs and seasonings and stir to combine.

5. Cover and bake for 1½ hours. Stir a couple of times during baking. If rice mixture becomes dry, add more broth during the last 20 minutes.

The Caviar of All Grains

Wild rice is referred to as the caviar of all grains. With its nutty textured seed and sweet taste it is definitely the rice of choice for creating very special dishes. It is truly one of the most versatile and flavorful grains.

Curried Rice

Eat curried rice on its own or add a bit of chicken or pork to bolster the flavor.

1. Combine ⅓ cup water and onion in a 1-quart casserole dish.

2. Cover and microwave on high for one minute.

3. Add another ⅓ cup water, rice, bouillon granules, curry powder, and pepper to casserole. Stir well.

4. Cover and microwave on high until water boils, about 3 minutes. Stir well.

5. Cover and microwave at 50 percent power until liquid is absorbed, about 10 minutes. Let stand 4 minutes before serving. Garnish with green onion fans if desired.

Serves 2

Calories: 119.40
Fat: 0.40 grams
Saturated Fat: 0.11 grams
Carbohydrates: 25.50 grams
Calcium: 21.74 mg
Lactose: 0.0 grams

⅔ cup water, divided
2 tablespoons chopped green onion
⅓ cup parboiled rice, uncooked
½ teaspoon chicken-flavored bouillon granules
¼ teaspoon curry powder
Dash of pepper
Green onion fans (optional)

Spanish Rice with Beef

Skillet meals are becoming more and more popular for good reason. They come together rather quickly, and it's all in one pan!

1. In a large, heavy skillet, cook ground beef, onion, and green pepper until meat is browned.

2. Drain in a colander and pat dry with a paper towel. Wipe pan drippings from skillet with a paper towel.

3. Return meat mixture to skillet.

4. Stir in tomatoes, water, rice, chili powder, oregano, salt, red pepper, and garlic powder. Bring to a boil.

5. Reduce heat, cover and simmer until rice is tender, stirring occasionally, about 30 minutes.

Serves 6

Calories: 314.72
Fat: 8.13 grams
Saturated Fat: 3.17 grams
Carbohydrates: 41.00 grams
Calcium: 50.94 mg
Lactose: 0.0 grams

1 pound lean ground beef
1 medium onion, chopped
1 medium-sized green pepper, chopped
2 16-ounce cans stewed tomatoes, undrained
1 cup water
1 cup uncooked rice
1½ teaspoons chili powder
¾ teaspoon dried whole oregano
½ teaspoon salt
¼ teaspoon red pepper
⅛ teaspoon garlic powder

Fiesta Rice

Viva la Fiesta!

Calories: 166.91
Fat: 2.42 grams
Saturated Fat: 0.47 grams
Carbohydrates: 29.93 grams
Calcium: 28.60 mg
Lactose: 0.0 grams

Nonstick cooking spray
1 teaspoon light olive oil
½ cup chopped sweet red pepper
¼ cup chopped onion
1 clove garlic, minced
1¼ cups chicken broth
½ cup long-grain rice, uncooked
½ cup frozen whole-kernel corn, thawed
½ cup salsa
½ cup drained canned black beans
1 tablespoon chopped fresh cilantro
¼ teaspoon salt
Orange slices (optional)
Fresh cilantro sprigs (optional)

1. Coat a large saucepan with cooking spray.

2. Heat olive oil over medium-high heat. Add red pepper, onion, and garlic. Sauté until crisp-tender.

3. Add broth, rice, corn, and salsa. Bring to a boil.

4. Reduce heat, cover and simmer for 20 minutes. Remove from heat. Let stand until liquid is absorbed, about 5 minutes.

5. Stir in beans, chopped cilantro, and salt. Garnish with orange slices and cilantro sprigs, if desired.

Seafood Risotto

Risotto is an elegant dish, perfect for entertaining.
Do all your prep work ahead of time and store ingredients in the fridge,
and the dish will only take about 30 minutes of cooking time.

1. In medium saucepan, combine water and broth and heat over low heat. Keep mixture on heat.

2. In large saucepan, heat olive oil over medium heat. Add onion and garlic; cook and stir until crisp-tender, about 3 minutes. Add rice; cook and stir for 3 minutes.

3. Start adding broth mixture, a cup at a time, stirring frequently, adding liquid when previous addition is absorbed. When only 1 cup of broth remains to be added, stir in celery, dill, wine, fish fillets, shrimp, and scallops to rice mixture. Add last cup of broth.

4. Cook, stirring constantly, for 5–7 minutes or until fish is cooked and rice is tender and creamy. Stir in butter and serve.

Arborio Rice

Arborio rice is a short-grain rice that contains a lot of starch. When cooked in broth and stirred, the rice releases much of that starch, which combines with the liquid to form a creamy sauce. If you can't find true Arborio rice, long-grain or medium-grain rice will work just as well. The risotto just won't be quite as creamy.

Calories: 397.22
Fat: 11.11 grams
Saturated fat: 3.20 grams
Fiber: 2.41 grams
Cholesterol: 94.39 mg
Lactose: 0.0 grams

2 cups water
2½ cups low-sodium chicken broth
2 tablespoons olive oil
1 onion, minced
3 cloves garlic, minced
1½ cups Arborio rice
1 cup chopped celery
1 tablespoon fresh dill weed
¼ cup dry white wine
½ pound sole fillets
¼ pound small raw shrimp
½ pound bay scallops
1 tablespoon butter

Herbed Rice Sauté

A little tip about rosemary: If it's possible to use "fresh" rosemary any time a recipe calls for rosemary, use it!

1. Coat a large, heavy skillet with cooking spray.

2. Add margarine and place over medium-high heat until margarine is melted. Add rice and onion, sautéing until rice is lightly browned.

3. Add water, rosemary, marjoram, whole savory, and bouillon cubes. Stir to dissolve bouillon. Bring to a boil.

4. Reduce heat and simmer, covered, until water is absorbed and rice is tender, about 25 minutes.

Brown Rice Pilaf

Brown rice is so good for you. In this recipe, brown rice soaks up these added flavors to please your palate.

1. Preheat oven to 350°F.

2. Combine broth, brown rice, onion, mushrooms, pepper, and thyme in a 1-quart casserole dish.

3. Cover and bake rice mixture for 1 hour.

4. Add celery to rice mixture. Cover again and bake until liquid is absorbed and celery is tender, about 15 minutes.

Italian Rice

Flavor-full and full of flavor! Artichoke hearts take center stage in this very different combination rice recipe. And this dish is full of color too!

1. Coarsely chop thawed artichoke hearts. Set aside.

2. Bring 1½ cups water to a boil in a medium saucepan. Stir in long-grain rice. Reduce heat and cover. Simmer rice until all liquid is absorbed and rice is tender, about 20 minutes.

3. In a large skillet, heat olive oil over medium heat. Add chopped artichoke hearts, red pepper strips, baby peas, green onions, and minced garlic. Sauté until veggies are crisp-tender, about 5 minutes.

4. Combine rice, sautéed vegetables, Italian dressing, and Italian seasoning.

5. Toss gently until evenly coated.

Serves 8

Calories: 121.77
Fat: 4.11 grams
Saturated Fat: 0.54 grams
Carbohydrates: 18.81 grams
Calcium: 20.79 mg
Lactose: 0.0 grams

1 9-ounce package frozen artichoke hearts, thawed
1½ cups water
¾ cup long grain rice, uncooked
1 tablespoon olive oil
⅔ cup sweet red pepper strips
½ cup frozen baby peas, thawed
½ cup sliced green onions
1 clove garlic, minced
3 tablespoons bottled Italian dressing
1 teaspoon dried Italian seasoning

Mexican Rice

Serves 8

Calories: 114.30
Fat: 0.45 grams
Saturated Fat: 0.10 grams
Carbohydrates: 23.80 grams
Calcium: 26.95 mg
Lactose: 0.0 grams

Nonstick cooking spray
1 cup long grain rice,
* uncooked*
¾ cup chopped dry sun-dried
* tomatoes*
½ cup chopped sweet red
* pepper*
¼ cup chopped green onions
1 4½-ounce can chopped
* green chilies*
2 teaspoons cumin seeds
1 clove garlic, minced
2½ cups beef broth

You be the judge of the green chilies; you don't have to use the whole can.
Decide for yourself how much or how little spice you want.

1. Preheat oven to 350°F.

2. Coat a 2-quart casserole dish with cooking spray.

3. Combine long grain rice, sun-dried tomatoes, sweet red pepper, green onions, green chilies, cumin seeds, and garlic in casserole dish.

4. Bring beef broth to a boil in a medium saucepan. Pour broth over rice mixture.

5. Cover and bake until liquid is absorbed and rice is tender, about 40 minutes.

Long Grain Rice Fluff

The kernel of long grain rice is long and slender. In fact, it's almost five times longer than its width! Long grain rice is known for its fluffiness when cooked. Basmati rice is one flavorful variety of long grain rice.

Oriental Wild Rice

This is good leftover the next day. Pop it in your lunch for an added treat.

1. Combine water and rice in a medium saucepan. Bring to a boil. Reduce heat, cover, and simmer until rice is tender, about 40 minutes. Drain and set aside.

2. Seed and cut red pepper into 1" pieces; cut onion into 1" pieces.

3. Coat a large skillet or wok with cooking spray. Drizzle sesame oil around top of wok or skillet, coating sides. Heat over medium-high heat.

4. Add red pepper, onions, broccoli, bean sprouts, carrots, sesame seeds, minced gingerroot, and soy sauce. Stir-fry all together for 3 minutes.

5. Cover and allow vegetables to steam until crisp-tender, about 6 minutes. Add rice. Stir-fry until mixture is thoroughly heated. Serve immediately.

Serves 6

Calories: 156.34
Fat: 4.32 grams
Saturated Fat: 0.62 grams
Carbohydrates: 25.19 grams
Calcium: 35.95 mg
Lactose: 0.0 grams

2½ cups water
1 cup wild rice, uncooked
Nonstick cooking spray
1 tablespoon dark sesame oil
2 cups broccoli flowerets
1 cup fresh bean sprouts
⅔ cup diagonally sliced
   carrot
1 small sweet red pepper
4 green onions
1 tablespoon sesame seeds
1 teaspoon peeled, minced
   gingerroot
2 teaspoons soy sauce

Minted Couscous

When this couscous hits your mouth you'll probably think that those green peas are delivering that minty flavor. Mint is one of those herbs that can be described as both warm and cool; in this rice dish it's very cool!

Serves 6

Calories: 123.16
Fat: 0.30 grams
Saturated Fat: 0.06 grams
Carbohydrates: 24.85 grams
Calcium: 11.50 mg
Lactose: 0.0 grams

1¾ cups water
2 teaspoons minced fresh mint
1 teaspoon chicken-flavored bouillon granules
⅛ teaspoon salt
1 cup couscous, uncooked
¾ cup frozen peas, thawed
Fresh mint sprigs (optional)

1. Combine water, fresh mint, bouillon granules, and salt in a medium saucepan. Bring to a boil.

2. Remove from heat. Add couscous and peas.

3. Cover and let stand until liquid is absorbed and couscous is tender, about 5 minutes.

4. Fluff couscous with a fork.

5. Transfer from saucepan to a serving bowl. Garnish with fresh mint springs, if desired.

Harvest Couscous

This dish has all the trappings of a favorite holiday dish.

Serves 6

Calories: 166.10
Fat: 0.34 grams
Saturated Fat: 0.05 grams
Carbohydrates: 38.18 grams
Calcium: 39.90 mg
Lactose: 0.0 grams

2 cups water
¾ cup peeled, diced sweet potato
¼ cup diced dried figs
⅓ cup diced dried apricots
½ teaspoon pumpkin pie spice
¾ cup couscous, uncooked

1. Combine water, sweet potato, figs, apricots, and pumpkin pie spice in a medium saucepan. Bring to a boil.

2. Reduce heat, cover, and simmer until potato is tender, about 15 minutes.

3. Remove from heat. Add couscous.

4. Cover and let stand until liquid is absorbed and couscous is tender, about 5 minutes.

5. Fluff couscous with a fork. Transfer to a serving bowl.

Chapter 18
Pasta

Pasta with Broccoli Tomato Sauce

This recipe delivers a Mediterranean flavor to pasta. Bon appetit!

Serves 4

Calories: 284.22
Fat: 6.13 grams
Saturated Fat: 0.87 grams
Carbohydrates: 44.03 grams
Calcium: 60.80 mg
Lactose: 0.0 grams

2 cups fresh broccoli flowerets
2 large ripe tomatoes
Nonstick cooking spray
1 tablespoon olive oil
2 garlic cloves, minced
½ teaspoon red pepper flakes
10 Greek olives, sliced
½ cup coarsely chopped parsley
Salt and pepper to taste
½ pound angel hair pasta
Freshly grated Parmesan cheese (optional)

1. Steam broccoli over boiling water until crisp-tender, about 3 minutes. Remove from heat. Rinse with cold water.

2. Immerse tomatoes in boiling water for 12 seconds to blanch them. Slip skins off tomatoes. Set aside. Coarsely chop tomatoes.

3. Coat a large skillet with cooking spray. Heat olive oil over medium-high heat. Add tomatoes, garlic, red pepper flakes, Greek olives, parsley, salt, and pepper. Sauté about 3 minutes. Add broccoli. Sauté for another 2 minutes.

4. Prepare pasta according to package instructions. Drain pasta and place on serving plate.

5. Ladle sauce over pasta. Sprinkle with freshly grated Parmesan cheese, if desired.

Under Cover Tomatoes

If you purchase tomatoes that aren't as ripe as you'd like, pop them in a paper bag and put them on the countertop for one or two days. This will speed the ripening process.

Chicken Spaghetti

Chicken just soaks up the wonderful seasonings in this dish.
Serve with a fresh garden salad and your meal is complete!

1. Coat a large skillet with cooking spray. Melt margarine over medium heat. Add onion and garlic. Sauté until lightly browned.

2. Cut each chicken breast into 8 pieces. Brown breasts with onion and garlic.

3. Add tomatoes and sauce. Bring to a boil.

4. Reduce heat and add basil, thyme, Italian seasoning, salt, and pepper. Cover and simmer until chicken is tender, about 25 minutes.

5. Serve over hot cooked spaghetti.

Serves 4

Calories: 434.56
Fat: 5.04 grams
Saturated Fat: 1.01 grams
Carbohydrates: 58.84 grams
Calcium: 55.75 mg
Lactose: 0.0 grams

Nonstick cooking spray
2 teaspoons margarine
½ cup onion, minced
1 clove garlic, minced
4 boneless, skinless chicken breasts
1 15-ounce can tomatoes, puréed
1 8-ounce can tomato sauce
1 teaspoon basil
¼ teaspoon thyme
¼ teaspoon Italian seasoning
½ teaspoon salt
½ teaspoon pepper
4 cups cooked spaghetti

Garden Pasta

Serves 8

Calories: 137.59
Fat: 2.06 grams
Saturated Fat: 0.31 grams
Carbohydrates: 24.62 grams
Calcium: 24.09 mg
Lactose: 0.0 grams

5 medium tomatoes,
    chopped
2 stalks celery, chopped
2 medium carrots, chopped
1 medium onion, chopped
1 teaspoon sugar
1 teaspoon basil
¼ teaspoon garlic powder
½ teaspoon salt
½ teaspoon pepper
½ teaspoon oregano
1 tablespoon olive oil
1 pound uncooked spaghetti

Bring the garden to your table every time you get a chance, even in pasta dishes!

1. In a heavy medium saucepan, add tomatoes, celery, carrots, and onion. Cover tightly. Cook over medium heat about 10 minutes, stirring occasionally and adjusting heat if too high.

2. Add sugar, basil, garlic powder, salt, pepper, and oregano. Cover and continue cooking over medium-low heat for an additional 5 minutes.

3. Add olive oil. Simmer until carrots are tender, about 30 minutes.

4. Cook spaghetti according to package directions. Drain.

5. Toss with sauce. Serve immediately.

Recipe Variation

Cut one or more of your favorite vegetables like broccoli, asparagus, or mushrooms into bite-sized pieces. Sauté veggies with minced garlic in lots of olive oil over high heat until crisp tender. Serve over cooked pasta with the oil, topping with freshly grated Parmesan if you like.

Spaghetti with Shrimp Sauce

There's something incredibly palate-pleasing about the combination of seafood with pasta. Shrimp lovers will love this recipe!

1. Coat a large skillet with cooking spray. Heat over medium-high heat.

2. Add onion, green pepper, green onions, celery, and garlic. Sauté until vegetables are tender.

3. Add tomato sauce, tomatoes, seasonings, and water. Cover and simmer 30 minutes, stirring occasionally.

4. Peel and de-vein shrimp. Rinse well. Add shrimp to skillet. Cover and simmer an additional 10 minutes.

5. Cook spaghetti according to package directions, omitting salt. Drain. Serve shrimp sauce over spaghetti.

Serves 4

Calories: 284.19
Fat: 2.92 grams
Saturated Fat: 0.52 grams
Carbohydrates: 33.12 grams
Calcium: 108.10 mg
Lactose: 0.0 grams

Nonstick cooking spray
1 medium onion, chopped
1 medium-sized green pepper, chopped
½ cup chopped green onions
¼ cup chopped celery
4 cloves garlic, minced
1 8-ounce can tomato sauce
½ 10-ounce can tomatoes with green chilies, undrained and chopped
¼ teaspoon salt
¼ teaspoon pepper
¼ teaspoon dried whole oregano
⅛ teaspoon dried whole rosemary
⅛ teaspoon dried whole thyme
¼ cup water
1 pound unpeeled fresh shrimp
4 ounces uncooked spaghetti

Eggplant Pasta

Serves 4

Calories: 343.33
Fat: 15.53 grams
Saturated Fat: 1.77 grams
Carbohydrates: 39.65 grams
Calcium: 52.55 mg
Lactose: 0.0 grams

2 tablespoons olive oil
3 cups eggplant, peeled, chopped
6 garlic cloves, minced
1 red bell pepper, cut into strips
6 large mushrooms, sliced
1 teaspoon dried oregano, crumbled
½ teaspoon dried crushed red pepper
⅓ cup dry red wine
1 large tomato, chopped
½ cup chopped pitted black olives
12 ounces freshly cooked penne
¼ cup toasted pine nuts
Freshly grated Parmesan cheese (optional)

The red bell pepper, eggplant, and black olives make this dish a delightfully beautiful presentation, and the flavor with the crunch of the pine nuts is sure to please!

1. In a large skillet or wok, heat olive oil over medium heat. Add eggplant and garlic. Cover and cook until eggplant is just tender, about 5 minutes, stirring occasionally.

2. Add red bell pepper, mushrooms, oregano, and dried crushed red pepper. Sauté until mushrooms are tender, about 4 minutes.

3. Add wine. Cook until mixture absorbs all the moisture, about 4 minutes.

4. Stir in tomato and black olives. Cook until mixture is just heated through. Transfer sauce to large bowl.

5. Add pasta and pine nuts. Toss until well combined. Serve immediately with freshly grated Parmesan cheese, if desired.

Eggplant Truths

Contrary to popular belief and practice, it is usually unnecessary to salt and press the juices from eggplant before cooking it. If an eggplant is firm and fresh, its flavor and consistency will be fine without any advance treatment.

Sun-Dried Tomato Pesto and Linguine

Sun-dried tomatoes just might become a staple in your pantry! They deliver an intense tomato flavor, and they are conveniently available all year round. They are truly an ideal cooking ingredient to complement your favorite LI meals.

1. Combine tomatoes and boiling water in a small bowl. Let stand for 5 minutes. Drain, reserving 1 cup liquid. Set aside.

2. Combine tomatoes, reserved liquid, cheese, parsley sprigs, slivered almonds, basil, olive oil, salt, and garlic in a food processor or blender. Process until smooth.

3. Prepare spinach by removing stems; wash leaves thoroughly and pat dry. Shred spinach.

4. Coat a large, heavy saucepan with cooking spray and place over medium heat until hot. Add spinach. Cover and cook until spinach wilts, stirring occasionally. Set aside.

5. Cook pasta according to package directions, omitting salt. Drain well. Combine tomato mixture and pasta. Gently toss. Add cooked spinach. Toss until well combined. Garnish with basil sprigs, if desired.

Serves 8

Calories: 257.48
Fat: 6.85 grams
Saturated Fat: 1.64 grams
Carbohydrates: 36.02 grams
Calcium: 171.57 mg
Lactose: 0.01 grams

20 dry sun-dried tomatoes
1½ cups boiling water
½ cup grated Parmesan cheese
½ cup tightly packed fresh parsley sprigs
¼ cup plus 2 tablespoons toasted slivered almonds
¼ cup chopped fresh basil
2 teaspoons olive oil
⅛ teaspoon salt
6 cloves garlic
Nonstick cooking spray
1 pound fresh spinach
12 ounces linguine, uncooked
Fresh basil sprigs (optional)

Greek Penne

Enjoy this healthy skillet meal with the creaminess of yogurt.

Serves 6

Calories: 280.20
Fat: 8.98 grams
Saturated Fat: 2.89 grams
Carbohydrates: 38.50 grams
Calcium: 170.18 mg
Lactose: 0.0 grams

2 teaspoons extra virgin olive oil
1 cup red onion, chopped
2 garlic cloves, minced
3 tablespoons roasted pine nuts
1½ pounds ripe plum tomatoes, coarsely chopped
1 tablespoon tomato paste
6 cups fresh spinach leaves, chopped
3 green onions, finely chopped
2 ounces feta cheese, crumbled (optional)
1 cup plain yogurt
Salt and pepper to taste
8 ounces penne pasta, cooked al dente

1. In a large heavy skillet, heat olive oil over medium-high heat. Add onion and sauté until tender.

2. Reduce heat to medium-low and add garlic and pine nuts. Stir in tomatoes and tomato paste. Cover and simmer for about 10 minutes to mingle flavors.

3. Add spinach and green onions to skillet. Place feta cheese and yogurt in blender. Process until smooth.

4. Remove the tomato mixture from heat. Stir in yogurt mixture. Season with salt and pepper.

5. Prepare penne according to package directions, cooking al dente. Drain. Pour penne in a large pasta bowl and top with sauce. Serve immediately.

Penne

Penne has a unique texture and, like all pasta, is loaded with energy. Use whole wheat pasta to get the full nutritional benefit.

Seafood Pasta Salad

*Plan to take this seafood pasta salad to your next gathering
and be ready for compliments and second helpings!*

1. Combine all ingredients in a large bowl. Toss until well combined.

2. Chill for at least an hour.

3. Garnish a large platter with lettuce leaves. Mound salad on platter. Garnish with strips of carrots and zucchini, if desired.

Serves 8

Calories: 338.86
Fat: 17.20 grams
Saturated Fat: 1.85 grams
Carbohydrates: 27.57 grams
Calcium: 68.28 mg
Lactose: 0.0 grams

½ cup barbecue sauce
Juice of 1 lemon
½ cup safflower oil
1 teaspoon prepared
    horseradish
½ teaspoon sugar
1 tablespoon chopped fresh
    basil
½ pound cooked crabmeat
½ pound cooked shrimp
½ pound spiral pasta, cooked
    and drained
1 cup frozen peas
1 cup thinly sliced zucchini
1 carrot, thinly sliced
½ green pepper, thinly sliced
½ cup chopped black olives
Lettuce of your choice

Italian Pasta Stir Fry

*When you think of stir fry, you probably think of rice or
chow mein noodles, but why not try spaghetti?*

Serves 6

Calories: 202.14
Fat: 4.45 grams
Saturated Fat: 1.19 grams
Carbohydrates: 30.73 grams
Calcium: 75.89 mg
Lactose: 0.01 grams

*8 ounces uncooked linguine
1 tablespoon olive oil
2 large cloves garlic, pressed
1 medium zucchini, sliced
1 medium onion, chopped
2 medium tomatoes, peeled
    and chopped
¼ cup fresh parsley, minced
1 teaspoon dried oregano
⅛ teaspoon salt
⅛ teaspoon ground black
    pepper
¼ cup grated Parmesan
    cheese*

1. Cook pasta according to package directions. Drain and keep warm.

2. Heat olive oil in a heavy skillet or wok. Add garlic and stir-fry for 15 seconds.

3. Add zucchini and onion. Stir-fry until crisp-tender, 2–3 minutes.

4. Add tomatoes, parsley, oregano, salt, and pepper to skillet. Gently stir until thoroughly heated, 1–2 minutes. Remove from heat.

5. Stir in warm pasta. Add Parmesan cheese, if desired. Serve immediately.

Oregano Trivia

Aromatic and pungent, oregano is very popular in Italian and Greek cuisines. It's used in seasoning sauces containing tomatoes and can be used dry or fresh. It's also one of the key seasonings in traditional pizza dishes.

Spaghetti Pancake

If you have leftover spaghetti, try making a spaghetti pancake. You may find yourself cooking extra spaghetti just so you'll have leftovers!

1. In a small bowl, beat together egg, thyme, garlic powder, pepper, and one tablespoon water. Set aside.

2. Spray medium skillet with cooking spray. Over medium-high heat, sauté green onion, mushrooms, and spaghetti, stirring frequently for about one minute.

3. Evenly spread mixture over bottom of skillet.

4. Reduce heat to medium-low. Pour egg mixture over spaghetti. Tilt skillet to distribute evenly.

5. Sprinkle cheese on top, if desired. Cover and cook for 1–2 minutes or until egg is set.

Serves 1

Calories: 228.76
Fat: 6.55 grams
Saturated Fat: 2.33 grams
Carbohydrates: 27.36 grams
Calcium: 95.61 mg
Lactose: 0.06 grams

1 egg
⅛ teaspoon dried thyme
⅛ teaspoon garlic powder
⅛ teaspoon pepper
1 tablespoon water
Nonstick cooking spray
1 green onion, thinly sliced
½ cup canned mushrooms,
* stems and pieces, drained*
½ cup cooked spaghetti
2½ teaspoons grated
* Parmesan cheese*

Linguine with Arugula and Pine Nuts

Calories: 446.72
Fat: 24.21 grams
Saturated Fat: 4.64 grams
Carbohydrates: 39.55 grams
Calcium: 185.02 mg
Lactose: 0.02 grams

1 pound linguine
½ cup olive oil
4 ounces arugula, trimmed
1 cup freshly grated
    Parmesan cheese
Salt and pepper to taste
½ cup toasted pine nuts

*Arugula gives this simple and quick recipe a delicious bite. You be
the judge on the amount of Parmesan cheese you include; it can be
just as tasty with half of the suggested 1 cup in the ingredients list.*

1. Cook linguine in large pot of boiling salted water until just tender. Stir occasionally.

2. While linguine is cooking, heat oil in heavy large skillet over medium heat. Add arugula and stir until wilted, about 30 seconds. Remove from heat.

3. Drain pasta and return to pot. Add arugula. Toss well.

4. Add Parmesan and salt and pepper to taste. Toss until well combined. Transfer to bowl.

5. Top with pine nuts and additional Parmesan, if desired. Serve immediately.

Pine Nut Trivia

You guessed it—pine nuts are the seeds of pine trees. However, not every pine tree will bless you with nuts for cooking. There are only about a dozen species of pine trees that will provide you with this crunchy addition to your pantry. In the United States the nuts are usually gathered in the wild.

Spaghetti with Zucchini Sauce

The key word here is fresh. Tomato sauce is often thought of as an all-day affair, but it doesn't have to be so. In fact, once you experience the fresh flavor of this tomato sauce, you may prefer it to all-day cooking.

1. Sauté oil and onion in a large skillet.

2. Add rest of ingredients except spaghetti and Parmesan cheese to onion. Cover and simmer for 15 minutes.

3. Uncover and continue to simmer for an additional 10 minutes. Discard bay leaf.

4. Cook spaghetti according to package directions. Drain.

5. Serve immediately with generous helpings of healthy, tasty sauce!

Zucchini and Italian Cooking

Pleasing and delicate, zucchini is one of the popular veggies in Italian cooking. It's an easy veggie to work with—all you need to do is wash it, cut off both ends, and slice it. However, zucchini will soften considerably after draining, so be careful not to overcook it!

Serves 6

Calories: 256.03
Fat: 10.16 grams
Saturated Fat: 1.44 grams
Carbohydrates: 32.52 grams
Calcium: 37.74 mg
Lactose: 0.0 grams

¼ cup olive oil
1 medium yellow onion, sliced
2 medium zucchini, sliced
3 cups sliced fresh tomatoes
½ teaspoon salt
1 bay leaf
¼ teaspoon pepper
¼ teaspoon basil
¼ teaspoon oregano
8 ounces uncooked spaghetti
Freshly grated Parmesan cheese (optional)

Fresh Mushroom and Asparagus Pasta

Serves 8

Calories: 354.36
Fat: 27.52 grams
Saturated Fat: 3.83 grams
Carbohydrates: 23.10 grams
Calcium: 13.99 mg
Lactose: 0.0 grams

8 ounces fresh asparagus
½ cup olive oil
2 cloves minced garlic
5 large fresh porcini
mushrooms, thickly sliced
Sea salt and freshly ground
pepper to taste
8 ounces fettuccine
Salted water
Freshly grated Parmesan
cheese (optional)

Use your imagination when it comes to pasta dishes. Combine different vegetables and sauces to create new combinations.

1. Cut asparagus into ¼" pieces. Set aside.

2. Heat olive oil in a large, deep skillet. Sauté garlic until crisp. Add sliced mushrooms to oil. Sauté until softened. Generously season with sea salt and freshly ground pepper.

3. Add asparagus to skillet mixture. Continue cooking until asparagus is crisp-tender. Set aside.

4. Prepare fettuccine according to package directions in salted water. Drain. Toss pasta with olive oil and mushroom mixture.

5. Sprinkle with grated Parmesan, if desired. Top with freshly ground pepper to taste. Serve immediately.

Angel Hair with Spinach and Almonds

*Cooking with both olive oil and margarine boosts
the flavor in this already delicious dish.*

1. Heat oil in a large skillet. Sauté garlic with cayenne pepper. Remove from heat.

2. Add chopped spinach to skillet. Toss over high heat for one minute, just enough to wilt spinach. Stir in margarine.

3. Cook pasta al dente. Drain well. Place in large bowl.

4. Add spinach, Parmesan, and nuts. Season to taste. Serve immediately.

Ah, Al Dente!

The literal meaning from Italian is "to the bite" or "to the tooth," which refers to the firmness of the pasta. It is believed that cooking pasta al dente is the best way for it to be served—with just a tiny bit of firmness in the center when you take a bite!

Serves 8

Calories: 533.39
Fat: 36.06 grams
Saturated Fat: 6.06 grams
Carbohydrates: 38.57 grams
Calcium: 228.02 mg
Lactose: 0.02 grams

½ cup olive oil
2 teaspoons minced garlic
Pinch cayenne pepper or to
    taste
7-ounce bunch of fresh
    spinach, coarsely
    chopped
4 tablespoons margarine
12 ounces angel hair pasta
1 cup grated Parmesan
    cheese
7 ounces toasted slivered
    almonds
Salt and pepper to taste

Garlic Broccoli Pasta for One

If you're cooking for one, this is a great recipe to whip up quickly after a long day at work. If you're cooking for more than one, then just do the math!

Serves 1

Calories: 223.09
Fat: 7.08 grams
Saturated Fat: 1.53 grams
Carbohydrates: 27.07 grams
Calcium: 92.96 mg
Lactose: 0.0 grams

1 teaspoon olive oil
1 clove minced garlic
1 tablespoon chopped onion
1 tablespoon white wine
4 tablespoons chicken broth
1 cup fresh broccoli, in small pieces
1 ounce pasta of your choice, cooked
Salt and pepper to taste
2 teaspoons freshly grated Parmesan cheese

1. Using a heavy skillet or wok, heat oil over medium-high heat. Add garlic and onion. Sauté over low heat until onion is translucent.

2. Add wine, chicken broth, and broccoli to skillet. Cover and cook until broccoli is crisp-tender.

3. Add pasta and toss all ingredients together. Cook until heated thoroughly.

4. Salt and pepper to taste. Serve on a warmed plate.

5. Sprinkle with freshly grated Parmesan cheese. Serve immediately.

Chapter 19
Veggies and Accompaniments

Old-Fashioned Potato Pancakes

*Potato pancakes are yummy for breakfast but can also
be a great accompaniment to beef or chicken.*

Serves 10

Calories: 57.26
Fat: 1.43 grams
Saturated Fat: 0.39 grams
Carbohydrates: 8.94
Calcium: 12.60 mg
Lactose: 0.01 grams

*2 cups raw grated red
     potatoes
2 whole eggs, beaten
1 onion, grated
1½ teaspoons salt
2 tablespoons flour
1 teaspoon margarine*

1. Peel large red potatoes. Soak in cold water for several hours.

2. Grate potatoes and place in a large bowl.

3. Add grated onion and beaten eggs, combining well. Stir in salt and flour.

4. Heat a griddle over medium-high heat and grease it with margarine. Let margarine warm and drop batter by spoonfuls onto hot griddle.

5. Cook pancakes until both sides are golden brown. Serve hot.

Apricot-Glazed Sweet Potatoes

When you're shopping for this recipe, be sure you buy the red sweet potatoes, not the yellowish ones. You'll be amazed at the distinct difference in the color of the meat and flavor of red sweet potatoes!

1. Preheat oven to 350°F.

2. Peel and chop sweet potatoes. Cook in boiling water until sweet potatoes are tender but not mushy.

3. Place sweet potatoes in a 12" × 9" × 2" baking pan. Set aside.

4. Combine brown sugar, cornstarch, salt, and cinnamon in a medium saucepan. Stir in apricot nectar, water, and orange peel. Bring to a boil, stirring constantly. Cook another 2 minutes.

5. Remove from heat. Stir in butter and pecans. Pour over sweet potatoes. Bake uncovered until heated through, about 20 minutes.

Suh-weet Potatoes!

This naturally sweet and high-fiber veggie can be prepared in so many ways. Sweet potatoes are packed full of nutrients in addition to great flavor. They are an excellent source of beta carotene, potassium, iron, antioxidants, vitamins C and B6, and folate. Suh-weet!

Serves 8

Calories: 329.44
Fat: 5.98 grams
Saturated Fat: 1.06 grams
Carbohydrates: 67.97 grams
Calcium: 81.69 mg
Lactose: 0.0 grams

3 pounds red sweet potatoes
1 cup packed brown sugar
5 teaspoons cornstarch
¼ teaspoon salt
⅛ teaspoon cinnamon
1 cup apricot nectar
½ cup hot water
2 teaspoons grated orange peel
2 teaspoons butter
½ cup chopped pecans

Garlic Mashed Potatoes

Make enough so you'll have leftovers to turn into potato pancakes, shepherd's pie—or just to eat again!

Serves 6

Calories: 335.17
Fat: 8.62 grams
Saturated Fat: 1.40 grams
Carbohydrates: 58.39 grams
Calcium: 66.70 mg
Lactose: 0.0 grams

10 large cloves garlic, peeled
¼ cup margarine
4 pounds russet potatoes, peeled and quartered
¾ teaspoon salt
1 cup warm soy milk
1 tablespoon chopped fresh flat-leaf parsley
⅛ teaspoon pepper

1. Thinly slice 3 cloves of the garlic. Reserve remaining cloves. Melt margarine in a small skillet over low heat. Add sliced garlic to margarine. Sauté until garlic is tender, about 10 minutes. Set aside.

2. Peel and quarter potatoes. Rinse potatoes. Place potatoes in a large pot. Add remaining 7 cloves of garlic and ¼ teaspoon of the salt. Cover potatoes with water.

3. Place potatoes over high heat and bring to boil. Cook potatoes until they break apart easily with a fork, about 30 minutes. Drain the liquid.

4. Combine potatoes and sautéed garlic in a large, deep bowl. Whip potatoes with an electric mixer. Add ½ cup of warm soy milk until garlic is mashed and well combined. Gradually add more soy milk until potatoes are fluffy.

5. Season with remaining ½ teaspoon salt, parsley, and pepper. Serve immediately.

Soy Savvy

Soy milk can be a bit tricky when heated. When you're including it in a recipe like the garlic mashed potatoes, keep in mind that they need to be served immediately. If you try to keep them warm for a long period of time, the soy milk has a tendency to begin to thin and leave the potatoes soupy.

Home-Style Gravy

This is a great basic lactose-free gravy recipe that you can use to ladle over meats, chicken, potatoes, and other veggies. Substitute beef broth for chicken broth if you're serving the gravy with beef.

1. Coat a medium saucepan with cooking spray and heat over medium-high heat. Add onion and dried thyme. Sauté until onion is tender, about 3 minutes.

2. Combine cornstarch and water in a small jar with a screw top. Shake until smooth and there are no lumps. Set aside.

3. Add broth to saucepan. Slowly stir in cornstarch mixture, stirring until smooth and well blended.

4. Add salt, pepper, and poultry seasoning to onion mixture. Bring to a boil, stirring constantly. Continue cooking until bubbly and thickened, stirring constantly.

Serves 12

Calories: 15.61
Fat: 0.31 grams
Saturated Fat: 0.08 grams
Carbohydrates: 2.47 grams
Calcium: 2.24 mg
Lactose: 0.0 grams

Nonstick cooking spray
½ cup chopped onion
1 teaspoon dried thyme
1½ tablespoons cornstarch
¼ cup water
1¼ cups chicken broth
¼ teaspoon salt
¼ teaspoon pepper
*¼ teaspoon poultry
    seasoning*

Roasted Asparagus with Onions

This recipe has a very eclectic combination of ingredients, and their flavors meld to produce an exquisite treat. This is even delicious served cold the next day!

Serves 6

Calories: 35.47
Fat: 0.87 grams
Saturated Fat: 0.15 grams
Carbohydrates: 6.00 grams
Calcium: 24.51 mg
Lactose: 0.0 grams

1 pound fresh asparagus spears
1 large red onion, thinly sliced
Nonstick cooking spray
2 tablespoons balsamic vinegar
1½ teaspoons grated orange rind
2 tablespoons fresh orange juice
1 teaspoon dark sesame oil
½ teaspoon freshly ground pepper
¼ teaspoon salt
¼ teaspoon sugar

1. Preheat oven to 400°F. Cut off tough ends of asparagus at an angle.

2. Spray two separate baking sheets with cooking spray. Arrange asparagus and onion separately on the two baking sheets.

3. Bake asparagus and onion in preheated oven until crisp-tender, about 15 minutes. Stir twice while baking.

4. Combine vinegar, orange rind, orange juice, sesame oil, pepper, salt, and sugar in a small jar. Cover and shake until thoroughly mixed.

5. Arrange asparagus and onion on a serving platter. Drizzle vinegar mixture over vegetables. Serve warm or at room temperature.

Asparagus Trivia

Did you know that asparagus is an edible member of the lily family? It grows in stalks that can reach up to 3 feet in height. Prized as a spring delicacy for eons, it's now available year round. The ancient Romans thought asparagus was able to cure everything from toothache to arthritis!

Green Beans with Pearl Onions

Fresh green beans are just the best. Be sure not to cook them to death. When green beans are overcooked they literally turn a grayish color. Bright green beans are best!

1. Remove strings from beans and wash. Cut beans into 2" pieces.

2. Combine beans, onions, water, and tarragon in a large saucepan. Bring to a boil.

3. Reduce heat, cover, and simmer until crisp-tender, about 20 minutes. Add tomato. Cover and continue cooking another 2 minutes.

4. Stir in vinegar and pepper. Toss until well combined.

Serves 6

Calories: 47.17
Fat: 0.17 grams
Saturated Fat: 0.04 grams
Carbohydrates: 10.91 grams
Calcium: 40.44 mg
Lactose: 0.0 grams

1 pound fresh green beans
18 pearl onions
1 cup water
1 teaspoon dried whole tarragon
1 medium tomato, coarsely chopped
1 tablespoon tarragon vinegar
¼ teaspoon freshly ground pepper

Creole Lima Beans

This dish gives you a hint of creole but is not hot-hot. If you want to kick it up, add some creole seasoning to please your taste buds!

1. Coat a large skillet with cooking spray. Melt margarine over medium heat.

2. Add celery, green pepper, and onion. Sauté until tender.

3. Stir in lima beans, tomato, and vegetable juice. Cover and bring to boil.

4. Reduce heat. Simmer until beans are tender, about 10 minutes. Serve immediately.

Serves 8

Calories: 81.18
Fat: 0.78 grams
Saturated Fat: 0.15 grams
Carbohydrates: 15.16 grams
Calcium: 25.04 mg
Lactose: 0.0 grams

Nonstick cooking spray
1 teaspoon margarine
½ cup chopped celery
½ cup chopped green pepper
½ cup chopped onion
1 16-ounce package frozen lima beans, thawed
1 cup diced tomato
1 cup spicy-hot vegetable cocktail juice

Sautéed Portobellos with Herbes de Provence

*The flavors of the herbs mingle through the fresh
mushrooms and a dash of balsamic vinegar.*

Serves 4

Calories: 87.26
Fat: 6.94 grams
Saturated Fat: 0.96 grams
Carbohydrates: 5.31 grams
Calcium: 12.64 mg
Lactose: 0.0 grams

*12 ounces Portobello
    mushroom caps*
2 tablespoons olive oil
4 cloves garlic, chopped
*2 teaspoons dried Herbes de
    Provence*
*1½ tablespoons balsamic
    vinegar*

1. Scrub mushrooms gently, removing stems. Rinse and pat dry with paper towels. Slice mushrooms into large bite-sized pieces.

2. Heat 1 tablespoon olive oil in a sauté pan over medium-high heat.

3. Sauté mushrooms until they begin to brown, shaking pan often. Add garlic and Herbes de Provence to mushrooms.

4. Continue to sauté another 3 minutes. Add vinegar. Continue cooking for another short minute.

5. Toss with remaining olive oil. Serve warm.

Blending Your Own Herbes de Provence

Herbes de Provence is a delectable blend of aromatic herbs that flourish in the hills of southern France. Make your own by combining the following herbs in a jar with a screw top and shaking to combine: 1 tablespoon dried basil; 1 tablespoon marjoram; 1 tablespoon dried summer savory; ½ tablespoon rosemary; 1 crumbled bay leaf. Add food-grade lavender buds, fennel seeds, and dried sage if you like. This also makes a great rub.

Cauliflower with Dijon Mustard Sauce

Creamy soy milk with the combination of Dijon mustard in this dish makes it an exceptional side dish. The mustard sauce is a nice color contrast to the cauliflower.

Serves 4

Calories: 272.01
Fat: 15.21 grams
Saturated Fat: 7.73 grams
Carbohydrates: 25.54 grams
Calcium: 101.00 mg
Lactose: 0.0 grams

¾ pound cauliflower, cut into
    florets
4 tablespoons butter or
    margarine
½ cup all-purpose flour
3 tablespoons Dijon mustard
2½ cups soy milk
Salt and pepper to taste

1. Steam cauliflower until tender, about 5 minutes.

2. Melt butter in a small saucepan. Add flour, stirring constantly. Continue cooking for one minute, still stirring. Add mustard. Stir until mixed thoroughly.

3. Gradually add soy milk, whisking continuously until it thickens into a smooth sauce. Bring to a boil. Reduce heat and simmer for 5 minutes.

4. Place cauliflower in a medium-sized ovenproof dish. Pour sauce on top. Place dish under a preheated broiler for 5 minutes. Top will become lightly browned.

Corn Soufflé

*Don't be intimidated by soufflés! They are delightful to
serve and to eat. This recipe is very easy to prepare and adds
elegance to your table alongside chicken or grilled veggies.*

Serves 6

Calories: 311.12
Fat: 15.83 grams
Saturated Fat: 3.21 grams
Carbohydrates: 30.12 grams
Calcium: 78.16 mg
Lactose: 0.06 grams

Nonstick cooking spray
3 cups vanilla soy milk
1 teaspoon salt
1 cup yellow cornmeal
*¼ cup margarine, cut into 4
    pieces*
2 tablespoons sugar
*¾ cup white corn kernels,
    fresh or frozen*
6 large eggs, separated
¼ teaspoon cream of tartar

1. Preheat oven to 375°F. Coat a 2-quart soufflé dish with cooking spray.

2. Combine soy milk and salt in a large saucepan over medium-high heat.
    Bring mixture to a simmer. Take care not to boil. Reduce heat to low.

3. Gradually add cornmeal, whisking constantly so that lumps do not
    form. Continue cooking until mixture begins to thicken, about 3 min-
    utes. Add margarine and sugar, whisking until the margarine melts,
    45–60 seconds. Stir in corn.

4. Remove from the heat. Allow to cool for 10 minutes, occasionally stir-
    ring. In a large bowl, whisk egg yolks until well blended. Gradually add
    cornmeal mixture to yolks, stirring to blend.

5. Beat egg whites and cream of tartar in a medium mixing bowl with an
    electric mixer on high speed until soft peaks form. Gently fold beaten
    whites into cornmeal mixture until just combined. Be careful not to
    over mix or the soufflé won't rise. Pour mixture into prepared soufflé
    dish. Bake about 40 minutes. Soufflé will puff up and turn a beautiful
    golden brown. Serve immediately.

Nutty Spinach

*Spinach never tasted so good—a touch of Italian gastronomy
with some Italian ham combined with crunchy pine nuts and almonds.
The flavors are bound together with the olive oil and garlic.*

1. Heat olive oil in a medium saucepan over medium heat. Add garlic.

2. Cook 2 minutes, stirring constantly. Remove garlic and discard.

3. Add pine nuts and almonds, cooking until lightly browned, about 3 minutes.

4. Stir in spinach, prosciutto, salt, and pepper. Toss to combine well. Continue cooking until just heated through.

5. Serve immediately.

Dark Green Nutritional Magic!

Thank the plant pigment carotenoids for the dark green color of spinach. In this magical group are beta carotene, vitamin A, and lutein. Spinach also contains antioxidants and bioflavonoids. All that can help prevent cancer.

Serves 4

Calories: 260.19
Fat: 23.93 grams
Saturated Fat: 2.89 grams
Carbohydrates: 6.81 grams
Calcium: 132.64 mg
Lactose: 0.0 grams

¼ cup olive oil
1 clove garlic, cut in half
¼ cup pine nuts
¼ cup blanched slivered
    almonds
1 pound fresh spinach,
    cooked, drained, and
    chopped
¼ cup chopped prosciutto
Salt and pepper to taste

Lemony Steamed Spinach

Serves 4

Calories: 257.28
Fat: 23.63 grams
Saturated Fat: 4.10 grams
Carbohydrates: 9.16 grams
Calcium: 233.94 mg
Lactose: 0.0 grams

2 pounds fresh spinach leaves
½ cup margarine, melted
2 teaspoons grated lemon zest
2 tablespoons fresh lemon juice
Salt to taste
White pepper to taste

This lemony spinach is a perfect side dish for any meal or can actually be a meal in itself! If you're a garlic lover, add some fresh garlic to the saucepan.

1. Wash spinach in cool water; shake off excess water. Remove any thick stems. Tear spinach leaves into bite-sized pieces.

2. Place in a large microwave-safe casserole dish. Cover casserole with thick plastic wrap. Cook on high for 2 minutes.

3. Stir and cook another short 2 minutes on high. Drain well. Squeeze out liquid.

4. In a small glass bowl, combine margarine, lemon zest, lemon juice, salt, and white pepper. Heat in microwave until warm.

5. Pour over spinach and toss to combine flavors.

Spinach with Jicama

Serves 4

Calories: 42.52
Fat: 2.51 grams
Saturated Fat: 0.35 grams
Carbohydrates: 4.19 grams
Calcium: 64.10 mg
Lactose: 0.0 grams

8 cups fresh spinach leaves
2 teaspoons olive oil
1½ teaspoons grated fresh ginger
2 cloves minced garlic
½ teaspoon soy sauce
½ cup sliced jicama
¼ teaspoon freshly ground black pepper

The ginger and garlic bring out the contrasts between the vegetables in this dish.

1. Wash fresh spinach thoroughly and drain well. Set aside.

2. In a large heavy skillet or wok, heat olive oil over medium heat. Add ginger and garlic. Sauté for a short minute.

3. Add soy sauce and jicama. Stir-fry for 2 minutes.

4. Add spinach to skillet. Stir-fry until spinach is just wilted, a quick 2 minutes.

5. Sprinkle with freshly ground black pepper.

Grilled Bok Choy

Bok choy has a delicate flavor all its own.

Serves 2

Calories: 74.45
Fat: 6.93 grams
Saturated Fat: 0.93 grams
Carbohydrates: 2.93 grams
Calcium: 31.74 mg
Lactose: 0.0 grams

1 tablespoon olive oil
2 sprigs fresh thyme
1 clove garlic, halved
1 8-ounce bunch bok choy,
*   rinsed and patted dry*
1 teaspoon lemon juice

1. In a small saucepan over medium heat, simmer oil, thyme, and garlic just until garlic begins to turn light brown. Remove from heat. Set aside and let cool for 5 minutes.

2. Strain the oil mixture. Using a basting or pastry brush, baste whole bok choy with the oil mixture.

3. Heat wok. Place bok choy in hot wok. Using tongs, turn bok choy until cooked on all sides. It will appear wilted.

4. Remove stem end of bok choy and slice in half lengthwise. Sprinkle with fresh lemon juice just before serving.

Bok Choy Bits

Bok choy is a variety of Chinese cabbage. Instead of forming a head as it grows, it's a group of white stems bunched together with thick, dark green leaves. It's often used in stir-fry dishes but can also be eaten raw.

Oriental-Style Broccoli

Options abound. If you'd prefer the broccoli minus the flank steak, just skip it!

Serves 4

Calories: 304.29
Fat: 21.71 grams
Saturated Fat: 4.08 grams
Carbohydrates: 13.33 grams
Calcium: 84.89 mg
Lactose: 0.0 grams

½ pound flank steak
1½ pounds broccoli
2 teaspoons sherry
⅛ teaspoon pepper
2 teaspoons soy sauce
½ teaspoon salt
½ teaspoon sugar
¾ cup water
¼ cup oil
2 teaspoons cornstarch

1. Place steak in freezer for a few minutes before preparing this recipe to make slicing it easier. Cut almost-frozen meat across grain into thin slices. Set aside. In a small bowl, combine sherry, pepper, soy sauce, salt, sugar, and ½ cup water.

2. Heat 2 tablespoons oil in a large, heavy skillet or wok. Add broccoli. Cover skillet and shake. Cook for 2 minutes or until broccoli is crisp-tender. Place broccoli on hot platter.

3. Place remaining 2 tablespoons oil in hot skillet. Add sliced meat. Brown quickly on both sides. Pour in soy sauce mixture. Cover and cook 2 minutes.

4. Dissolve cornstarch in remaining ¼ cup water, making sure mixture is smooth. Gradually add to skillet mixture, stirring constantly. Mixture will begin to thicken.

5. Add broccoli back to skillet, stirring to combine all ingredients well. Make sure it is heated through. Serve immediately.

Broccoli with Almonds

*Versatile broccoli can team up with so many ingredients
for delicious outcomes. Make sure to check those labels
on the mustard that you choose for hidden lactose!*

1. Preheat oven to 375°F. Cut stems from broccoli florets.

2. Steam florets until crisp-tender. Immediately pour broccoli into a medium bowl. Toss gently with the wine. Allow to rest for 15 minutes.

3. Meanwhile, blend 1 tablespoon oil and Dijon mustard in a small bowl. Drain liquid from the broccoli. Toss gently with mustard and oil mixture, coating well.

4. Place broccoli mixture into ovenproof baking dish. Toss almonds with 1 teaspoon remaining oil in a small bowl. Sprinkle on top of broccoli.

5. Bake at 375°F until thoroughly heated, about 15 minutes. Almonds will be a toasty light brown color.

Bro-calcium!

Broccoli matches milk in calcium. Calcium is essential to keep your body running. It assists muscle coordination and nervous system communication, among other vital functions. If your body doesn't get enough calcium from the food you eat, it starts to steal it from your bones.

Serves 6

Calories: 98.40
Fat: 5.16 grams
Saturated Fat: 0.59 grams
Carbohydrates: 8.10 grams
Calcium: 59.79 mg
Lactose: 0.0 grams

1 head fresh broccoli
½ cup dry white wine
1 tablespoon plus 1 teaspoon olive oil
1 tablespoon Dijon mustard
1½ ounces slivered almonds

Summer Veggie Rainbow Sauté

*The bright veggie colors in this dish make it truly
inviting as well as colorfully presentable.*

Serves 4

Calories: 43.03
Fat: 1.41 grams
Saturated Fat: 0.22 grams
Carbohydrates: 7.34 grams
Calcium: 22.85 mg
Lactose: 0.0 grams

1 teaspoon olive oil
½ yellow onion, sliced
½ green pepper, sliced
1 yellow squash, thickly sliced
1 zucchini, thickly sliced
1 chopped tomato
½ teaspoon dried oregano
1 teaspoon basil
*Freshly ground pepper to
    taste*

1. Heat olive oil in a large, heavy skillet over low heat.

2. Add onion and sauté until soft.

3. Add green pepper. Cook until pepper wilts.

4. Add yellow squash, zucchini, and tomato. Cover and cook for 10 minutes.

5. Stir in oregano, basil, and pepper.

Honey Harvard Beets

*Beets are quite tasty but are too often overlooked. This recipe is simple to
prepare and the taste is simply delicious! Freeze the beets to enjoy later.*

Yields about 5 cups

Calories: 72.64
Fat: 0.12 grams
Saturated Fat: 0.02 grams
Carbohydrates: 17.95 grams
Calcium: 67.53 mg
Lactose: 0.0 grams

1 tablespoon cornstarch
1 teaspoon salt
½ cup cider vinegar
½ cup water
½ cup honey
2 whole cloves
4 cups sliced boiled beets

1. Stir cornstarch, salt, vinegar, and water in a medium saucepan. Place over low heat.

2. Stir in honey and cloves. Boil for 5 minutes until thick and clear. Add beets.

The Beet Beat

*Beets are low in calories, but they have the highest natural sugar content
of any vegetable! Beets get their beautiful color from the bright red pigment betacyanin, which is extracted as a natural dye or food coloring.*

Snow Pea Stir Fry

*This recipe says it serves four, but if you love
peas change it to more like two servings!*

1. Combine cornstarch and chicken broth in a jar with a screw top lid. Shake well until lumps disappear. Set aside.

2. Coat a large skillet or wok with cooking spray. Place over low heat. Add garlic to skillet and sauté until lightly browned.

3. Add soy sauce, snow peas, bamboo shoots, and water chestnuts. Stir-fry over high heat for 1 minute.

4. Reduce heat to medium. Add chicken broth mixture gradually, stirring constantly. Bring to a boil.

5. Cook, stirring constantly for a short minute until sauce begins to thicken.

Stir Fry Flexibility

Stir-fried fresh veggies can be a treat when you're hungry at midnight. It's a great cold healthy snack. The possibilities of stir fry combinations are unlimited, and they can be totally lactose free. Stir fry is a great family meal when you're cooking for both family members with LI and those without.

Serves 4

Calories: 84.08
Fat: 0.84 grams
Saturated Fat: 0.21 grams
Carbohydrates: 16.28 grams
Calcium: 47.72 mg
Lactose: 0.0 grams

1 teaspoon cornstarch
½ cup chicken broth
Nonstick cooking spray
2 cloves minced garlic
1 teaspoon soy sauce
2 cups fresh snow peas
1 8-ounce can sliced bamboo
    shoots, drained
1 8-ounce can water
    chestnuts, drained

Orange Braised Tofu

*If you don't have Chinese five-spice powder in your pantry,
it's about time you experience its essence. You'll find yourself
reaching for it to prepare dishes besides this one!*

Serves 8

Calories: 180.62
Fat: 8.28 grams
Saturated Fat: 1.71 grams
Carbohydrates: 13.22 grams
Calcium: 402.98 mg
Lactose: 0.0 grams

½ cup water
¼ cup soy sauce
¾ cup fresh orange juice
2 tablespoons orange zest
2 tablespoons rice vinegar
2 tablespoons honey
½ teaspoon Chinese five-spice
  powder
¼ teaspoon salt
2 14-ounce blocks firm tofu,
  halved horizontally

1. In a large sauté pan combine water, soy sauce, orange juice, orange zest, rice vinegar, honey, Chinese five-spice powder, and salt. Bring to a boil.

2. Add tofu to hot mixture, laying it flat in pan.

3. Reduce heat and simmer for 15 minutes. Turn tofu once halfway through simmering.

4. Remove from heat. Cool tofu in its liquid, turning a few more times.

5. Cover and chill.

Tofu Trivia

Tofu is also known as bean curd—and for good reason! It is made by curding the mild white milk of the soybean. High in protein, tofu contains no cholesterol and is lactose free. When you're shopping, look for calcium-fortified tofu. Keep tofu refrigerated in water until you're ready to use it.

Chapter 20
Desserts

Apple Yogurt Coffee Cake with Streusel Filling

Serves 6

Calories: 531.50
Fat: 25.56 grams
Saturated Fat: 11.94 grams
Carbohydrates: 67.93 grams
Calcium: 74.52 mg
Lactose: 0.02 grams

¼ cup sugar
1 tablespoon melted
    margarine
1 tablespoon flour
1 teaspoon ground cinnamon
¼ cup chopped walnuts or
    pecans
1 tablespoon melted
    margarine
1 tablespoon packed brown
    sugar
¼ teaspoon ground
    cinnamon
2 apples, cored and sliced
2 cups flour
1 teaspoon baking powder
1 teaspoon baking soda
½ teaspoon salt
½ cup butter
½ cup sugar
2 eggs
1 8-ounce carton plain yogurt

*Warm apples with cinnamon is always a combination
that's hard to beat. This coffee cake has an easy sprinkle-in
filling that comes out of the oven in divine fashion!*

1. Preheat oven to 350°F. In a small bowl, combine ¼ cup sugar, 1 table-spoon melted margarine, 1 tablespoon flour, 1 teaspoon cinnamon, and pecans or walnuts for filling. Mix well. Set aside.

2. Combine second tablespoon melted margarine with brown sugar and cin-namon in 9" × 9" × 2" square baking pan. Smooth mixture evenly over bottom. Slice apples and arrange on top of brown sugar mixture.

3. In a medium bowl, combine flour, baking powder, baking soda, and salt. Set aside. In medium mixing bowl, cream butter and sugar with mixer. Add eggs one at a time, beating well after each addition. Reduce mixer speed. Alternately add dry ingredients with yogurt, scraping bowl when necessary.

4. Spread half of batter over apple slices. Sprinkle filling mixture over bat-ter in pan. Spread remaining batter over filling.

5. Bake until a toothpick inserted in the center comes out clean, about 30 minutes. This is delicious served warm!

Strawberry Yogurt Scones

*Try this recipe with other fruits such as fresh
blueberries, red raspberries, or peaches.*

Serves 4

Calories: 333.08
Fat: 12.92 grams
Saturated Fat: 2.58 grams
Carbohydrates: 48.05 grams
Calcium: 54.48 mg
Lactose: 0.0 grams

Parchment paper
1½ cups all-purpose flour
2½ tablespoons sugar
1 tablespoon baking powder
½ teaspoon baking soda
½ stick margarine
½ cup plain yogurt
*½ cup fresh coarsely
    chopped strawberries*

1. Preheat oven to 350°F. Line bottom of baking sheet with parchment paper. Set aside.

2. In a medium bowl, combine flour, sugar, baking powder, and baking soda. Add margarine. Blend with a fork until mixture resembles coarse cornmeal.

3. Add yogurt and strawberries. Gently mix to create dough.

4. Pat dough into a 6" circle. Cut into quarters. Place on the parchment-lined baking sheet about an inch apart.

5. Bake scones until tops are golden brown, about 15 minutes. Make sure scones are cooked all the way through.

Baking with Yogurt

In traditional baking you can very quickly learn to substitute yogurt in place of milk and buttermilk. The blandness of yogurt is a perfect complement to other ingredients such as brown sugars, dried fruits, and molasses, and you'll get feather-light baked goods when you bake with it. Yogurt should become a "staple ingredient" in your LI lifestyle cooking.

Baked Apples

This recipe is an exceptional treat with a dollop of honey-cinnamon yogurt.

1. Preheat oven to 350ºF. Spray 8" × 8" baking dish with nonstick cooking spray. Set aside.

2. Core and thinly slice apples. Toss apples with apple juice in a medium bowl.

3. In a small bowl, combine brown sugar, cornstarch, cinnamon, nutmeg, and salt. Mix well. Sprinkle brown sugar mixture over apples. Stir gently until apples are well coated.

4. Pour apples into prepared baking dish. Bake until sauce is bubbling and the edges of apples begin to brown, about 40 minutes.

5. In a small bowl, combine yogurt, honey, and cinnamon. Stir until well mixed. Divide apples into four dessert dishes and top with yogurt topping.

Banana Citrus Trifle

*A trifle makes a beautiful centerpiece presentation for a special occasion,
and this one is a very easy recipe. If presentation isn't what you need,
just use a large plastic bowl to make the trifle and dig in!*

1. Cut cake into ¼"-thick slices. Set aside. In a medium bowl, pour lime juice over banana slices. Set aside.

2. Peel and section oranges over a small saucepan, reserving juice. Set orange sections aside in a small bowl.

3. Combine sugar and water with juice in saucepan. Stir well. Bring to a boil over medium heat. Cook uncovered until mixture is reduced to ⅓ cup, about 5 minutes. Remove from heat. Stir in grated orange and lime rinds.

4. Pour mixture over banana slices. Toss gently, combining well. Arrange half of cake slices in a 2-quart trifle bowl. Spoon half of banana mixture over cake slices. Spread half of the yogurt over banana mixture; then arrange half of orange sections over yogurt.

5. Repeat layering procedure with remaining cake, banana mixture, yogurt, and orange sections. Cover tightly. Chill for at least 6 hours.

Serves 8

Calories: 218.53
Fat: 1.13 grams
Saturated Fat: 0.49 grams
Carbohydrates: 49.95 grams
Calcium: 146.05 mg
Lactose: 0.0 grams

8 ounces commercial angel food cake
1 tablespoon lime juice
3⅓ cups sliced banana
3 oranges
¼ cup sugar
¼ cup water
1½ teaspoons grated orange rind
1½ teaspoons grated lime rind
1½ cups vanilla yogurt

Berry Pear Clafouti

This combination of pears and raspberries in a fancy-sounding dessert is actually very easy to put together! For the full experience of this dish, serve it warm.

Serves 8

Calories: 192.55
Fat: 4.73 grams
Saturated Fat: 1.10 grams
Carbohydrates: 33.22 grams
Calcium: 35.29 mg
Lactose: 0.03 grams

Nonstick cooking spray
2 tablespoons plus ½ cup sugar
½ cup all-purpose flour
4 large eggs
1 cup soy milk
1 tablespoon margarine, melted
2 teaspoons grated lemon zest
1 teaspoon vanilla extract
2 ripe but firm pears
1 cup fresh raspberries
Powdered sugar for dusting

1. Preheat oven to 400°F. Coat a 9½" round deep-dish pie pan with cooking spray. Sprinkle 1 tablespoon sugar across bottom of pan. Tilt pan to coat as evenly as possible. Set aside.

2. In a large bowl, whisk together ½ cup sugar, flour, eggs, milk, margarine, lemon zest, and vanilla. Peel, core, and thinly slice the pears.

3. Arrange the pear slices in prepared pan. Scatter raspberries on top of pears. Pour batter over fruit.

4. Sprinkle remaining sugar over batter. Bake until clafouti is puffy and firm to touch, about 45 minutes.

5. Remove from oven and allow to cool slightly. Dust top of clafouti with powdered sugar. Serve warm.

Clafouti Trivia

Can you say "kla-foo-tee"? Clafouti is a baked custard-like French dessert. It's typically prepared with fresh fruit and a batter similar to pancake batter, and it resembles a mouthwatering pudding cake! Originally from the Limousin region, clafoutis apparently spread throughout France during the nineteenth century.

Pumpkin Custard

*The tofu and pumpkin combo in this recipe makes
it a very smooth custard. The flavorful custard and crunchy
gingersnap topping is sure to be a keeper for your LI lifestyle!*

Serves 6

Calories: 383.87
Fat: 10.56 grams
Saturated Fat: 2.26 grams
Carbohydrates: 65.54 grams
Calcium: 188.61 mg
Lactose: 0.01 grams

Nonstick cooking spray
12 ounces firm tofu, drained
1 15-ounce can pumpkin
⅔ cup packed brown sugar
1 teaspoon rum extract
1½ teaspoons cinnamon
¾ teaspoon ginger
½ teaspoon cloves
3 egg whites
8 gingersnap cookies
1 tablespoon white sugar
2 tablespoons margarine

1. Preheat the oven to 350°F. Spray six 6-ounce custard cups with nonstick vegetable spray.

2. Purée tofu in blender until smooth. Add pumpkin, brown sugar, rum extract, cinnamon, ginger, and cloves to blender. Purée until well blended. Add egg whites. Mix quickly until just blended. Be careful not to over mix. Pour mixture into the six custard cups. Bake for 20 minutes.

3. While custard is baking, prepare gingersnap topping. Place gingersnaps in a plastic bag and crush with a rolling pin. Stir gingersnap crumbs and sugar together in a small bowl. Cut margarine into small bits and add to the gingersnap mixture. Using a fork or pastry blender, cut in margarine until the mixture resembles coarse crumbs.

4. After baking for 20 minutes, remove custard cups from oven. Sprinkle the gingersnap topping over pumpkin custard.

5. Return custard to the oven. Bake until the edges of the custards separate from the cups, about 20 minutes.

Green Tea Tofu Flan

This recipe blends the Asian flavor of green tea with the European texture of flan. As always, you can substitute rice milk if soy isn't your "cup of tea."

⚜

Serves 6

Calories: 189.23
Fat: 5.18 grams
Saturated Fat: 1.32 grams
Carbohydrates: 28.56 grams
Calcium: 74.53 mg
Lactose: 0.04 grams

1½ cups plain soy milk
1 bag green tea
7 ounces firm tofu, patted dry
4 eggs
¾ cup sugar
1 teaspoon vanilla extract
Boiling water

1. Preheat the oven to 350°F.

2. Bring soy milk just to bubbling around the edges in a small saucepan over medium-high heat. Don't allow it to boil. Remove from heat. Add green tea bag. Steep for 6 minutes. Remove tea bag.

3. Place tofu in blender. Purée until smooth. Add eggs and sugar to blender. Process until smooth.

4. Add the tea-infused soy milk and vanilla to blender mixture. Process until well combined. Pour mixture into six 8-ounce custard cups.

5. Place cups in 1" boiling water on a baking pan. Bake until just set, about 45 minutes. Cool flan to room temperature. Chill. Invert on small plates to serve.

Green Tea Is Qi-Boosting!

The Chinese refer to green tea as "liquid jade." Green tea is considered a drink of longevity. Containing minimal caffeine, it gives your mind and spirit a gentle lift. Green tea, with its polyphenol compounds, appears to act as an antioxidant in the prevention of cancer.

Creamy Apricot Mousse

*It's like an apricot cloud! And it's floating right into your
LI lifestyle with a ton of calcium benefits for you!*

Serves 4

Calories: 231.79
Fat: 5.52 grams
Saturated Fat: 3.50 grams
Carbohydrates: 27.27 grams
Calcium: 433.57 mg
Lactose: 0.0 grams

*1 16-ounce can apricots,
   packed in juice
1 envelope unflavored gelatin
¼ teaspoon almond extract
½ teaspoon vanilla extract
2 cups yogurt cheese*

1. Drain apricots. Reserve juice in a clear measuring cup. Set aside apricots. If apricot juice does not measure up to 1 cup, add enough water to equal 1 cup.

2. Pour apricot juice into a heavy 1-quart saucepan. Sprinkle gelatin over top. Let sit and soften for 5 minutes.

3. Over medium heat, stir constantly to dissolve gelatin. Do not allow mixture to boil. Remove from heat. Cool for 5 minutes.

4. Purée apricots, almond extract, vanilla extract, and gelatin in blender until smooth.

5. Place yogurt cheese in a large bowl. Gradually whisk in the apricot purée. Pour into four individual dessert dishes. Refrigerate until firm, at least 60 minutes, before serving.

Chocolate Brownies

You can make these already healthy brownies a tad healthier by substituting whole wheat pastry flour for some of the all-purpose flour, which will make the texture even smoother!

Yields 24 brownies

Calories: 127.74
Fat: 1.35 grams
Saturated Fat: 0.52 grams
Carbohydrates: 29.41 grams
Calcium: 20.32 mg
Lactose: 0.0 grams

Nonstick cooking spray
2¼ cups sugar
1½ cups all-purpose flour
1½ cups unsweetened cocoa powder
1½ teaspoons baking powder
1½ teaspoons baking soda
⅛ teaspoon salt
1 cup unsweetened applesauce
1 cup soft tofu
¾ cup chocolate soy milk
2 teaspoons vanilla extract

1. Preheat oven to 350°F. Coat a 9" × 13" baking dish with cooking spray.

2. In a large bowl, combine sugar, flour, cocoa powder, baking powder, baking soda, and salt.

3. In a blender, combine applesauce, tofu, soy milk, and vanilla. Process until well blended.

4. Add tofu mixture to dry ingredients. Mix well. Scrape batter into prepared pan.

5. Bake until top is dry, about 45 minutes. Leave in pan to cool. Cut into bars.

Cocoa Rocks!

There have been many studies linking cocoa and dark chocolate with health benefits. Cocoa and chocolate contain a large amount of antioxidants that may keep high blood pressure down, reducing the risk of heart attack and stroke. The darker chocolate with the most concentrated cocoa proves to be the most beneficial.

Blueberry Yogurt Crumble

*This lactose-free delight is comparable to old-fashioned blueberry buckle.
It's yummy served warm, but it's also tasty as it cools down!*

1. Preheat oven to 350°F. Grease and flour a 9" × 13" baking pan.

2. Combine sugar, cinnamon, and nutmeg in a small bowl. Blend margarine into sugar mixture with a fork. Large crumbs will form.

3. In a medium mixing bowl, cream butter and brown sugar with electric mixer. Add egg, mixing well. Stir baking soda into flour in a measuring cup.

4. Reduce mixer speed, adding flour gradually, scraping sides of bowl as necessary. When flour is well blended, add yogurt, vanilla, and lemon zest. Mix well at medium speed for 4 minutes.

5. Pour batter into prepared pan. Sprinkle fresh blueberries over top, pressing them very lightly into batter. Sprinkle crumbly topping across top. Bake for 45 minutes. Cool on a rack. Serve warm.

Serves 12

Calories: 379.74
Fat: 10.94 grams
Saturated Fat: 5.75 grams
Carbohydrates: 67.81 grams
Calcium: 58.78 mg
Lactose: 0.0 grams

1 cup sugar
2 teaspoons cinnamon
¼ teaspoon nutmeg
2 tablespoons margarine
1 stick butter
1½ cups brown sugar
1 egg
1 teaspoon baking soda
2½ cups flour
1 cup plain yogurt
1 teaspoon vanilla
½ teaspoon lemon zest
*2 cups fresh blueberries
(frozen may be
substituted)*

Zucchini Yogurt Cake

Zucchini does wonderful things to baked goods. In this recipe it provides an oh-so-natural moistness.

Calories: 404.36
Fat: 21.61 grams
Saturated Fat: 1.97 grams
Carbohydrates: 48.37 grams
Calcium: 51.54 mg
Lactose: 0.01 grams

2 cups flour
2 teaspoons baking powder
2 teaspoons cinnamon
1 teaspoon baking soda
½ teaspoon salt
3 eggs
1¼ cups packed brown sugar
¼ cup honey
¾ cup oil
½ cup plain yogurt
1½ cups shredded unpeeled zucchini
1 cup chopped walnuts
½ cup finely diced banana
1 teaspoon grated orange peel
Powdered sugar for garnish (optional)

1. Grease and flour 10" fluted tube pan. Set aside. In a medium bowl, stir together flour, baking powder, cinnamon, baking soda, and salt. Set aside.

2. In large mixing bowl, beat eggs with electric mixer until light. With mixer running, gradually add sugar and honey until mixture is light and fluffy. Slowly beat in oil.

3. Reduce speed to low. Fold in flour mixture alternately with yogurt, scraping bowl as necessary. Fold in zucchini, walnuts, banana, and orange peel.

4. Turn batter into prepared tube pan. Bake for 50 minutes or until cake begins to crack on top. Don't allow to get too brown!

5. Invert on a rack to cool. Remove from pan while still warm. Cool completely. Sprinkle with powdered sugar, if desired.

Zucchini's Kissing Cousin

Zucchini is related to pumpkin. Zukes happen to be the most popular of summer squash. Being about 94 percent water makes zucchini one of the lowest calorie veggies. With its unobtrusive taste, zucchini complements other ingredients that it's paired with in tasty recipes!

Chocolate Layer Cake

Cooking with coffee is becoming quite the rage, so here's a recipe with cold coffee. You won't even know the tofu is there; it soaks up the coffee flavor and adds to the smooth texture of this chocolate delight!

1. Preheat oven to 350°F. Grease and flour two 8" round cake pans.

2. In a large bowl, whisk together tofu, syrup, coffee, and vanilla until well blended and smooth. Sift together cocoa powder, flours, baking powder, baking soda, and cinnamon.

3. Add dry ingredient to tofu mixture in mixing bowl. Beat with electric mixer until smooth, about 3 minutes. Divide batter between cake pans. Bake until cake springs back to touch, about 15 minutes.

4. Cool in pans on wire racks for 10 minutes, then invert cakes onto racks. Cool completely. Frost with Tofu Chocolate Frosting recipe (page 274).

Serves 12

Calories: 142.85
Fat: 2.09 grams
Saturated Fat: 0.80 grams
Carbohydrates: 31.06 grams
Calcium: 72.71 mg
Lactose: 0.0 grams

1 cup puréed firm tofu
1 cup maple syrup
¾ cup brewed strong coffee, cold
2 teaspoons vanilla extract
1 cup unsweetened cocoa powder
¾ cup whole wheat pastry flour
½ cup all-purpose flour
1 teaspoon baking powder
1 teaspoon baking soda
½ teaspoon ground cinnamon
Tofu Chocolate Frosting (page 274)

Tofu Chocolate Frosting

*There's something luxurious about the combination of chocolate
with raspberries when the two hit your palate together.*

Serves 12

Calories: 90.47
Fat: 5.70 grams
Saturated Fat: 2.65 grams
Carbohydrates: 9.44 grams
Calcium: 47.95 mg
Lactose: 0.0 grams

10.5 ounces extra-firm tofu
2 teaspoons vanilla extract
6 ounces semisweet
 chocolate, melted
Fresh raspberries for garnish
 (optional)

1. Place tofu, vanilla, and chocolate in blender. Process until smooth

2. Place one cake layer on serving plate. Spread with ½ cup frosting.

3. Top with second cake layer. Frost top and sides.

4. Garnish with raspberries, if desired.

Tofu Is a Friendly Ingredient

*You're going to find as you experiment with your own recipes in con-
verting them to lactose free that tofu can "fill in" so many places to
provide both the texture and consistency you crave. Don't let tofu intim-
idate you! Tofu is not only a friendly ingredient but it is very LI-friendly!*

New York Style Cheesecake

Versatile yogurt cheese will surprise you in this recipe! Who would have thought that cheesecake would be on your list of things to enjoy in your LI lifestyle?

Serves 12

Calories: 269.72
Fat: 4.91 grams
Saturated Fat: 2.72 grams
Carbohydrates: 44.02 grams
Calcium: 286.73 mg
Lactose: 0.01 grams

Nonstick cooking spray
4 cups yogurt cheese
2 cups sugar
3 egg whites
1 tablespoon fresh lemon juice
1 teaspoon fresh lemon zest
1 teaspoon vanilla extract
3 tablespoons sifted cake flour

1. Preheat oven to 325°F. Spray the sides and bottom of a 2-quart soufflé dish with cooking spray.

2. In a medium bowl, whisk yogurt cheese with sugar, egg whites, lemon juice, lemon zest, vanilla, and cake flour. Be careful not to over beat.

3. Pour into prepared soufflé dish. Set dish into a large pan of hot water. Bake in preheated oven until cake is browned and begins to crack, about 90 minutes.

4. Turn oven off. Leave cake in oven for 60 minutes longer.

5. Remove cheesecake from water bath. Place dish on a wire rack for one hour to completely cool. Invert on serving platter. Refrigerate until serving time.

Cheesecake Trivia

It is believed that cheesecake originated in ancient Greece. The first recorded mention of cheesecake was in 776 B.C., when it was served to the participating athletes during the first Olympic Games. However, New Yorkers insist that cheesecake wasn't really cheesecake until it was New York cheesecake!

Lemon Cheesecake

The longest part of this recipe is waiting for your cheesecake to chill. The addition of yogurt cheese makes it a decadent treat to satisfy your LI cheesecake cravings!

Serves 8

Calories: 141.94
Fat: 2.77 grams
Saturated Fat: 1.75 grams
Carbohydrates: 19.11 grams
Calcium: 211.20 mg
Lactose: 0.01 grams

Nonstick cooking spray
2 cups yogurt cheese
¼ cup plus 3 tablespoons sugar, or to taste
1 tablespoon cornstarch
4 egg whites
Juice of 1 lemon
1 teaspoon vanilla
½ teaspoon grated lemon peel

1. Preheat oven to 325°F. Spray a 7" springform pan with cooking spray. Set aside.

2. Whisk yogurt cheese, sugar, and cornstarch together in a large bowl.

3. Beat egg whites until stiff. Fold into yogurt cheese mixture with lemon juice, vanilla, and lemon peel. Whisk until well blended.

4. Pour into prepared springform pan. Smooth top with a rubber spatula.

5. Bake until center is set, about 45 minutes. Cool slightly on a wire rack. Refrigerate until chilled.

Frozen Peanut Butter Pie

This dessert is easy to make and beautiful to serve!
The creamy, peanut buttery texture is delicately delightful!

1. Combine all ingredients except pie shell and chocolate curls in blender.

2. Process on medium-high speed until mixture is very smooth and creamy.

3. Pour into prepared pie shell. Freeze overnight.

4. Allow to thaw for about 10 minutes before serving.

5. Garnish with semi-sweet chocolate curls, if desired.

Peanut Butter Trivia

Around 1890, a physician supposedly encouraged the owner of a food products company to process and package ground peanut paste as a nutritious protein substitute for people with poor teeth who couldn't chew meat. The physician had previously experimented with the process by grinding peanuts in his hand-cranked meat grinder. The price for peanut butter was about 6 cents per pound.

Serves 8

Calories: 454.13
Fat: 26.80 grams
Saturated Fat: 5.06 grams
Carbohydrates: 42.63 grams
Calcium: 131.91 mg
Lactose: 0.0 grams

1 pound firm tofu, drained
¾ cup peanut butter
½ cup honey
¼ cup oil
1 teaspoon vanilla
⅛ teaspoon salt
1 graham cracker pie shell
Semi-sweet chocolate curls
for garnish (optional)

Minty Raspberry Sorbet

Make your own fresh sorbets and you won't ever miss ice cream!
Experiment to make your own varieties; the possibilities are endless.

Yields 7 servings

Calories: 129.79
Fat: 0.17 grams
Saturated Fat: 0.01 grams
Carbohydrates: 20.49 grams
Calcium: 9.68 mg
Lactose: 0.0 grams

2 cups burgundy wine
1 cup water
½ cup sugar
⅓ cup minced fresh mint
1⅓ cups fresh raspberries
2 tablespoons unsweetened orange juice
1½ tablespoons lemon juice

1. Rinse cheesecloth and squeeze dry. Fold and set aside.

2. In a heavy saucepan, combine wine, water, sugar, and fresh mint. Bring to a boil over medium heat, stirring constantly until sugar is dissolved. Boil 3 minutes without stirring.

3. Remove from heat. Allow to cool completely. Line a colander with a double layer of cheesecloth, allowing cheesecloth to extend over edge of colander. Place colander in a large bowl.

4. Pour mixture into colander, allowing liquid to drain into bowl. Discard mint. Place raspberries in blender. Process until smooth. Strain purée. Discard seeds. Add purée, orange juice, and lemon juice to wine mixture. Stir until well mixed.

5. Pour into freezer can of a 2-quart electric freezer. Freeze according to manufacturer's instructions. Scoop sorbet into individual dessert bowls. Serve immediately.

Peachy Tofu Ice Cream

Smooth and fresh, peach ice cream is definitely tasty. You'll be more than pleased with this recipe that allows you to have your ice cream and eat it too!

1. Peel peaches and chop. Squeeze juice from lemons.

2. In a small bowl combine chopped peaches, fresh lemon juice, and 1 cup sugar. Cover tightly and refrigerate for at least an hour, allowing flavors to mingle.

3. In a large bowl, combine peach mixture with soy milk, tofu, additional sugar, vanilla, and salt.

4. Divide mixture in four equal batches. Process each batch in blender until consistency is smooth and creamy.

5. Pour into freezer cans of two 4-quart electric freezers. Freeze according to manufacturer's instructions.

Fresh, Ripe Peaches

Not only do fresh, ripe peaches smell like a fruity perfume, they are versatile fruits. Just slicing one for a snack is truly a treat, and there are endless ways to use them in cooking, canning, and freezing! Add to that the high nutritional value—this low-calorie fruit is a rich source of antioxidants, vitamin A, vitamin C, potassium, and fiber.

Yields 26 servings

Calories: 138.81
Fat: 2.93 grams
Saturated Fat: 0.41 grams
Carbohydrates: 23.84 grams
Calcium: 196.75 mg
Lactose: 0.0 grams

8 medium peaches
2 lemons
1 cup sugar
3 cups soy milk
1½ pounds tofu
1¼ cups sugar
4 tablespoons vanilla
½ teaspoon salt

Appendix A
Lactose-Free Menus

Planning routine family dinners or extravagant celebration meals is a snap with the recipes in this book. Be creative when you plan, and don't be afraid to experiment. Choose recipes with ingredients you like, and substitute ingredients you like for ones you don't. The following are some suggested menus to get you started.

Breakfast Menu
Eggs En Cocotte (page 33)
Deluxe Daybreak Smoothie
    (page 24)
Blueberry Muffins (page 51)
Blueberry Fruit Spread (page 140)

Dinner Menu 1
Chinese Coleslaw (page 97)
Oven-Fried Sesame
    Chicken (page 178)
Orange Rice (page 217)
Apricot-Glazed Sweet
    Potatoes (page 245)
Banana Citrus Trifle (page 265)

Dinner Menu 2
Fruit Fondue Sauce (page 149)
Grilled Salmon with Creamy
    Tarragon Sauce (page 199)
Roasted Asparagus with
    Onions (page 248)
Green Tea Tofu Flan (page 268)

Dinner Menu 3
Cherry Tomatoes with Bean
    Stuffing (page 162)
Linguine with Arugula and
    Pine Nuts (page 238)
Creamy Apricot Mousse
    (page 269)

Dinner Menu 4
Honey Curry Dressing (page
    119) with fresh salad greens
Basil Orange Chicken (page 184)
Orange Braised Tofu (page 260)
Baked Apples (page 264)

Dinner Menu 5
Cold Blueberry Soup (page 94)
Papaya Dream Vinaigrette (page
    121) with fresh salad greens
Poached Salmon and Yogurt
    Dill Sauce (page 199)
Fig Bars (page 63)

Dinner Menu 6
Snapper with Lemon Dill
  Spinach (page 200)
Green Beans with Pearl
  Onions (page 249)
Strawberry Yogurt Dip (page
  128) with fresh strawberries

Dinner Menu 7
Pasta and Fava Bean
  Soup (page 90)
Oven-Fried Trout (page 203)
Cauliflower with Dijon Mustard
  Sauce (page 251)
New York Style Cheesecake
  (page 275)

Dinner Menu 8
Cool-as-a-Cucumber
  Salad (page 108)
Skillet Lemony Lamb
  Chops (page 192)
Corn Soufflé (page 252)
Lemon Cheesecake (page 276)

Dinner Menu 9
Tex-Mex Black Bean Dip (page
  159) with tortilla chips
Tomato Pesto (page 130)
  with fresh vegetables
Tomato Fresca Sauce (page
  151) with spaghetti squash
Herbed Rice Sauté (page 222)
Zucchini Yogurt Cake (page 272)

Potluck Favorites
Overnight Coleslaw (page 96)
Onion Spinach Spread (page 137)
Layered Four-Bean
  Salad (page 160)

Appendix B
Resources

This appendix contains a wealth of resources to help you explore a lactose-free lifestyle.

National Digestive Diseases Information Clearinghouse
http://digestive.niddk.nih.gov/ddiseases/pubs/lactoseintolerance/
The National Digestive Diseases Clearinghouse (NDDIC) is a service of the National Institute of Diabetes and Digestive and Kidney Diseases (NIDDK). The NIDDK is part of the National Institutes of Health under the United States Department of Health and Human Services. This Web site contains a thorough explanation of lactose intolerance in easily understandable terms, complete with figures of the digestive system.

American Dietetic Association
www.eatright.org
The American Dietetic Association's Web site has information dedicated to educating people about lactose intolerance and nutritional information for children with lactose intolerance.

International Foundation for Functional Gastrointestinal Disorders
www.iffgd.org
The International Foundation for Functional Gastrointestinal Disorders, Inc. (IFFGD) has information on lactose intolerance and other digestive disorders.

Soy Foods Association of North America
www.soyfoods.org
This Web site has all kinds of charts and information about the nutritional content of common foods and soy products.

Soy Foods' Primer on Soy
http://www.soyfoods.org/health/primer-on-soy/
This link will take you to a lengthy introduction to soy that will probably answer any and all questions about soy you could ever dream up.

Index